THE AFRICAN DIASPORA IN THE
UNITED STATES AND EUROPE

Research in Migration and Ethnic Relations Series

Series Editor:
Maykel Verkuyten, ERCOMER
Utrecht University

The Research in Migration and Ethnic Relations series has been at the forefront of research in the field for ten years. The series has built an international reputation for cutting edge theoretical work, for comparative research especially on Europe and for nationally-based studies with broader relevance to international issues. Published in association with the European Research Centre on Migration and Ethnic Relations (ERCOMER), Utrecht University, it draws contributions from the best international scholars in the field, offering an interdisciplinary perspective on some of the key issues of the contemporary world.

Other titles in the series

Cities and Labour Immigration
Comparing Policy Responses in Amsterdam, Paris, Rome and Tel Aviv
Michael Alexander
ISBN 978 0 7546 4722 5

Diversity Management and Discrimination
Immigrants and Ethnic Minorities in the EU
John Wrench
ISBN 978 0 7546 4890 1

Minority Rights in International Law
The Roma of Europe
Helen O'Nions
ISBN 978 0 7546 0921 6

**EUROPEAN RESEARCH CENTRE
ON MIGRATION & ETHNIC RELATIONS**

The African Diaspora in the United States and Europe

The Ghanaian Experience

JOHN A. ARTHUR
University of Minnesota, USA

ASHGATE

Published by
Ashgate Publishing Limited
Gower House
Croft Road
Aldershot
Hampshire GU11 3HR
England

Ashgate Publishing Company
Suite 420
101 Cherry Street
Burlington, VT 05401-4405
USA

Ashgate website: http://www.ashgate.com

British Library Cataloguing in Publication Data
Arthur, John A., 1958-
    The African diaspora in the United States and Europe : the
    Ghanaian experience. - (Research in migration and ethnic
    relations series)
    1. Ghanaians - United States - Social conditions
    2. Ghanaians - Europe - Social conditions 3. African
    diaspora 4. Ghana - Emigration and immigration 5. Ghana
    Social conditions 6. Ghana - Economic conditions 7. Ghana -
    Politics and government 8. United States - Emigration and
    immigration 9. Europe - Emigration and immigration
    I. Title
    304.8'09667

Library of Congress Cataloging-in-Publication Data
Arthur, John A., 1958-
    The African Diaspora in the United States and Europe : the Ghanaian experience / by
John A. Arthur.
        p. cm. -- (Research in migration and ethnic relations series)
    Includes bibliographical references and index.
    ISBN-13: 978-0-7546-4841-3
    ISBN-10: 0-7546-4841-9
    1. Ghana--Emigration and immigration. 2. Ghanaians--United States. 3. African
diaspora. I. Title.

    JV9022.3.A78 2008
    304.8'730667--dc22
                                                                    2007031231

ISBN 978 0 7546 4841 3

Printed and bound in Great Britain by TJ International Ltd, Padstow, Cornwall.

Contents

This book is dedicated to the celebration and the still flaming and living memories of Agnes Djomorkor Tagoe (Nii Ami), Kenneth Konuah Arthur (K.K.), and my dearest Uncle Benjamin Yarboi Akuetteh (B.Y.).
Nii Ami, thank you for your genteel, candor, and calming influences.
To Uncle Benjamin, thank you for shepherding and anchoring me, and for always teaching me by precept. In your collective dreams we all continue to strive and aspire in the global African diaspora. I am also indebted to the effervescence of Nana Adufua Makeeba Arthur for marking the continuity of these dreams, hopes, and aspirations.

Preface

Ghanaians wander and they are no strangers to migration. From time immemorial, they have wandered throughout Africa for purposes of trade, to look for work, improve upon their lives, or escape from the harsh and unforgiving economic and political morass at home. Today, a new form of their migratory behavior can be found in what is commonly referred to as the new global migration and transnational border crossings. This migration is characterized by the voluntary, and at times involuntary movement of skilled and unskilled population principally from the emerging nations of Africa, Latin America, the Caribbean, Asia, and the former Soviet Republics to the advanced industrial nations in the West, particularly the United States, Great Britain, France, Germany, the Netherlands, Canada, and Australia.

Responding to push-pull economic and political factors at home in Ghana and abroad, the Ghanaians who are featured in this study are fairly recent arrivals to the international labor market scene but their growing accomplishments and contributions in every aspect of human endeavor are enviable and noteworthy. Their strong work ethic, entrepreneurial acumen, cooperative familial spirit, and altruistic sense of community anchored in traditional Ghanaian ethos and mores provides them with the strategies to confront and deal with uncertainties such as racism, marginality, discrimination, and the status of being a foreigner, black, African, and outsider-looking-in. Their respective immigrant journeys and the accompanying niches that they carve for themselves give Ghana a strong presence in the transnational labor market. And the lessons that they learn while domiciled abroad, the assets, innovations, and skills, that they acquire ultimately transforms Ghana.

The majority of the Ghanaian émigrés intend for their sojourn abroad to be temporary. Once they have attained economic and cultural goals, most of them will repatriate to Ghana and assume various roles in tackling the monumental task of nation-building. In this process, they become change agents whose immigrant contributions enrich the social, cultural, and economic tapestries of Ghana; contributions that outweigh foreign bilateral and multilateral assistance to the country.

The major focus of this book is to present a sociological exposé of the Ghanaian diaspora in the United States and Europe. At the cusp of independence, Ghana enjoyed a period of economic stability. Buoyed by receipts derived from gold, cocoa, bauxite, and aluminum, the country was in a period of boom relative to other countries in the West African sub-region. Primary and secondary schools proliferated; so did post-secondary or tertiary institutions of learning. Many Ghanaians were sponsored abroad mainly to Great Britain and later to the United States by the government. Several also went on their own to pursue advanced degrees. The expectation was that those who went abroad will return and contribute their quota toward national development. Some returned, albeit briefly, but the majority stayed as economic and political conditions in the country deteriorated culminating in successive military interventions. Those who cannot afford to go to the West headed to oil-rich Nigeria. The saga of the worldwide Ghanaian brain drain had commenced. Part of the growing number of the contemporary black African community and diaspora that has formed in the West, the lived experiences of the Ghanaian émigrés resonates in the close-knit but often fragmented communities and identities that they create in their adopted countries to reflect their blackness, their Ghanaian, and by extension their African cultural heritage. When they have gone abroad to settle permanently or temporarily, Ghanaians have always created their cultural communities often accompanied by the panoply of their celebrated and colorful cultures. In this book, I unravel the contents of the diaspora communities that Ghanaians create and forge with members of the host societies where they are domiciled and the transnational links and networks that they establish with their kin folks at home.

In living among the immigrants and participating in the daily routines of their social world (weddings, funerals, parties, child-naming ceremonies, or the celebration of Independence Day on March 6), I have sought to bring individual and collective meanings as to why they left Ghana, the processes involved in undertaking their sometimes arduous journeys to the West, the formation of their families and kin group, institutional and benevolent organizations, their work and labor force participation, how they construct and express religious, racial, and ethnic global identities, the social world of the second generation youth, why they send remittances home, and their eventual repatriation.

From the northern plains of Minneapolis-St. Paul, Minnesota, in the heartland of America to Columbia, South Carolina, and Atlanta, Georgia to Houston in the American Southeast and Southwest; to the British West Midland cities of Coventry, and Warwick to the fertile farmlands of southern Italy to interview Ghanaian migrant farm workers, I tell the stories of some of the immigrants, giving voice to the unique circumstances that define the contextual nuances and vicissitudes of the respective communities that the immigrants engender to build thousands of miles away from home. In the end, the portrait that I seek to present is of a growing transnational community of Ghanaians in the diaspora who leave Ghana but never abandon the pride and shared sense of loyalty and nationalism that they share with their place of birth.

Considering that the majority of them leave home in the prime of their productive years, their continued departure and settlement away from home is bound to have manifest and latent consequences for the central government as it strives to implement economic and social development initiatives and schemes to ameliorate the massive problems confronting the country and improve upon the living standards of Ghanaians. In this book, I explore the role of the central government in the management of this brain drain and how the skills, resources, assets and the human capital that the immigrants create can be incorporated and integrated into the gigantic and often daunting process of nation-building. The management of international migration and its incorporation into the planning of economic development are delineated.

In writing this book, I benefited from numerous friends and colleagues. I owe a debt of gratitude to Geraldine Gomes Hughes for reading earlier drafts of this book and sharing with me her insightful and superb editorial skills. Her personal immigrant experiences brought with her from Malaysia to the United States often enabled me to see the cross-currents that shape and define the common threads that all immigrants, including myself, weave far away from home. Special thanks to Brandy Hoffman and LeAnne Rutherford, Department of Composition and Instructional Development Services respectively, for their insightful editorial comments and suggestions. I am very grateful to my friend, Bruce Mork who read and provided useful comments for the initial proposal. I convey my heartfelt gratitude and appreciation to all the Ghanaians that I met and interviewed in the course of collecting the information for this book. Thank you for opening up your homes to me, for letting me share in your various life-changing events; whether it was at the child-naming ceremonies, the celebration of the lives of your departed relatives, the parties that you organized to honor Ghana's Independence day, and for inviting me to your places of work and worship. I extend a special appreciation to all the immigrant children for sharing with me notions about the place of immigrant youth identity in the Ghanaian diaspora. I stand in awe of your energy, promise, courage, and forbearance. I am indebted and heartened by the Ghanaian migrant farmers in Southern Italy who broke bread with me under the shade made by the trees. One day we shall meet and break bread again under the same tree. I am thankful to the immigrant taxi drivers who took me to the homes of fellow Ghanaians. As we say in Ghana, to all of you, when morning breaks and you hear the cock crow, I say a big thank you. I am particularly thankful to Dr. Linda Krug, Dean of the College of Liberal Arts and Dr. Vince Magnuson, Vice-Chancellor for Academic Administration both at the University of Minnesota Duluth for providing me with research support.

John A. Arthur, Professor,
Former Head, Department of Sociology and Anthropology, and
Director, University of Minnesota Study in England Program,
Minnesota, USA

Chapter 1

The Ghanaian Diaspora in the United States: Setting, and Overview of Chapters

Throughout history, major migratory streams of people have left their countries of birth to seek better fortunes in far away lands. Sometimes, the mass migratory flows have been precipitated by religious persecution, famine, war, genocide, discrimination, economic dislocations, and diseases. Often, domestic and international schisms or natural disasters serve as push-pull factors to influence mass population outmigration. The saga of the Irish migration to the United States illustrates how domestic pressures set in motion by English conquest in the twelfth century resulted in bloodiness and repression that certainly contributed to Irish outmigration to North America.

During the first 50 years after the United States of America (USA) attained independence in 1776, the country admitted about 710,000 immigrants, chiefly from Western Europe. In a period spanning 108 years (1776–1884), America admitted approximately two immigrants per day. Between 1820 and 1880, most of the immigrants who settled in the USA came from Northern and Western Europe. At the beginning of the twentieth century, the bulk of immigrants to the USA continued to come from Europe, this time from Eastern Europe. During the 1990s, America admitted two immigrants per minute. The sheer magnitude of the flow of immigrants into the country is staggering. In 2001 alone, the USA admitted about one million legal immigrants as permanent residents.

Today, Africans are increasingly becoming a visible part of the migration of skilled and unskilled people leaving the developing countries to settle in the USA. However, as Kennedy (1996) pointed out, the voluntary and involuntary migration of peoples of black African descent to North America is not a recent event. Kennedy noted that after the discovery and settlement of the New World, Africans were brought in large numbers by the Europeans and settled in the Americas (as cited in Konadu-Agyemang et. al., 2006). During the Transatlantic slave trade, about 10 to 20 million Africans were forcefully transported to the USA in what is now described as the genesis of the black African diaspora in North and South America, and the Caribbean. For three hundred years, Africans were brought to the Americas as slaves and indentured workers in the agricultural plantations and mines (Gordon, 1998; Takougang, 1995). However, after slavery was abolished in the early nineteenth century, few Africans settled in the USA. Gordon indicates that between 1900 and 1950, only 31,000 Africans migrated to the USA.

According to immigration figures, from 1820 to 2000, only 689,084 Africans were lawfully admitted as immigrants (Table 2: United States Immigration and

Custom Enforcement Statistical Yearbook, 2000). During the same period, nearly nine million Asians, 17 million immigrants from Canada and Mexico, and 38 million Europeans were admitted as legal immigrants. Sanford Ungar (1995) attributed the low migration of Africans to the USA to the financial difficulties encountered in qualifying for visas, persistent racism toward people of color in America, the preference for immigrants of European stock over non-Europeans, and the sheer physical distance between Africa and North America which made it difficult, if not impossible, for Africans to engage in illegal border crossings. As a result of the difficulties Africans often encounter in migrating to the USA, their migration patterns have been highly selective. Those who are fortunate to be granted visas are some of the Continent's best and brightest, including the highly educated (usually those holding tertiary and post-secondary credentials), a professional and occupational cadre, and their families or dependents. In addition to the flux of educated and skilled immigrants, since 1980, several African refugees mainly from Somalia, Ethiopia, Eritrea, Liberia, Sierra Leone, and Sudan have settled in the USA. Forced to flee from their respective countries due to political and economic instability, the African refugees were admitted under the Refugee Act of 1980 which broadened the qualification for entry as a refugee to make it possible for stateless and uprooted persons from non-communist countries to enter the USA for resettlement.

Numerous factors gave impetus to a rise in African immigration. Following the attainment of political independence after World War II, several African countries started sponsoring students to pursue higher education in the USA. Now in control of their political and economic destinies following the demise of foreign colonization, these countries, including Ghana, saw the need to train a cadre of civil service personnel abroad to assist in the task of development and to manage bourgeoning social institutions and organizations. Furthermore, during and after the war, the USA rekindled its interests in the rich mineral and agricultural resources of Africa. Consequently, American institutions of higher learning granted scholarships under bilateral and multilateral agreements with several African countries to sponsor students to come to America. Africa became part of the USA's policy of containing global communism during the Cold War between East and West. The USA hoped the Africans sponsored by their governments would return home and occupy senior level government positions and assist in forging strong bonds of cooperation between the two continents (Takougang, 1995).

Ghanaian migration to the USA is also influenced by the Hart-Celler Act of 1965. The Hart-Celler Act of 1965 abolished the highly restrictive national origins quota system that had formed the fulcrum of American immigration policy since the 1920s. This legislation paved the way for prospective immigrants from non-European regions such as Africa, Asia, and Latin America to apply for visas to come to the USA. For Africans desirous of coming to the USA, this was a significant development. The opening up of visas for immigrants coincided with the end of foreign colonization in Africa and the subsequent attainment of independence by some of the countries of Africa. This meant that more Africans could immigrate to the USA. Even so, African migration was a mere trickle of the total number of immigrants who were coming from non-European countries.

Since the nineteenth century, the proportion of Africans who have been allowed to settle in the USA has not exceeded three per cent of the total number of immigrants who come to the country. However, despite this small number, the African-born population continues to show phenomenal increases. The peak period in the African-born immigrant population in the USA coincided with an overall surge in immigration to America. African migration to the USA peaked between 1981–1990 and 1991–2000. During these two decades the number of legal immigrants admitted into the country from Africa doubled, from 176,893 to 354,939 respectively. From 1980 to 2000, the African immigrant population grew fivefold with the peak period in this wave occurring in 1991 when a record 1.8 million people were granted legal status. According to the Census of the USA for 2000, the number of Africans (naturalized and unnaturalized citizens) living in the country increased to reach about 701,000 people. The majority of Africans entered the country after 1980. For those who are now naturalized citizens, 44.2 per cent entered before 1980; another 25 per cent entered between 1980 and 1984, and nearly 11 per cent entered between 1994 and 2000 (Table 7-1: United States Bureau of the Census, Current Population Survey: March 2000).

In particular, the growth in the sub-Saharan African-born immigrant population in the USA can be attributed to the continued political destabilization of the Continent often resulting in civil wars, ecological disasters, ethnic turmoil, incessant military coup d'état, erosion of civil society coupled with the absence of rule of law, still-born economic policies, and the internal and external involuntary uprooting or displacement of massive number of Africans from their homelands. Other factors spurring this migration include the proliferation of secondary and tertiary institutions of learning across Africa, information technology and exchanges, and the global incorporation of Africa into the world's economic system. In addition, the civil wars in the Horn of Africa during the 1980s involving Somalia, Ethiopia, and Eritrea, including the Sudanese crisis, brought thousands of Africans to the USA under the Refugee Act of 1980.

Ghanaian immigrants form a significant part of the total number of Africans who settle in the USA. During the decade of 1990 to 2000, the majority of African immigrants who were lawfully admitted to the USA came from Nigeria, Ethiopia, Egypt, Ghana, Somalia, Cape Verde, Sudan, Kenya, and South Africa (Table 3: United States Immigration and Customs Enforcement Statistical Yearbook, 2000). Ghanaian immigrants rank in the top five of the African immigrants who are legally admitted as permanent residents of the USA. From 1990–2000, immigration admitted a total of 40,104 Ghanaians as legal residents. Nearly a third of all Ghanaians admitted during the decade of 1990–2000 were admitted in fiscal years 1996 and 1997. Like other newcomers to America, Ghanaians are usually admitted as permanent residents under the lottery or Diversity Program, as immediate relatives (spouses, children, and parents) of American citizens, under family-sponsored preferences, and as political refugees and asylum seekers. Ghanaians have also been admitted as permanent residents under the third preference provision in immigration law which allows for foreign-born persons with exceptional skills to apply for employer sponsorships to become permanent or legal residents. Ghanaians also benefited from the Immigration Reform and Control Act (IRCA) of 1986, commonly known as the Simpson-Mazzoli

Act. Enacted to stem the tide of illegal migration from Mexico and Central America, and to impose sanctions on employers who knowingly hired illegal aliens, the IRCA made it possible for 2.7 million illegal aliens, including some Ghanaians, to gain amnesty by becoming permanent residents and eventually citizens of the USA. For Ghanaians who had acquired American citizenship, Congress offered an opportunity to allow the subsequent immigration of their well-educated and skilled relatives. Four years after the IRCA became law and in response to concerns from American business leaders that the USA was losing its competitive edge to other countries and to address a looming labor shortage, Congress passed the Immigration Act of 1990 which allowed the relatives of American citizens to be put on a fast track for permanent residency.

According to immigration and census data, Ghanaian immigrants admitted to the USA rank in the top one-quarter of the immigrant population and foreign-born stock of major metropolitan areas like Atlanta (Georgia) and the District of Columbia, including Baltimore (Maryland). In Minnesota, for example, the state's new foreign-born residents more than doubled in the 1990s, and Africans, mainly from Ghana, Sudan, Somalia, Liberia, and Ethiopia, are included in the phenomenal growth of the immigrant population who have recently moved to the state. Often these immigrants choose to reside in the Minneapolis-St. Paul metropolitan area and its surrounding suburbs and counties, including the St. Cloud and Rochester corridors. Minnesota's African immigrants come to the state to take advantage of the state's buoyant economy, its low rates of unemployment (a little over three per cent as opposed to five per cent at the national level), better educational opportunities, and the state's longstanding ethos of liberalism, tolerance, and diversity.

The geopolitical, economic, and social conditions of countries are important to the understanding of the reasons why people choose to leave their native lands and take up residence in another country. In the case of Ghana, the dynamic nature of push-pull factors in spurring large-scale international migration provide the contextual nexus within which to situate the ongoing wave of outmigration to foreign destinations, particularly to the West. Ghana's recent economic and political history and her status as an emerging nation certainly provide the prism through which we see why Ghanaians are leaving their homeland in unforeseen numbers.

Formerly known as the Gold Coast, Ghana occupies an area of about 92,100 square miles, roughly the size of Oregon in America. Formed from the merger of the British colony of the Gold Coast and the trust territory of Togoland, Ghana is bounded on the north by Burkina Faso, Togo to the east, the Ivory Coast to the west, and on the south by the Atlantic Ocean. The country derived its name from the ancient empire of Ghana. During the nineteenth century, the Ashanti Empire was a powerful kingdom state, virtually controlling the Akan people of the interior region of Ghana. The empire and its federation dominated the political and economic systems of the coastal regions as well and, at its zenith, controlled the bulk of trade that took place in the Gulf of Guinea.

Gold brought several European powers to the shores of Ghana, in particular, and the Gulf of Guinea, in general. The first to arrive by the end of the fifteenth century were the Portuguese, who set up a trading post and castle in 1482 at Elmina near Cape Coast. The Portuguese remained on the Gold Coast for almost a century. They found so much gold between the rivers Ankobra and the Volta that they named the place Mina, meaning "gold mine." The aim of the King, John II of Portugal, was to trade in gold, ivory, and slaves. The Portuguese were followed by the Dutch who in 1598 built forts at Komenda and Kormantsil. At the beginning of the sixteenth century, the slave trade slightly overshadowed the gold trade as the slave plantation economies expanded in the Americas and the Caribbean. Gold and the slave trade brought other Europeans to the coast of Ghana. The Dutch, Danes, and English all joined the Portuguese in the area known as the Gold Coast. The entire coastline of the Gold Coast was dotted by forts and castles all built by various European powers. In 1642, the Portuguese lost Elmina to the Dutch and left the Gold Coast permanently.

The Dutch and the British formed trading companies, the Dutch West Indian Company and the British African Company of Merchants. These companies were given licenses by the British and Dutch governments to trade overseas, especially in the Far East. By the early part of the nineteenth century, the British had managed to drive away the other European countries, leaving it as the sole European power in the Gold Coast. In 1874, the British established the Gold Coast Colony following the withdrawal of the Dutch from the Gold Coast. With the establishment of the colony, Britain started to gain a permanent foothold in the country by expanding its territorial sphere of influence into the interior. Using wars and treaties, the British were able to gain complete control over the country at the beginning of the twentieth century. Following a policy of indirect rule, the British colonial administration used local chiefs and traditional leaders to administer the colony of the Gold Coast.

During the period of British colonial rule, the Gold Coast made remarkable progress in economic and industrial activities. By 1948, the colony of the Gold Coast was described as a model colony with an economy and educational system that was the envy of British, French, and Portuguese Africa (Birmingham, 1998). The production of cocoa for export, the commercial mining of gold, the harvesting of timber, and an abundant supply of agricultural raw materials provided the resources for developing the infrastructure of the colony. The colony also became a supplier of raw materials to the factories of the British colonizers. Recognizing the importance of cocoa to the country's economy, the Cocoa Marketing Board (CMB) was created in 1947 to assist in the marketing of the country's major cash crop on the world commodity market and to provide production and marketing services to the farmers. By 1950, the Gold Coast had become the world's major supplier of cocoa, producing more than one half of the world's supply.

Receipts from the sale of cocoa on the world commodities exchange provided the country with ample foreign reserves to launch various capital projects such as the mass construction of primary and secondary schools. In 1948, the University College of the Gold Coast (later to become the University of Ghana) was established. Graduates from the secondary and tertiary educational system filled the jobs that were created by the colonial administration. Railroads and trunk roads were constructed to connect the major regional centers of commerce. By the beginning of the Second World War, the country boasted a cadre of well-educated statesmen and women, either educated locally or abroad in Great Britain. Among these were Dr. J.B. Danquah, John Mensah Sarbah, Dr. James Kwegyir Aggrey, George Ferguson,

William Ofori Atta, Obetsebi Lamptey, George Grant (Paa Grant), and Otumfuo Osei Agyeman Prempeh I. The Gold Coast had become the "Star of Black Africa."

The colony provided troops and military logistics to assist Britain in both World War I and II. The Gold Coast Regiment, numbering over 40,000 recruits, served with distinction in battles against German forces during World War II; soldiers from the Gold Coast also fought in Burma and Ethiopia. The post-war period represented a watershed in the political development of the Gold Coast. The returning soldiers who had fought alongside the British and European troops came home only to be confronted with poverty, unemployment, ill-health, and colonial racism. While serving in the war effort, the soldiers came to realize that their participation in the two wars was meant only to quell German and Japanese domination of Europe and Asia and provide self-determination for the people on the two continents. The moral pontification of the colonizers did not feature the liberation of Black Africa from European colonial domination or the need to grant self-determination to Africans.

The returning war veterans came to realize that colonization and its appendages were oppressive and dehumanizing. Suddenly, the ex-servicemen, joined by the local intelligentsia, recognized foreign colonization as a form of oppression, similar to the oppression they had fought against in Europe and Asia on behalf of the British. The soldiers won the war and returned home only to become perpetual paupers. Post-war wages lagged behind post-war prices of consumer items. Aided by an Accra sub-chief, the veterans helped stage a boycott of foreign goods. In 1948, they started to agitate for constitutional reform by staging a peaceful march to the Osu Christianborg Castle near Accra, seat of the British colonial administration. The purpose of the march was to call the governor's attention to the economic problems confronting the ex-servicemen. Near the entrance to the governor's residence, the colonial security forces opened fire, killing Sergeant Peter Adjetey, Corporal Attipoe, and Private Odartey Lamptey. The colonial administrators blamed the leaders of the United Gold Coast Convention (UGCC) party for the riots that ensued. They arrested the party's top leaders, known as the "big six:" Kwame Nkrumah, Obetsebi Lamptey, Akuffo Addo, Ako Adjei, J.B. Danquah, and Ofori-Atta. Riots, accompanied by looting, broke out in Accra and other regional centers in protest against the shooting incident. For the first time the British colonial administrators had been challenged openly in Africa. The irreversible struggle for independence from colonial domination had begun in black Africa. The shooting and the subsequent arrest of the "big six" galvanized local elites against imperial domination, exploitation, and empire building. The British government appointed a commission to investigate the shooting of the three ex-servicemen on February 28, 1948, but the investigation did not silence the agitation for political independence in the Gold Coast. It radicalized the leadership of the UGCC to demand an end to British political hegemony and grant the Gold Coast self-rule. Kwame Nkrumah, who had been educated in the USA and was serving as the secretary-general of the UGCC, recruited youth and cocoa farmers into the ranks of the UGCC. The youth movement of the party, consisting of young men and women who had little or no education, rallied around Nkrumah's slogan of "Africa for the Africans." They organized rallies and political education for urban and rural folks. The cocoa farmers were concerned that the British colonial government paid them far less for their produce than what the colonial government was paid overseas for selling the cocoa on the world market. The fortunes of the cocoa farmers started to wane as the cocoa swollen shoot disease and falling prices decimated their profits. Their disenchantment was capitalized upon by Nkrumah who mobilized the farmers, farm laborers, and the traditional chiefs to confront the colonial administration over the prices paid to farmers. While this mobilization was going on, Nkrumah expanded the base of his political protest movement against the colonial government by bringing in the powerful "Makola" women traders, the trade unions, and the railroad and transportation workers. By widening his political sphere of influence, Nkrumah succeeded in putting pressure on the British colonial government for constitutional reform by advocating for "positive action" or civil disobedience, strikes, and demonstrations.

The British yielded to Nkrumah's populist approach and called the first-ever elections in Black Africa in 1951 in the Gold Coast. Nkrumah's Convention People's Party (CPP) won. Following Nkrumah's election victory, the British were compelled to release him from prison and made him Leader of Government Business. In becoming leader of government affairs, Nkrumah acquired the political legitimacy and the skills that he needed to become a national leader. This position also accorded him an opportunity to negotiate the political and economic future of the Gold Coast with the British colonial administration.

The agitation for political independence continued throughout the early part of the 1950s. Finally on March 6, 1957, the Gold Coast became the first country in colonial Africa to gain independence from a major European power, Great Britain. The country was renamed Ghana, its original name. Ghana's hard-won fight for self-determination spread like wildfire to British West Africa as Nigeria, Sierra Leone, and Gambia gained their independence. The political agitation spawned by the independence movement also swept across British East Africa, forcing the British to grant independence to Kenya, Tanzania, Uganda, and Malawi.

Post-Independence and the Modern Era

Ghana's new leaders faced the monumental tasks of national reconstruction and the integration of diverse ethnic and tribal groups into the new nation-state. Equally daunting was the task of building the country's economy and infrastructures. The period following independence was marked by the construction of roads, schools, and hospitals. To cater to the healthcare needs of its citizens, community health centers known as polyclinics were constructed throughout the country. Feeder roads to connect major agricultural produce centers were built. The central government established produce marketing boards such as the Cocoa Marketing Board (CMB) to purchase and market the country's agricultural commodities on the world market and to provide farmers with the financial resources they needed to improve their yields. Two ports, Tema and Takoradi, were built and later expanded to facilitate the country's export and import sectors. The educational infrastructure of the country improved and expanded with the construction of secondary and tertiary institutions of learning. Primary schools became free to all. At the regional levels, Polytechnics were set up in every administrative region of the country. Teacher training institutions also proliferated. At the university level of education, Kwame Nkrumah University of Science and Technology and the University of Cape Coast were constructed. The country's flagship institution, the University of Ghana at Legon was expanded to accommodate an increase in student placements. And for more than two decades after independence, the country's universities and training colleges were among the best in Black Africa, supplying teachers and experts to countries such as Nigeria in the West and Kenya and Uganda to the East. The country was viewed by the international community as the "Gateway to Africa," and the country's domestic economy was also among the most productive in Black Africa.

The post-independence momentum that the country had enjoyed came to a halt less than ten years after the British left the country. On February 24, 1966, a group of army cum police personnel led by Colonel Emmanuel Kotoka, Major Akwesi Amankwa Afrifa, Lieutenant-General Joseph Arthur Ankrah, and Inspector General of Police John William Harlley overthrew the civilian and democratically elected government of Nkrumah in a coup, and formed the National Liberation Council (NLC), which reigned from 1966–1969. This first military coup of its kind in Black Africa was staged in response to perceived economic corruption, thefts of state properties by top government officials, and political abuse of power on the part of the Nkrumah regime. Before the NLC could consolidate its power, attempts were already underway to stage coups and counter coups to destabilize the new government. Two abortive coups were staged by the military in 1967 and 1968 in an attempt to forestall the Nkrumah government's return to office. The coup plotters were tried, found guilty, and executed. In 1969, the NLC returned the country to civilian rule under Prime Minister Dr. Kofi Abrefa Busia, but Busia's civilian regime was short lived. The military did not give Busia's government enough time to address the mounting economic problems confronting the nation. In 1972, Colonel Ignatius Kutu Acheampong seized power in a military takeover and established the National Redemption Council (NRC) which became the ruling government of the country.

Under Acheampong's tenure (1972–1978), the economic, social, and political fortunes of the country worsened. Shortages of essential commodities posed serious threats to stability. Prices skyrocketed and citizens had to queue for essential commodities and consumer goods such as bread, toilet paper, and other items such as milk and sugar. Corruption permeated the entire fabric of the culture. Meanwhile, the intelligentsia and university students organized to protest the policies of the government, which brought them into violent contact with the military and police forces. Acheampong's regime was marked by a militarized order. In his attempt to end party politics in Ghana and create a unified government, Acheampong alienated the rank and file of the country, leaving only the Supreme Military Council (SMC) that he had formed as his main political ally.

The domination of the military in the political life of the country continued into the late 1970s with another aborted coup led by Flight Lieutenant Jerry John Rawlings on May 15, 1979. The leaders of this coup were arrested, brought before a court martial, and imprisoned. On June 4 of that same year, military personnel entered Burma Camp (military headquarters), freed Rawlings, and launched a successful coup d'état. The Armed Forces Revolutionary Council (AFRC), led by Rawlings, became the new government of the country. This government stayed in power from May 15 to June 4,

1979 before handing over power to another civilian government headed by Dr. Hilla Limann. As in the past, Limann's civilian government did not have enough time to buckle down to the business of running the country. Rawlings intervened again on December 31, 1981, seized power in a coup (the eighth military takeover since 1966) and formed the Provisional National Defense Council (PNDC).

The second Rawlings government was very popular with the rank and file Ghanaians though the populism style of the government did not prevent coup attempts throughout the 1980s, all which were foiled. Rawlings's PNDC government attempted to forge a government of national unity comprising military and civilians. Noble as this gesture was, it fell short of silencing opposition to PNDC rule which came from students, professional bodies like the Ghana Bar Association, the trade unions, and the Popular Front Party and People's National Party. Some opponents of the PNDC fled into exile, accusing the Rawlings government of human rights violations, rigid control of the press, and political terror. Many Ghanaians became fearful of the PNDC as it became more militarized in spite of adopting a populist governance style. Under the PNDC, institutions to mobilize grassroots support for the government were created to involve ordinary Ghanaians in running the affairs of the state. Committees such as the Citizen Vetting Committee, the Worker's Defense Committee, and the People's Defense Committee were established to serve as watchdogs against political and economic corruption and to bring to justice those found guilty. However, the members of the citizen vetting committees, including the public tribunals, were not adequately schooled in matters of political governance. They intimidated many Ghanaians at all levels of society. The rule of law and civil democratic principles were sacrificed, and a dark cloud of political cynicism and threats came to dominate the national character and discourse of Ghana.

The political uncertainties aggravated the myriad of problems facing the economy which still remained mired in hyperinflation, near empty foreign reserves, and low production capacity. To grow the economy, the PNDC took a number of initiatives. Notable among these was the Economic Recovery Program (ERP), launched in 1983 to address the country's economic stagnation. By all accounts, the PNDC made substantial progress with this initiative, reducing inflation, paying down the national debt, and growing the economy by increasing agricultural exports. This initial success revived international confidence in the PNDC, thus paving the way for massive infusions of international development assistance and loans which were used to improve roads, boost agricultures, restructure the civil service, and implement fiscal reforms. This assistance also enabled the reorganization of state-owned corporations under a divestiture policy which was aimed at their privatization. Under the privatization program, the government's shares in state-owned limited liability companies were to be sold to private interests. The structural adjustments that arose from these initiatives proved to be economically burdensome for ordinary Ghanaians; lay-offs from the civil service and redeployment of state workers caused trepidation, for example. Hardest hit by the structural alignment of the country's economy were wage earners, civil servants, farmers, and rural folks. Even the elites were hit hard as well.

Angered by the extent of the reforms, Ghanaians started calling on the PNDC to return the country to civilian and constitutional rule. In response to this pressure, the PNDC set up the National Commission for Democracy (NCD) headed by Justice Daniel F. Annan. The commission was given the mandate to draft a workable democratic system that would include all Ghanaians in the political decision process. One of the recommendations of the NCD was the call to organize district assemblies to make it possible for local districts to involve their members in political decision making. With this move, the PNDC's grip on power began to loosen. In 1988, district assembly elections were held throughout the country. A consultative assembly was appointed to draft a new constitution for the country. The momentum toward constitutional and political party rule in Ghana had begun, once again. A national referendum was held on April 28, 1992 to approve the new constitution.

Under the new constitution, an Executive President would be chosen to govern the country for a four-year term with eligibility to seek a second and final term. In the ensuing national elections that took place on November 3, 1992, Rawlings' party, National Democratic Congress (NDC), garnered almost 60 per cent of the votes. With the subsequent parliamentary elections held on December 29, 1992, a new era dawned in Ghana politics. Rawlings became the new President assisted by Kow Nkensen Arkaah as Vice-President, and Justice Daniel F. Annan as the Speaker of Parliament. With the Fourth Republic inaugurated, Ghana was once again on the road to parliamentary and constitutional democracy. Rawlings's NDC party sought and successfully won another four-year term in 1996, defeating the main opposition party, the New Patriotic Party (NPP). Again, moderate improvements occurred in the infrastructure of the country, especially on road construction in rural and urban areas. The perennial problem of food supply, always a politically volatile issue, was abated. Public confidence in social institutions to ameliorate pressing social problems started to improve. On December 7, 2001, democracy and constitutional rule were again given another opportunity to thrive as Ghanaians went to the polls to elect a new President and members of parliament. The opposition party NPP were swept to office, replacing Rawlings' NDC party. The NPP which was led by Dr. John Agyekum Kufuor became the new government, thus bringing to an end almost 20 years of Rawlings's tenure as a political figure in Ghana politics. Following the national elections in that year, the NPP was elected to power, winning one hundred of the two hundred parliamentary seats with the NDC taking 92 seats. The remaining eight seats went to the small parties. Ghana had endured a smooth political transition through the ballot box, a positive affirmation of democratic and representative governance. Kufuor was sworn into office on January 7, 2001, and became the first Ghanaian president to unseat another president elected at the polls.

In a sense, Ghanaians are still grappling with how to transform their naturally rich nation to the status of an economically self-sufficient, politically free, democratic, and civil society. The geopolitical environment of Ghanaian society since political independence in 1957 reveals that for almost twenty-one years, the country remained under military tutelage and hegemony. True multi-party politics is in its infancy, only in place for sixteen years since the country attained political autonomy from British rule. The current constitutional and political environment of Ghana is, indeed, very fragile. Lack of confidence in the country's political and economic systems continues to threaten an already fragile experimentation with democracy. The short- and long-term effects of the political and economic instability that has plagued the country since 1966 have been devastating to a once thriving and buoyant economy. Those who can afford to leave the country have done so and, for those remaining, the possibility of future emigration continues to dominate the lives of thousands more. For most Ghanaians, going abroad, mainly to the West, has come to assume a strategic significance, a way of coping with economic depression and political insecurity, thus making Ghana an immigrant-sending country.

Overview of Chapters

The over-arching theme of this book is the formation and continuity of the Ghanaian immigrant diaspora in the West. The book is predicated on the basic premise that like other developing countries, Ghana has become incorporated into the global economic system of which international migration of skilled and unskilled labor is an important dimension. The tone of each chapter points to one fundamental reality: that for a growing number of Ghanaians, international migration has become the dominant means whereby people achieve social mobility, acquire the resources and human capital to economically sustain themselves and their families, and at the same time forge a cross-national identity whose primary goal is to link Ghanaians to the centers of global labor markets in the West.

Chapter Two examines the aims of this study and provides an in-depth analysis of the methods and techniques used in collecting the data for this study. Chapter Three discusses the proximate causes of Ghanaian migration to the United States and the West as a whole. The chapter highlights the social and cultural processes influencing the decision to travel abroad. The chapter positions the causes of Ghanaian migration within the framework of extended family relationships and the collective efforts that have come to form the culture of going abroad in Ghana. In particular, the push-pull factors that operate in Ghana and the United States are ascertained, including the cultural, economic, and political environments that have come to dominate and shape the imperative of going abroad among Ghanaians. The section examines the normative and cultural phenomena that Ghanaians have come to associate with going abroad: the factors that prospective immigrants weigh before undertaking the journey to the West, the role of family-sponsored migration, and the use of collective resources to maximize the economic fortunes of the migrants' extended family unit.

Chapter Four highlights the structure and composition of the Ghanaian immigrant families. Case studies of selected immigrant families are used to present a portrait and the inner workings of the families. Specific focus is placed on the gender relations and the formation of social networks to confront economic and social realities brought upon by living in a new cultural setting. The chapter highlights the sociological continuity of family roles among the immigrants and the power and status relations that are forged in the interactions between women and men. It accentuates the role and impact of international migration and education on women's lives and how migration affords Ghanaian immigrant women the opportunity to define new identities for themselves, to renegotiate new familial relationships with their husbands, and at the same time to affirm their traditional feminine roles.

Chapter Five is about the carving of identity. It examines the processes involved in the shaping of the immigrants' ethnic and racial identities, and the institutional apparatus that they form to negotiate entry into the affairs of the host society. Negotiating and expressing racial and ethnic identity among the immigrants is framed not only by how they define and bring meaning to their subordinate, outsider-looking-in, and foreigner status, but also to the immigrants' notions about their blackness, African-ness, and transnational status. The chapter stresses the coping strategies used by the immigrants to confront and deal with racism and discrimination. In staying connected to their Ghanaian and African roots as well as defining identities that transcend national borders, immigrants to America and the West have succeeded in lessening the deleterious impact of experiences with denigration and racial discrimination.

Like other immigrants to the USA, the Ghanaians who have settled in the West form institutions and organizations to connect them to their homeland and at the same time assist their integration and incorporation into the affairs of the host societies. These institutions and organizations are sometimes formed across ethnic, religious, and educational lines. They also include immigrant mutual aid, benevolent associations, and secondary group networks that form to anchor the immigrants in Ghanaian cultural heritage and provide economic and psychological support to the immigrants. The Ghanaian immigrants spend a significant portion of their time attending Ghanaian-based social functions like weddings, funerals, parties, celebration of Ghana's Independence Day, and child-naming ceremonies. Collectively, these social activities serve to affirm the cultural panoply of the immigrants while garnering the resources and social capital of the immigrants as they forge and define their membership in foreign societies. Chapter Six highlights the nature of these immigrant associations and institutions, stressing their role in the formation and continuity of the Ghanaian diaspora. The chapter also unravels the pathways of naturalization and citizenship among the immigrants and the formation of transnational spaces and identities among the immigrants.

Chapter Seven focuses on the construction and negotiation of identity among the second generation immigrant youth. The chapter highlights how the youth define, represent, and bring meaning to their own identities. The chapter explores the social and cultural nexus of the relationships that immigrant youth form with other teenagers, including their first-generation parents, and the society at large. The overlapping nature of the multiple identities that the youth form and sustain are explored within the broader contexts of minority–majority youth interactions in a race and identity-conscious society such as the USA. Narratives and personal experiences from some of the youth are used to illustrate the multiple and ever-shifting identities of the immigrant youth.

Chapter Eight provides an exposé of remittance flows and their role in the formation of the Ghanaian diaspora and national economic and social development. The majority of Ghanaian immigrants come to the USA to fulfil predetermined economic and cultural goals. The economic and cultural goals are intended to raise their standard of living and build upon the immigrants' human capital potential. The immigrants seek for themselves and their families back home in Ghana a standard of living that is higher than the one they were accustomed to while living in Ghana.

Toward this end, the benefits that accrue from migration are shared with family members at home through remittance flows. The chapter notes that the Ghanaian immigrants' perception about prevailing social and economic conditions at home, their economic status, and individual and family attributes (age, educational attainment, marital status, length of stay abroad) determines the frequency and amount of money remitted home, the uses of the remittance, and the short- and long-term repatriation plans of the immigrants.

When people migrate, it is usually assumed that the settlement is permanent. However, a common theme in the migratory experiences of Ghanaians is the temporality or sojourner status that the immigrants portray. Home looms very large in the minds of Ghanaian immigrants abroad. In the Ghanaian psyche, international migration is seen as a temporary journey to escape the grinding economic malaise confronting the country. Ultimately, the immigrants desire to return home either for a permanent or temporary resettlement. Chapter Nine describes the determinants of return migration and repatriation to Ghana. It focuses on the relationship between return migration and economic and social development in Ghana by highlighting the role of immigrant returnees in Ghana's development efforts. The chapter identifies and discusses the factors that facilitate and constrain the re-entry and reintegration of returnees into the body polity of Ghanaian society.

Ghanaians have become active participants in the new global migration. Chapter Ten expands on the transnational and immigrant journeys of the Ghanaian diaspora to the West. It draws upon the life experiences of Ghanaians in the British West Midlands and Southern Italy. The purpose of the chapter is to present a portrait of the Ghanaian diaspora in the European Union and identify any commonalities with the Ghanaian migration to the USA. In broadening the scope of the Ghanaian diaspora to Europe, the chapter seeks to unravel how the immigrants encounter and confront racial and ethnic discrimination in Europe, their attitudes toward improving upon the socioeconomic conditions in Ghana, including the prospects for future repatriation and implications for the reversal of the Ghanaian brain drain. It provides a preliminary sketch of the Ghanaian migrant farm workers, several of whom entered Italy by crossing the Sahara desert to reach the Mediterranean and, ultimately, Southern Italy. The chapter ends with a brief discussion of the theoretical and methodological implications of the Ghanaian diaspora for the development of meta-theories of international migration.

Chapter Eleven presents a summary of the key findings from this study and examines the Ghanaian government's policies on the international migration of its citizens. When migrants cross international boundaries and seek to establish a temporary or permanent residency in another country, the process often triggers a response from the governments of the immigrant-receiving countries. The responses may take the form of restrictive policies and tougher immigration policies designed to limit the number of both legal and illegal immigration. Successive governments of Ghana have looked at Ghanaian migration as an individualistic decision which people make in order to seek better economic and cultural opportunities for themselves and their families outside the country. Historically, the economic ramification of the brain drain and the loss of the country's professional cadres have not been incorporated into economic development planning schemes. With a fragile economy, high population growth rate, massive debt problem, and acute foreign reserves due to a weak export-driven manufacturing base, the management of the economic aspect of the country's migration policies assumes a critical importance. As Afolayan (2001) points out, the formulation and management of policies to deal with emigration from the developing countries may lie at the heart of resolving some of the structural imbalances in countries like Ghana that are losing much of their skilled labor to the West. The chapter highlights the measures and policies that the Ghana government can implement to stem the flow of its skilled and unskilled workers to the West. Measures taken by the government to assist in the repatriation and resettlement of Ghanaians are discussed. The chapter examines the goals of Ghana's migration policy and seeks to illuminate the processes involved in managing international migration as a vital component of Ghana's economic and political development.

Chapter 2

Aims of Study and Data Collection

As risk takers, people who leave their countries of origin to become immigrants become the focus of scholarly attention. Whether they are welcomed with open arms as legal residents or forced by legal and political considerations to remain underground as illegal aliens, immigrants who come to America have always been very fascinating people. Immigrants enrich the American immigrant cultural quilt, and bring added value to the economy of the country through the variety of skills that they contribute to American society and the West as a whole. As they engage in the affairs of their new societies, immigrants provide cultural and economic enrichment and add to the tapestry of life. Intellectual curiosity pervades their sometimes effervescent and ambitious fervour, their triumphs, hopes, sorrows, and unmet needs. Wave after wave of immigrants from Europe have come to the shores of the USA seeking economic, cultural and political freedom. Africans who migrate to the USA are no different.

Part of the contemporary African diaspora in the USA, the immigrant experiences of the Ghanaian-Americans currently living in the USA have yet to be systematically documented. Past and current studies on the "old" and "new" immigration have focused on European immigrants, and recently on Asians and immigrants from South and Central America. The rapid increase in the number of Ghanaians lawfully admitted into the country as permanent residents since 1980 provides an opportunity to investigate the varying degrees of the historical experiences of Ghanaian immigrants in the USA, focusing on their immigrant journeys, the ways they seek membership in their new society, and how they express their individual and collective social and cultural identities. In highlighting the diasporic and immigrant sojourn of Ghanaians in the USA, this study seeks to investigate the factors that shape and influence the outcomes of international migration among Ghanaians and to underscore the broader socioeconomic changes in Ghana that underlie the growing trend of out-migration of Ghanaians to the Western world.

A central theme of this book is the attention it gives to the experiences of the immigrant and transnational journeys of Ghanaians who have settled in the USA. The aim is to provide a sociological exposé of the Ghanaian immigrant diaspora. The international migratory behavior of Ghanaians is cast within a perspective that recognizes the varied and multiple socioeconomic, cultural, and political contexts in which the immigrants connect with their host societies and communities as well as the ones they left behind at home. Their migration journeys and experiences are not seen as isolated and singular events that are characterized by moving or relocating to a specific location or country. Rather, their migratory experiences are conceived as an attempt to forge a transnational identity that links them to many countries. Though the primary emphasis is on the immigrants who have settled in the USA, attention is also focused on the experiences of Ghanaian immigrants living in the European Union (British West Midlands and Southern Italy). One of the goals is to provide a lens through which to document the contents of the cross-national immigrant journeys of the Ghanaians who have settled abroad and to delineate differences and similarities in the diaspora experiences of the Ghanaians who have settled in the USA and Europe.

The study seeks to provide a systematic exposé of the macro-level factors that spur Ghanaian migration to the West by highlighting the sociological, political, cultural and economic determinants or the push-pull factors of Ghanaian migration. The Ghanaian-American immigrant experiences are extremely dynamic in form, continually unfolding, and shaped by forces that operate in both the USA, and Ghana, and at the global level. International migration is a major component in the global exchanges of human and natural resources, and of capital transfer. It is triggered, in part, by technology, greater international interdependency, the expansion in economic and industrial activities, growing global inequalities in consumption patterns and standards of living, improved communications and transportation, and the relationships that are forged when people enter into marital unions with persons outside of their countries of origin. The underlying motivational factors that spur migratory and population mobility flows across international boundaries are as varied as the individuals and the groups they represent.

The study delineates the incentives and disincentives that operate at the local, regional, and international levels in Ghana as well as the destination source that motivates the migratory flows of Ghanaians to the USA. The push-pull factors are cast within broad theoretical formulations that enable the identification of paradigms to describe the full spectrum of the international migratory experience from the Ghanaian and African perspectives. Ultimately, the analysis seeks to explain the migration flow of Ghanaians to the West as a complex set of inter-relationships that link nations characterized by economic interdependency and technological transfer of human and natural resources from one region of the world to another. The aim is to situate the major formation and development of Ghanaian immigration and the forces that influence this migration. The expectation is that, by bringing out the sociological determinants about how Ghanaians create and are recreated by the global process of migration, I will be able to show the specific and broad relationship Ghanaian immigrants have with the growing foreign-born population residing in the USA and Europe.

The Dynamic Nature of the Ghanaian Diaspora

The realities of the Ghanaian-American immigrant life are forever changing. These changes are spurred by a myriad of internal factors and conditions in Ghana such as the economic, political, and social systems of the country. In addition, global economic factors such as the transnational movement of skilled labor from developing to developed countries as well as changes occurring in immigration policies in the West also affect the changing nature of Ghanaian migration. To document the processes that shape these changes, this book uses the Ghanaian immigrant community as a unit of analysis to track the experiences of immigrant families and individuals who have settled in the United States and give voice to what it means to be Ghanaian-American. The study articulates the migratory experiences of the immigrants' household, along with the daily decisions and processes involved in how the immigrants negotiate entry into the affairs of their newly adopted society. The analysis depicts the dynamic interactions between the immigrants and the community contexts within which immigrants' expectations, hopes, aspirations, and fears become actualized. It links Ghanaian immigrants to the "new" global migration and documents the intervening variables that define and characterize the formulation of the intent to migrate, as well as the actualization of that motivation. The voices and faces of these Ghanaians, less often heard or seen in national media discourses, resonate in tones that are vivid and lucid. They speak with a rich range of accents and voices, of diverse encounters, experiences, and expectations, capturing the fullness of the black African kaleidoscope in the West. Altogether, these voices and immigrant conversations reveal the rich cultural melody that dominates the creation of the Ghanaian (African) spirit, character, and essence. In the end, these voices all speak to a common unity of purpose: the celebration of the continuity of Ghanaian and African immigrant diaspora in the West.

In this book, the international migratory process is seen as a rational and calculated behavior that is designed to improve upon the human capital and standards of living of the Ghanaians who have undertaken the journey to America. Recognition is given to the fact that migration is not a static or fixed process, but rather is very dynamic in its complex forms. Understanding the forces that motivate people to migrate to other destinations must be balanced with the expectations, if any, that accompany the return migration or repatriation process. This study directs attention to the phenomena of reverse or return migration to Ghana. The issues that are addressed include the following: the determinants of return migration among Ghanaians who have settled in the USA, whether return migration is influenced by the same factors that trigger migration in the first place, the factors that hamper or facilitate the reintegration of the returnees into the mainstream of Ghanaian society, how the returnees resolve these constraints, and the impact that the returnees have on their communities. The answers to these questions are important in delineating the contextual factors inherent in the return migratory process. The information that is collected speaks to the critical relationship between the international migration of Ghanaians and the brain drain, that is, the impact of heavy migration on a developing country like Ghana's economic and social progress as it continues to lose a large share of its skilled and unskilled population to the West. At the same time, the discussion of Ghanaian immigrant return migration sheds light on the micro and macro elements in accounting for why people move or stay. Central to the above considerations is the role of the national government in the management of return migration. The Ghana government is committed to harnessing the potential and skills of the immigrants who do repatriate because it has economic and social implications in defining specific modalities of national development and possible course(s) of action. These modalities are needed to implement policies aimed at the short- and long-term transformation of Ghana's staggering economy into a vibrant, advanced economy. Increasingly, returning Ghanaian migrants are becoming an important cog in the wheel of national development. A systematic approach to understanding the dynamics of return migration to Ghana and the role that returnees play in assisting Ghana's development is imperative.

This book also explores the processes involved in the individual and collective forms of how Ghanaian immigrants abroad construct and negotiate racial, ethnic, and class identity. For a majority of the Ghanaians who have settled in the West, central questions exist as cross currents influencing the social construction and depiction of Ghanaian immigrant identity. What does it mean to be a Ghanaian-American in the racial, class, and ethnic mosaics of the USA? To what extent are the immigrants able to assimilate into the mainstream society, and what do they stand to risk or gain by forging and creating their distinctive identities? My interest is to highlight the processes by which racial, class, and ethnic categorizations are established, asserted, or reproduced to confront immigrants' perceived sense of marginalization, denigration, and alienation. Ultimately, my goal is not only to highlight the process of racial, class, and ethnic identity formations from an individualistic basis but instead, from a perspective that appreciates the larger identities Ghanaians construct for themselves or that have become assigned to them on the basis of their membership in an ever-changing American ethnic mosaic. Racial, class, and ethnic identities, once constructed, have ramifications, intended and unintended, that are bound to be epiphenomenal for any social group. A source of pride, identity, and nationalism, racial and ethnic characterizations in a mosaic and multicultural society are a major site for conflict, division, social strain, cooperation, or accommodation. This book investigates strategies for coping with the fragmented racial and ethnic polarizations in the USA and the contents of the new multiethnic intersections that arise from these constructions. As Milton Vickerman (1999) points out, for black Caribbean and blacks in the diaspora who settle in the USA, the strategies for coping with the realities of *de facto* and *de jure* discrimination become significant in light of the continued legacies and vestiges of discrimination in the USA. As minorities in a race conscious society, the social and cultural processes involved in how the new black immigrants construct and interpret race identities ultimately determine the form(s) of inclusion and incorporation that the new immigrants will form with the majority society.

Immigrant institutional adaptation is an important facet in the making of immigrant identities in host nations. As more and more Ghanaians enter the USA, they begin to develop their own institutions which they sometimes transplant from home and bring to the USA and the West as a whole. These institutions include the immigrant mutual benefit and benevolence societies, religious institutions, and other immigrant social organizations designed to assist them to adapt to their new lives. They fulfil a dual purpose—to help the immigrants adapt to the expectations of the new society, and at the same time anchor the immigrants in the values and traditions of Ghanaian society. The social constructions of these organizations and immigrant-based institutions are discussed and their role in the integration of the immigrants assessed.

In addition, attention is focused on the contexts of the relationship Ghanaians establish with other immigrants of the new global migration in general, and with members of the native-born black diaspora in the USA. Attitudes and sentiments of the immigrants regarding racial stratification and the black and white split are cast within the broader contexts of racial and ethnic policies in the USA. Like any other immigrant group attempting to gain a foothold in a race-conscious society, Ghanaians living in the USA, to some extent, are like ethnographers attempting to unravel the contents of the community of America in its rudimentary and complex social and cultural forms. The knowledge that the immigrants gain about America become recipes for action to fulfil unmet needs in their individual and collective lives.

This book seeks to map out the multiple representations of the Ghanaian immigrant in the body polity of American society. It explores sociological continuities and a broad range of themes in the Ghanaian immigrants' journey to America (family and religious formations, work and occupational participation, immigrant social networks, education, and human resource utilization. By highlighting the immigrants' patterns of adaptation, acculturation, assimilation, settlement, social network support systems, mutual aid, family formation, gender-centered roles, and second-generation youth identities, this book is an attempt to understand the complex ways by which the Ghanaians who come to the USA and the West mix or remix their lives with those of the host society and in so doing, carve out new lives for themselves and make America more diverse.

A major focus of this book is the historical, social, political, and economic processes which have created the structures within which the decision to migrate is made. This approach allows for the consideration of the internal conditions that spur international migration from Ghana. It also sheds light on the broad social changes generated by local, international economic, and political exigencies, and how these changes influence the international migratory decision-making process of Ghanaians. For Ghana and many developing countries, international migration has become the dominant strategy whereby skilled and unskilled persons move to the Western economies in search of higher paying jobs and better standards of living. The sociological explanation of how these global contexts and modes of incorporation are formed via migration becomes significant in the understanding of the relative contributions that migrants make to the development of the host and sending countries respectively.

The expectations and responsibilities associated with coming to the USA are great and pose a daunting challenge for the immigrants. The immigrants' families at home depend on the goodwill and generosity of the Ghanaian immigrants who are domiciled abroad to remit funds and alleviate the harsh economic conditions and poverty that characterizes the lives of most Ghanaians. Remittance flows from abroad to the families of the immigrants in Ghana have become an important component of economic consumption as well as production in Ghana. This study highlights the role of remittance flows in the national reconstruction effort in Ghana and how foreign remittance is changing the multiple landscapes of Ghanaian lives in areas such as gender relations, economic development, and community social change. A common theme is how the remittance behavior of the Ghanaian immigrants is formed by their individual and collective perceptions of their international and diasporic experiences, and identities. The focus on remittance flows is important in delineating the impact of international migration on Ghanaian social structure especially the household unit, and how households in turn utilize the remittances they receive from their kin folks abroad to fulfil their economic needs.

The focus on the interlocking transnational relationships and identities of the migratory experiences of the Ghanaian immigrants is significant because it introduces a new dimension in the study of the new African diaspora to the West. The Ghanaians shape and are shaped by the global process of migration. The images and networks Ghanaians who have migrated to the West form across borders continue to provide them with alternatives and options to deal with and confront the myriad of social, economic, and political problems plaguing their country. As Steven Gold (2001) points out, "transnationalism proposes that by retaining social, cultural and economic connections with many settings, people can surmount the impediments traditionally associated with long distances and international borders." The complexities involved in the creation and nurturing of these transnational immigrant networks are such that they highlight a fundamental aspect of human nature: the need or desire to shape new patterns of existence and adaptation, and to organize collective resources to ensure survival in a global economy and geopolitical world system that is increasingly characterized by competition, conflicts, and occasionally cooperation. With the Ghanaians who come to the West, the forging of this identity takes the form of the connections and interconnections they form with their host societies as well as the home country. Pointedly, the new identities Ghanaians continue to carve become contextualized within the framework and vicissitudes of structured global processes and transplanted diasporic communities.

Data Collection and Field Ethnography

Multiple data techniques were used to collect the information for this book. Standardized and semi-standardized face-to-face interviews were administered to a non-random probability sample of 1200 Ghanaian immigrants living in seven major areas of the United States: the Midwest (Minneapolis-St. Paul, Minnesota); the Northeast (Newark, New Jersey); the mid-Atlantic region (Washington, D.C.); the Southeast (Fairfax and Alexandria, Virginia; Columbia, South Carolina); and the Southwest (Houston, Texas). Demographic considerations influenced the decision to focus on these particular urban and regional centers. Official USA Census and immigration service data reveal that the Northeast, mid-Atlantic, Southeast, Southwest, and Midwest regions are the preferred residential settlements of the majority of African émigrés, including those from Ghana. As their numbers increase, some of the Africans are settling away from the northern and Southeast corridors of the USA by moving to the heartland of America, particularly Minneapolis-St. Paul, Chicago, Columbus, Cleveland, and Milwaukee.

The data collection phase lasted for three years. The purpose of the interviews was to collect baseline qualitative and quantitative information about the Ghanaian immigrants. Aside from basic classificatory and demographic information such as the age, gender, educational background, marital status, and the occupation of the respondents, the interviews focused on a wide range of issues designed to tap the total immigrant experiences of the Ghanaian immigrants in the selected cities and regions of the country.

The open-ended questions were designed to elicit broad responses for the subjects. Open-ended, unstructured questions prompted introspection from individual immigrant respondents, regarding their subjective experience as defined by themes such as status formation; labor force participation; family formation; the negotiation of racial, class, and ethnic identities; the pathways for the expression of transnational identity; and the creation of institutional structures as well as immigrant group networks. The open-ended research process allowed for the possibility of investigating multiple dimensions of the immigrants' perspectives and experiences about their migratory encounters with the USA. By probing into the institutional structures that the immigrants have created to minimize the apprehensions associated with having a foreign status, one is able to tease out the specific nuances of the Ghanaian immigrants' diasporic experiences in the USA.

The information gathered from the structured face-to-face interviews was supplemented with in-depth focus group interviews. The focus group method of data collection is designed to gather information from a small group of research participants about life events, processes, experiences, and attitudes. Group interviewing allows the researcher to observe and record social interactions, often of profound importance to qualitative investigations. Focus group sessions give greater attention to the participants' perspectives and provide access to both actual and existentially meaningful or relevant interactional experiences (Russell Bernard, 1994). The focus groups discussed a wide range of issues such as the attributes of their individual migrations to the USA (including the impact of socioeconomic and political conditions in Ghana on international migration, issues of immigrant integration, the perceived social psychological meanings that the immigrants attach to their individual and collective migratory experiences, and the creation of multiple and fragmented transnational linkages). Respondents explored themes concerning education, employment, family relationships, immigrant social network and support systems, construction and formation of racial and ethnic identities, gender roles, and problems confronting the second generation immigrant youth. Other issues that guided the focus groups discussion sessions included citizenship and naturalization; the psychological value, meanings, and attitudes that the immigrants attach to their immigrant journeys and experiences; the role of the immigrants in the social, political, and economic development of Ghana; repatriation; and the future of Ghanaian migration to the West.

As the moderator and facilitator of the focus sessions, I framed and guided the majority of the issues that were discussed. I had formed some preconceived notions about African immigrants and their experiences in the USA. While these biases guided the selection of the topics and themes that I moderated, I was also conscious of these preconceptions and did not allow that to interfere with the groups' perspective(s). At times, the groups defined the discussion issues that were central to the groups' subjective and objective immigrant experiences. In allowing the focus groups to sometimes define the issues that were discussed, I was able to discover continuities and convergences in their immigrant stories. The focus group data elucidated and validated aspects of the survey data I had previously collected, unmasking the normative complexities inherent in the global migratory process. In addition, the focus groups yielded valuable insights into how the immigrants form and interpret new realities in their diaspora away from home. In the end, the focus group sessions expanded the substantive boundaries and contents of my findings.

To ensure that the focus group members were as homogeneous as possible, I organized the groups according to thematic issues representing various phenomenological contexts that capture the subjectivity and group dynamics of the immigrants' experiences. For example, one focus group was comprised of only Ghanaian immigrant women and taxi drivers in the Washington, D.C. metropolitan area. Another focus group session was devoted to second-generation immigrant youth, nurses and allied healthcare workers, and migrant farmers. The essence of this was to ensure that group members who were similar or shared experiences were given the opportunity to frame and discuss issues that were critical and germane to their professional, occupational, or youth experiences. To assess cohort effects, I organized a focus group representing three immigration waves from Ghana. The three waves consisted of those who arrived in the United States before 1980, between 1981 and 1990, and post-1991. To facilitate interactions among the group members and minimize the possibility of one person controlling the direction of the discussions, I decided to keep each focus group small, limiting membership to an average of eight members.

The data on the immigrant returnees were collected during research visits to Ghana. A non-random probability design method was used to select the returnees. There is a paucity of data on international migration returnees in Ghana. Officially, the Government of Ghana does not maintain a record of Ghanaian citizens who return home from travel abroad after a protracted stay since there is no official designation of "returnee migrant." But returnee associations have recently formed in Ghana to provide returnees with a sense of shared identity. These associations serve one main function: to assist the returnees in mobilizing their resources to ease the transition from living abroad to living in Ghana. Second, these associations form mutual benefit and benevolent trusts to provide financial, technical, and psychological support for their registered members. Some of these associations located in the Accra-Tema metropolitan area were of immense assistance in identifying prospective respondents for the study by allowing for information about the study to be disseminated to their members. Aided with information provided by some of the associations, I developed a register of potential focus group members who were then contacted and asked to participate in the focus group sessions. In Ghana, I visited with returnees living in communities located near East Legon, McCarthy Hill, Cantoments, the Ridge Hospital area, and residential communities near Spintex Road, the motorway, and Tema.

Once I had obtained permission from the returnee associations and the returnees themselves to collect information from them for the study, I met with a small group of returnees to conduct a pilot test and preliminary focus group session to become acquainted with the respondents. I informed the respondents how they were selected, stressed that participation was voluntary, and addressed any concerns that the subjects had about the study. A venue was selected for perspective respondents to meet. The bulk of the returnees had settled in Ghana after 1995. Equal representation of male and female returnees and different age groups were included in the focus groups. Responses were solicited from a wide range of questions, including the reasons for returning to Ghana, problems experienced in readjustment and post-repatriation, strategies used to cope with repatriation, community reaction, negotiating and forging inclusion in the civic polity of Ghanaian society, returnee perceived role of the repatriated in Ghana's development, and the permanence of the return.

This book also benefited from secondary data compiled by government and social service agencies. Census data were used to supplement the information collected from the interviews and the focus group sessions. In addition, statistical records on immigrants collected by the Immigration service proved valuable in gaining insights about the Ghanaian immigrant population. The official immigration data of the United States provided information such as type of immigrant visa, year of entry, gender, labor force participation, ports of entry into the USA, naturalization, and educational attainment. I used these data to supplement the interview and census data. The use of multiple data sources is designed to provide a comprehensive portrait of the Ghanaian immigrant community in America.

Perhaps the richest source of data I collected came from my participation in various social and cultural evens organized by the Ghanaian community in several cities, particularly Minneapolis-St. Paul, Chicago, Columbia, Houston, and Washington, D.C. I played the role of participant observer directly participating in the affairs of the immigrant community. Several ceremonies hosted by the Ghanaian immigrant communities across the USA which I attended offered me access to the "heart" of the immigrant community. I was invited to attend child-naming ceremonies, parties hosted by the Ghanaian immigrant association, and Independence Day celebrations. Weddings, funerals, and religious ceremonies hosted by the immigrant community also gave me access to the community's fabric. In addition, access to the activities of various Ghanaian immigrant ethnic groups and associations (Ashanti, Ga-Adangbe, Fanti, Okuapeman, Ewe, and Dagomba) representing a cross section of Ghanaian ethnic societies that have formed in the USA enabled me to sketch the sociocultural contours of the immigrants' territorial spaces. Various alumni associations representing a broad section of secondary and post-secondary institutions from Ghana that have formed in America, as well as the Ghana national immigration associations, including the immigration associations that have formed along tribal and ethnic lines, all provided a listing of their members from their registries. From the listing provided by these associations and groups, I was able to initiate contacts with individual immigrants, their families, and their network of friends and associates, who all shared with me their migration experiences, which enabled me to gain insight into the Ghanaian diaspora.

As indicated, one of the goals of this study is to broaden the understanding of the Ghanaian diaspora and immigrant experiences by drawing parallels between the immigrants who have settled in the USA and the European Union. Toward this end, a focus group session and telephone survey was conducted in the United Kingdom and Italy. In all, a total of 120 Ghanaians living in the British West Midlands cities of Coventry and Warwick, Wolverhampton, and Leicester (United Kingdom), and in the Southern Italian towns of Reggio di Calabria, Sicily, Naples, and Brindisi were interviewed. The British West Midlands cities are located outside of Birmingham, the United Kingdom's second largest city, and all of the cities have been transformed by the migration of people from the Commonwealth countries in Africa, Asia, and the Caribbean. As such, they represent a melting pot of cultures interlaced with British ethos and normative systems. Part of the Black Country and located at the heart of the industrial revolution, the West Midland cities are home to businesses and industries specializing in automotive production, and light and heavy manufacturing, including factories producing boots, hosiery, and shoes. The focus group sessions and the telephone survey asked the respondents to describe their migratory experiences in the UK. Key aspects of this experience include education attainment, labor force participation, family life, race and ethnic identity formation, British–Ghana ties, immigrants' long term aspirations, and perceptions and attitudes about their role in the economic and political development of Ghana. Other sources of information came from newspaper archives and in-depth autobiographical interviews with selected émigrés.

My background as an African immigrant in the diaspora also framed the questions and issues that are addressed in this book. In collecting the data for this study, I have sought to map out the contours of the lived experiences of the Ghanaian immigrants and at the same time provide a forum for the shared voices representing the core contents of the immigrants' lives. In that regard, I have played the role of a storyteller, merely modelling other people's experiences. In drawing upon both micro and macro-level data, I have tried to focus the narratives on the immigrants themselves, often reflecting on their individual and group perceptions and providing an evaluation of their transnational immigration journeys using their own words. Sometimes, I have found similarities in the voices of the immigrants with my own immigrant story. When I listened to immigrant returnees engage in a discourse about the reasons for returning home, the role that returnees expect to play in national development, and the problems that they encounter as they attempt to reintegrate themselves into the affairs of their home country, I found myself often interjecting, attempting to form and select the full spectrum of the issues involved in my exchanges with the returnees. After all, I share in their immigrant realities, being a product of the twin forces of globalization and international migration and their impact on my homeland. In essence, though it was difficult to remain neutral, I had to be guided by the basic reality that there are tensions and at times contradictions in the individual and collective representations of the experiences of the immigrants I came into contact with. These tensions and contradictions are sometimes played out in forums that resemble a typical African market scene. There are multiple voices that have to be heard, sometimes simultaneously. The immigrants speak passionately about the transforming influences of migration in their lives. In their individual and collective voices, they all seem to be reflecting poignantly on the same theme: the relegation and marginalization of people of African descent in the ongoing discourses pertaining to globalization, technology, international border crossings, spatial and transnational identities, and the accompanying social changes wrought by these transformations.

Chapter 3

Crossing the Atlantic to Ablotsi and Mansε: The Exodus of Ghanaians to the West

According to the Ga people, going to *ablotsi* or to *mansε*, means to travel to a far and distant land for a temporary or permanent sojourn. In the cultural ethos of Ghanaian society as a whole, usually to say that one is going abroad is to imply that he or she is traveling to the West, particularly to the USA, Great Britain, Canada, Germany, or Australia. These have been the historical places of destination for the majority of Ghanaians who embark upon foreign travel. It is to these destinations that most prospective candidates for travel abroad refer to when they ponder on foreign travel. More recently as economic and political conditions have deteriorated, *ablotsi* and *mansε* have also come to signify the global dispersion of Ghanaians to destinations in Asia, the Middle East, and the former Soviet Republics. Still, the preferred destinations are the USA or the G8 countries. Going abroad has become a national cultural epic and phenomenon. The social pressure to go abroad has created its own subculture, its own sense of comradeship and community of people who view international migration as the mechanism to fulfill a goal: to ameliorate the economic despair facing many Ghanaians today. This profound phenomenon involves every spectrum of Ghanaian society, from youth to the aged, skilled to unskilled, rural and urban dwellers, and men and women.

Once initiated, the migratory process does not end with the arrival of legal and illegal immigrants alike at their various destinations in the USA and other countries in the West. Concerns about the well-being of relatives left behind dominate the lives of the immigrants. In fact, family reunification is by far the most common form of Ghanaian immigration to this country. Students who come to pursue tertiary education and update their credentials form the next highest group of Ghanaians coming to settle in America.

The urge to come to America or to the West stems from the recognition among Ghanaians that somehow it is possible through hard work, determination, and maybe, even luck to forge a new and better life in this country than the one they have left behind. In their eagerness to come to the USA, the Ghanaian immigrants are not deterred by the growing public antipathy about legal and illegal immigration. They know that once they have entered, they can get a piece of the pie and possibly achieve their dreams. Irrespective of the era of immigration, one thing remains certain: The impact of immigration continues to be felt in all aspects of American society. The rapidity, extent, and volume of immigrant flows into the USA continue to overwhelm a large segment of the American population. Indeed, the internal policies and global forces that trigger the migration of skilled and unskilled labor to America are very complex. To the average American, the rising levels of legal and illegal immigration cannot be sustained. Many Americans would like the government to put in place a comprehensive reform of immigration policies. Public antipathy about uncontrolled immigration resonates as a political issue. Yet, few Americans are aware of the interdependency of the American economy and the supply of cheap immigrant labor for segments of the economy such as agricultural production, food processing, construction, and the hospitality industry.

For Ghanaian immigrants as well as immigrants in general, the opportunity to find jobs in these sectors is behind the motivation to come to the United States. Coming to America is an adaptive response to the depressing economic plight of Ghanaians. As Owusu (1998) pointed out, for several Ghanaians, "the apparent prosperity in the West and the flashy trappings that returning and visiting Ghanaians bring home, including the construction of expensive homes" continue to serve as strong motivation for the need to go abroad. Prospective Ghanaians who desire to travel abroad do so often guided by the notion that they have to acquire and bring to Ghana the commercial symbols or trappings of the West. With the relatively higher wages that they hope to receive upon arrival, the immigrants expect to be able to afford to save and purchase Western consumer items.

Ghana has seen its economic and political fortunes rise and fall. Most Ghanaians perceive that persistent economic depression serves as a major catalyst for international migration. Ghana is richly endowed in natural and human resources relative to other countries in sub-Saharan Africa. At its zenith in the late 1950s through the early 1970s, Ghana's universities, teacher training colleges, and hospitals were among the best in Africa. The certificates, diplomas, and degrees awarded by secondary and tertiary institutions of learning were accorded international recognition. Before and after independence, Ghana became a destination point for migrants from other parts of Africa and the Middle East, particularly Nigeria, Liberia, the Ivory Coast, Sierra Leone, Syria, and Lebanon. From Asia, she attracted Chinese, Indian, and Pakistani merchants and traders to her shores. Chinese, Russian, and Cuban entrepreneurs and political activists came to the country to offer political leadership and guidance in steering the country along the path to socialism and economic self-sufficiency.

The era of the country's first President and Prime Minister Kwame Nkrumah ushered in a period of relative economic stability following the departure of the British colonial administrators in 1957. But the political stability of the country was short-lived as Nkrumah's administration came under criticism for economic corruption and political abuse of power. Political dissent against the Nkrumah regime was met with stiff resistance. In the face of mass protest and under the pretense of maintaining national security, the Nkrumah government passed the Preventive Detention Act. With this law, the government silenced the opponents, sending most of them into exile. Those who stayed and continued to challenge the government ended up at Usher Fort Prison. With the purge of political foes completed, Nkrumah's political party, the Convention Peoples Party (CPP), emerged as the nation's sole political voice. But this phase of Ghana's political development was ephemeral. In 1966, Nkrumah's government was toppled by a military-cum-police alliance. The Ghanaian dream of independence and prosperity began to fizzle. By the end of 1970, the dream was over. Something had gone awry with Ghana. The once thriving country and shining star of Black Africa was plunged into economic and political morass. Hope replaced despair and the concern that for the first time the country was on the wrong course. Democratic institutions faltered. The moderate but enviable success that the country had enjoyed came to a sudden end. People started to look for ways to leave the country. Following the 1960s exile of dissenters during the Nkrumah administration, the 1970s saw tens of thousands of Ghanaians move to Nigeria, fleeing the unpopular rule of General Acheampong. Professionals and non-professionals alike sought to take advantage of Nigeria's booming economy, principally in the oil, industrial, and manufacturing sectors, and to participate in higher education. This was known in the local ethos as the *agege* phenomenon. Ghanaian secondary school teachers, university lecturers, technicians, nurses, skilled artisans, and even including those who did not have any marketable skills flocked to one of Africa's largest and most populated countries. Even before the exodus to Nigeria, several Ghanaians engaged in inter and intra regional migration in the West African sub region. Seasonal labor mobility in the cocoa producing areas of the region often spurred the migration of young men who would leave their families for months at a time to travel to the cocoa production centers in search of jobs (Arthur, 1991; Zachariah and Conde, 1981).

More than 40 years after it started, the emigration of Ghanaians has yet to subside. Ghanaians continue to look for greener pastures in foreign lands. Mounting economic problems caused by decades of economic mismanagement coupled with political dislocations and the erosion of civic and public cultures have caused hundreds of thousands of Ghanaians to become discontent about the destiny of their country. Emigration has become part of the national psyche, the expectation that, in order for individuals and families to survive economically, travel abroad is necessary. The sustained and prolonged saga of the brain drain had begun. Intra-regional migration of Ghanaians to other destinations in Africa as well as international migration to distant destinations all across Europe, North America, and Asia now became and still is the norm, thus making Ghana a major immigrant-sending country

Situating the Causes of Ghanaian Migration to the USA: Push and Pull Factors

In identifying the reasons why people move from one place to another, social scientists often rely on the push-pull factors of migration developed by Ravenstein (1885; 1889). Central to this theory are economic, social, and political characteristics of immigrant sending and immigrant-receiving countries, structured global inequities in living standards, economic productivity, income levels, and cultural factors such as education and the arts (Weiner, 1992; Fuchs, 1992; and Watkins, 1995). In this regard, places with high standards of living and economic production are seen as magnets that attract a cadre of skilled and unskilled workers from places where the standard of living is very low. The study of the sociological and psychological processes involved in the voluntary movement of labor, the transfer of skills, and the dispersion of people from places of less capital and industrial concentration to the more economically advanced societies have yielded a number of significant findings.

A dominant finding is that migration is a rational decision undertaken to enhance the human capital potential of the migrant. Prospective migrants are "pulled" from rural, predominantly agricultural, peasant and non-industrial-based economic production social systems and "pushed" to the more developed, differentiated economies characterized by industrial and manufacturing production. The goal is to achieve a standard of living that is relatively higher than one the migrants are accustomed to in their place of origination. The migrant is merely responding to the comparative advantage that the industrial, manufacturing, and technologically-based capitalist system has over the underdeveloped agrarian and rural economies of the developing countries. In this equation, migrants are risk takers, often having to weigh the costs and benefits to be derived from the migratory process before they undertake the journey. Migration is conceived as an investment calculated to provide the maximum payoff for the migrant (DaVanzo, 1976; Suval, 1972).

The Todaro (1970) model of migration can be applied to Ghanaian migration. One of the most important reasons why people migrate is to seek a better economic life. The goal is to tap into and take advantage of relatively higher wage differentials in the urban industrial and manufacturing economy. The expectation among Ghanaians is that upon making the journey to the West and to the centers of economic production, they can position themselves in a favorable environment to tackle and ameliorate their individual and societal economic problems. Again, the main goal is pecuniary gain. In the case of Ghanaians, migration is the strategy implemented to alleviate grinding poverty and deprivation. In a migrant-sending society like Ghana, blocked economic opportunities, lack of industrial diversification, a mass of rural and semi-rural proletariat who eke out an existence in subsistence farming, and low wages and remuneration converge to create economic conditions that are conducive for the out-migration of people to more favorable economic production and employment centers. In addition, the intended migrant destination is as important as the economic goals that the migrants seek to accomplish. In this respect, place utility attributes (such as higher standards of living in America, technological innovations, and governmental policies regarding population mobility) work to define and shape the environment of international migration among Ghanaians. The concept of place utility in migration studies was developed by Wolpert (1965). Wolpert explained the concept as the composite of utilities which are derived from the individual's integration at some position in space. That is, people will move to those places whose overall utility (jobs, prospects for high income, education, and housing) provides the prospective migrant with the optimum economic advantage or benefit. Migrants therefore select their destinations based on the comparative advantage of place and destinations (Brown and Moore, 1970; Brown and Longbrake, 1970).

Mabojunge (1970) offers some useful insights into the causes of African migration. Mabojunge's (1970) systems approach model of migration discerned four components that have a significant effect on population mobility. These factors are economic, technological, social, and governmental. From Mabojunge's perspective, migration is seen as a circular, interdependent, progressively complex, and self-modifying system (Pryor 1983). The interdependency between global centers of commerce, manufacturing, and industry in the developing countries and abundant and cheap sources of labor in the developing countries operate to influence the transfer of labor from the developing (peripheral economies) to the advanced (core economies). From Mabojunje's theoretical perspective, structured unequal economic relationship between the developed and developing countries is a major determinant of migration. In this regard, Ghanaian migration to the USA and the West can be viewed as an inevitable outcome of the structural economic and cultural dependency and inequality between varying systems of economic and industrial production. The opportunity to earn higher wages, have a better standard of living, and access to cultural institutions and technological innovations (education, healthcare, the arts), is the motivating force behind the quest among Ghanaians to seek a better lifestyle for themselves in the West. The circularity of this movement involves the rotation of skilled and unskilled labor between underdeveloped economic systems and more advanced economic centers and systems of capital production. The cumulative strength in terms of the economic opportunities in the North (rich and advanced countries) relative to economic conditions in the Southern countries (poor, and underdeveloped countries) serves to push and pull Ghanaians to the West (Cohen, 1992; Adepoju, 1991; and Arthur, 2001).

The global status of Ghana as a developing nation shapes the international migratory behavior of its citizens. From the perspective of core-periphery theory, Ghana as a periphery country enters the world economy as a supplier of agriculturally-based raw materials which are sent to the core countries where they are processed into consumable commodities for internal and external consumption. The peripherization of the domestic economy of Ghana and that of Africa as a whole makes it very difficult for the developing countries to build a manufacturing-base economy as the bulk of the raw materials are shipped for processing in the West (Nkrumah, 1970; Amin, 1974). And as Ouattara (1997) pointed out, increased world trade and globalization continue to push people from the less developed countries to the developed countries in search of work and better economic opportunities. The dependency of Ghana's economy on the production of agricultural raw materials for export worsens the job prospects for Ghanaians who desire to work in manufacturing. Ghana specializes in the production of specific cash crops such as cocoa and the mining of minerals such as gold and bauxite for export with little local processing of these raw materials into finished or semi-finished products for domestic and foreign consumption. Following independence, Ghana's political regimes followed in the same direction of the colonizers by focusing the country's economy on the extraction of minerals and the production of agricultural raw materials in exchange for Western consumable items. The agricultural and raw materials extraction economy of Ghana makes the country's economy vulnerable to the price fluctuations of commodities on the global market. This means that the country does not derive the full economic benefits from the marketing and sale of its natural resources. In addition, the advanced countries set commodity prices so low that the foreign receipts that the producing countries receive is not nearly enough to enable the governments to finance social service projects or develop the necessary infrastructure for industrial and economic take-off.

In Ghana, the dire economic conditions associated with low productivity include high unemployment and underemployment rates, massive rural to urban internal population shifts and transfers, arrested economic and industrial development, and population growth. Cheap and surplus labor competes for jobs that are often scarce and low-paying. The displaced rural workers become semi-proletarian, often forced to drift to the urban centers where they eke an existence as street hawkers. Traditionally, the civil service-and-government-controlled corporations (for instance the Ghana Industrial Holding Corporations, GIHOC) have been major employers, but structural adjustment and divestiture (both preconditions for World Bank assistance) have led to the displacement of hundreds of thousands of workers. The erosion of the national currency and starvation wages (the minimum wage is less than $2 a day) prevent most Ghanaians from meeting their basic economic needs. As a highly-indebted poor country, the short and long term economic fortune of the country is inexorably linked to aid from donor countries in the West.

The inability of the central government to find lasting solutions to the economic woes of the country has created an atmosphere of restlessness, frustration, and anger. Unmet needs and the lack of confidence in social institutions to preserve a normative system have made many Ghanaians skeptical about any promises made to them by their leaders. As one immigrant noted, "You work all your life, you get paid nothing, maybe about the equivalent of a dollar a day, you can't keep body and soul together, and meanwhile, the politicians want you to tighten your belt for more economic austerity." The result, as another immigrant noted, is "savage poverty and a normalization of abnormal living conditions that no human being should be subjected to in the twenty-first century. If you stay in Ghana, the poverty will choke the life out of you. One has to go abroad." In the northern tier of the country in particular, the poverty is pernicious and gut wrenching, sometimes defying human comprehension. Steps to ameliorate the vicious economic plight of the people in this region of Ghana as well as other areas of the country have, for the most part, proved daunting and futile. To better their lives, many resort to internal migration which is often the first stage of a series of migratory moves designed to arrest the problem of poverty and deprivation. Ultimately, this migratory move would lead to international migration to the West.

Differences in skill levels and the opportunity structures between the developed and developing nations is a primary determinant of population mobility. The developing regions of the world have come to rely heavily on the developed countries for trade, education, healthcare, transportation, and capital formation and utilization. This creates a dependency and promotes unequal access to and distribution of global resources between the affluent and economically deprived nations. This reliance also creates a pool of transnational skilled workers who drift to the more affluent countries to seek better lifestyles for themselves and their families. As a demographic process, the global transfer and movement of skilled labor is influenced by the interconnectedness of world economies, the cultural and economic incorporation of the economies of the developing countries into the global capitalist production system, and the dwindling labor pool in the economically advanced countries in the Western hemisphere. The transformations resulting from this demographic process have changed the cultural and economic landscapes of both the migrant sending and receiving countries. The urgency to escape the poverty and pessimistic outlook for the economic future of the nation, coupled with the confluence of global economic restructuring and the gradual dismantling of international barriers have had a major influence on the flow of Ghanaians to relatively affluent countries.

The institutionalized bias in the location of economic and social development projects is another cause of internal and international migration in Ghana. During the colonial era, the bulk of development projects were located in the capital city of Accra, including Tema. Regional capital centers such as Kumasi also benefited from this policy. The entire northern tier of the country was almost left out. Its economic and social infrastructures were not developed. The Brong-Ahafo, Volta, Central, and Western regions and the southern tier of the country benefited from the centrally planned economic policies adopted by the post colonial governments of Ghana. But their level of economic development does not compare to that of Accra or Kumasi. The continuation of the colonially-induced policy whereby development projects were centered in the southern tier of the country meant that for the bulk of the rural population of the northern tier, economic deprivation, poverty, and massive unemployment became the order of the day. Motivated youth seeking but cannot find employment in the rural sector often end up coming to Accra or Kumasi. The inequalities in education, incomes, and standards of living between the northern and southern tiers have persisted. The result is mass migration to the urban centers and ultimately emigration to the West.

Short and long-term economic policies designed by the government and international organizations have sometimes worsened the plight of the urban and rural poor in the country. During the 1980s, the government implemented Structural Adjustment Programs (SAP) suggested by the World Bank and the International Monetary Fund to ameliorate the economic hemorrhage of the country. The goal was to create the necessary conditions conducive for attracting foreign investments into the country, divesture the country's private sector, curb excess redundancies in the public sector, remove government subsidies on utilities, and currency devaluation. The effect of SAP was that it led to a massive layoffs and retrenchments of civil service and private sector workers, raised the prices on imported commodities, cut back government investments in education and denied the majority of Ghanaians the opportunity to afford utilities. The result was more of the same: the persistence of impoverishment at every level of Ghanaian society and what Ayitey (1992) referred to as "betrayal." The cumulative effect of decades of the economic morass has created the pressure on many Ghanaians to emigrate, often forcing the educated and uneducated to respond to deteriorating economic conditions by resorting to international migration.

In short, the primary push factor accounting for Ghanaian migration is economic. The lack of employment prospects, chronic deprivation, poor resource management, a stymied private sector, and corruption all converge to push out many Ghanaians to look abroad for opportunities. In the survey of the Ghanaian immigrant population, respondents highlighted economic motivation as the dominant reason for leaving Ghana. Among the majority of Ghanaians in the USA, international migration is perceived as a form of economic pilgrimage, a necessary journey to be undertaken given the myriad of problems associated with the stagnation of the political and economic systems in Ghana. The post-independence economy of the country has yet to build a solid economic and industrial infrastructure for providing a meaningful and sustained improvement in the quality of life for Ghanaians. Promises to improve upon the economic lives of the people have been made by past and current politicians. None have panned out. The result is the mass out-migration of Ghanaians who persistently keep knocking on the doors of the West seeking to enter as economic migrants.

Political Motivations to Migrate

By all accounts, Awudu is a successful Ghanaian-American immigrant and the owner of an auto parts dealership in the USA. From his perspective, the most compelling reason for leaving Ghana was his utter discontent with the reign of General Acheampong. Educated at the Kumasi Polytechnic and with credentials from City and Guilds in London, he was one of the pioneers of the drift of skilled Ghanaians to Nigeria where he taught at a secondary school and a polytechnic institute. For nearly eight years, he followed the downward spiral of Ghana's political culture. His hopes were to return to Ghana after the military rule ended. On one of several visits he made from Nigeria to Ghana to visit with relatives, he and two dozen other Ghanaians were stopped by military and border guard officials at a check point just before they entered Ghana. The soldiers confiscated without cause large sums of money he and the other passengers were bringing to Ghana. Those who resisted were manhandled, handcuffed, and beaten. Most came to Ghana empty handed. The dream of going to Nigeria to seek better economic opportunities to improve upon his standard of living suddenly came to an abrupt end.

In spite of the mistreatment, Awudu never wavered, and he continued believing in the future of his country. He yearned for a return to civilian and constitutional rule. But his hopes were dashed when Rawlings came to power. Awudu immediately concluded that his sojourn in Nigeria was going to be permanent. Then he began thinking more broadly: perhaps he could find his way to the United States. He saved enough money to support his visa application, migrated to America, and decided to study automotive engineering; he became certified as a trained auto mechanic and worked tirelessly to save for the down payment to finance his automotive shop where he deals in remanufactured and used auto parts. For Awudu, the primary reason for leaving Ghana was the fear and uncertainties that dominated the political culture of Ghana for almost a quarter of a century. In his experience, the advent of military rule created a culture which legitimized violence as a means of conflict resolution in the country. This new order was vicious in its intentions, lacked political legitimacy, and was the harbinger of organized political corruption and state-controlled thievery that characterized the country's political landscape for decades. The erosion of Ghana's political institutions became the force that pushed many Ghanaians out of the country to seek refugee and asylum status in America and elsewhere. In seeking political asylum in the USA, Awudu and several other Ghanaians who have sought a safer haven abroad to escape the country's political strife during the 1960s to the early 1980s are united by one common objective: the desire to begin a new life free from political intimidation, violence, and persistent civil unrest.

Political factors that have operated in Ghana since 1966 have pushed many natives out of the country. The deterioration of democratic institutions led to a climate of despair and fear. The erosion of rule of law and the lack of confidence in the government to offer political security to its citizens is a major consideration for leaving. The immigrants believe that these insecurities became magnified under the country's previous military regimes, particularly under Acheampong's rule which according to one immigrant "was the most disruptive and chaotic periods in the recent history of the country. The erosion of civil liberties, coupled with the absence of rule of law engendered feelings of insecurity and apprehension on the part of many Ghanaians. The country's institutions of justice failed to provide adequate protection, equity, and due process to ordinary Ghanaians. Those who felt the frustration and who had the means fled the country."

The Acheampong government's open warfare with the intelligentsia, the middle-class, the rank and file of Ghanaian society, and with the National Union of Ghana Students (NUGS), which represented students from the country's universities and training colleges, created disenchantment and stoked tension in every segment of Ghanaian society. The universities were frequently shut down due to mass student demonstrations and collective resistance to Acheampong's attempt to hold on to power longer than he had initially promised. A clampdown by the government on political demonstration brought the students in direct conflict with the military who often used violence to dispel the student demonstrators. This sort of instability caused many Ghanaian professionals to leave the country.

Despite the precarious political situation of the country, the central government did not intervene or thwart the efforts of those who wanted to leave the country. This freedom to leave Ghana became a *sine qua non* factor that subsequently legitimized the imperative of overseas travel among Ghanaians and fostered a cultural expectation among the Ghanaian populace that international migration is a viable alternative to the precarious political conditions that confronted the nation. Thus, the concomitant recognition on the part of the various political regimes of the country was that the creation of an environment where people are free to move about or transfer their skills to another foreign location if need be, is a basic human right which must be nurtured in accordance with the rule of law and international charter agreement. The institutionalization of the political freedom that the government accorded to Ghanaians to travel abroad and seek legal residency or citizenship in other countries ultimately served the country well in that it helped to develop the notion that it was normatively acceptable for Ghanaians to look abroad to satisfy or meet their political and objectives. These political objectives would not have been met if the government had clamped down on the free movement of people and prohibited Ghanaians from traveling abroad. When Rawlings became the leader of Ghana, he stabilized the political and economic situation of the country. Moderate improvements occurred in food production, but intractable political and economic problems still persisted. A new democratically elected government led by Kufuor took over from Rawlings in 2000, but it is too soon to assess the impact of this government on the domestic scene. Meanwhile, the mass migration of skilled and unskilled talents has yet to abate.

Leaving Ghana for the West: The Role of Transnational Family Networks

According to the pioneering studies of Uhlenberg (1973), Goldscheider (1971) and Johnston (1971), the attachments that people form within the contexts of their family relationships are critical to the understanding of the reasons why people move. These studies point to the fact that family networks and the attachments and bonds that are fostered in these networks may impede or enhance the probability that one is going to migrate. The institution of the family in Ghana is based on strong bonds and networks of people who are related by blood, marriage, or adoption. Ghanaians stay involved in the affairs of the extended family system at home and abroad. Family members maintain close contact with one another and share information about family matters including life changing events such as births or deaths. In most cases, going abroad does not sever the bonds among family members. Those abroad have come to depend on relatives at home for support (spiritual and psychological) to confront and cope with the uncertainties of living far away from home. On their part, those remaining at home come to depend on relatives abroad for economic support. The migratory experience to the West is viewed as a family affair. For those who are living abroad, the expectation is that they will be generous in assisting the family at home to meet their obligations. More importantly, they are supposed to pave the way for other family members to follow. This is an unwritten code in Ghanaian cultural ethos: the cooperation and organization of extended family resources at home and abroad to meet cultural and economic goals. In American immigration history, several immigrant groups form these transnational networks to facilitate their integration into the host society and at the same time maintain links with home. Steven Gold's (2001) study of Israeli immigrants in the United States and Great Britain, and Luin Goldring's (1996) work on Mexicans domiciled in the United States illustrates the growing significance of transnational networks in facilitating migration. Ghanaians in the diaspora are no exception in the collective mobilization of transnational resources to implement international migration strategies.

The case of Efua illustrates the roles of immediate and extended family in transnational migration. When Efua was accepted as a graduate student to study microbiology at a southern institution of higher learning in the USA, her family was elated. But this elation was ephemeral. The consternation was how to raise the thousands of dollars it would take to help her become established. Although she had never attended school, Efua's grandmother summoned family members who quickly contacted other extended family members to raise some money to assist Efua meet her educational expenditures. Relatives of Efua living in the Brong Ahafo region of Ghana traveled several times to Accra to contact well-established relatives to contribute money and assist in securing an airline ticket and passport for Efua. The involvement of the family culminated in a meeting that was held at Efua's house and which was attended by several close relatives. At this meeting, logistics about her travel to America was made. Relatives who had contacts in the United States were contacted for assistance. The relatives responded very generously. Their collective resolve made it possible for her to afford the ticket, and provided sufficient proof of her ability to meet the financial requirements to qualify for a student visa. The few relatives Efua had in the United States provided her with pre-and-post-departure information about the imperative of choosing a specialty of study that would make it possible to find an employer to sponsor her for labor certification so that she might eventually obtain a green card (permanent residency) to enable her to live and work in the United States.

The expectation is that Efua will assist other family members to enter America upon the completion of her education. International migration has become a strategy which is adopted by a growing number of Ghanaian families to shore up their economic resources and maintain a decent standard of living. For Ghanaians who are eager to leave the country to travel to the United States, several ways are found to finance the journey to the West. Money, no matter how small, is borrowed from extended family members. Sometimes family treasures (gold and trinkets) are sold to raise money to support enterprising family members for sponsorship to the United States and to other Western capitals. The strong kinship bonds fostered by extended family members greatly facilitate the process of going abroad. The same networks are used to send letters of invitation to American consulates to certify financial support for prospective migrants or to pay for educational expenses in the United States enabling a relative to obtain a visa.

In large urban areas, networks of contacts are formed to implement the travel abroad. Information about expectations of coming to the West (how to obtain work permit papers, find work in the underground labor market, save money, remit money home) are offered to prospective immigrants to the West. Issues pertaining to becoming a potential immigrant in America or Great Britain are gleaned from various media and newspaper accounts as well as from returned immigrants, including tips on the following: job prospects in the West, how to secure employment and social security documents, which parts of the United States provide the optimum economic and cultural opportunities, and where to locate established concentrations of Ghanaians already living in the United States.

Ghanaians are of the mind set that the local economy of Ghana holds no future for anyone who does not have access to foreign currencies, especially the American dollar and the British pound sterling. Again, it is expected that Ghanaians who are sponsored by their families to go abroad to study or work will ultimately have to provide economic support for extended family members. The *ablotsi* or *mansε* resident becomes the family's safety net, responsible for fulfilling all the social and economic needs of the family. He or she becomes the welfare system that is lacking in Ghana. The old, the young, the needy, and those in ill-health all depend on their relatives to remit funds home regularly to alleviate the worsening economic plight facing the citizens of Ghana. The psychological motivations influencing the decision to leave Ghana are very strong. As Atkinson (1964) pointed out, the motive or the goals that migrants expect to achieve following their arrival in the receiving country are formed prior to departure. Ghanaians imagine the benefits they and their family members will derive from going to the West. This motivation is supported by the fact that Ghanaians at home see the outcome of foreign travel when those who are sojourned in the West come home. They often bring gifts, money, and consumer goods which they share with family members.

The Ghanaian family has become a sponsoring agency of international migration. The household and extended family structure make decisions about going abroad.

Ghanaian migration to the United States is influenced by the level of education of family members prior to and after migration, skill level, the presence of kin group and networks of mutual aid and support, the attitudes of the host society toward immigrants and immigration policies, access to labor markets and fluency in English. The expected value that accrues to households who have members or relatives living abroad and remitting to other family members who stay behind undergirds the family decisions as who will go abroad and when. In households with relatives and extended kin members who have undertaken the journey abroad, particularly to the United States and Great Britain, the material and cultural symbols of the West (imported cars and very nice clothing), are displayed, consciously or unconsciously, thus creating a bandwagon effect which serves to motivate the continued mass out-migration of Ghanaian youth to the West or to other countries where they can work, save money, and buy consumer items for shipment to Ghana.

The collective effort of Ghanaian families to ensure that they have family members who live abroad is also rationalized in terms of securing access to foreign consumer goods. Having access to foreign consumer goods and the foreign exchange to purchase those commodities that are always in short supply in Ghana constitutes a special form of social currency in four related ways. First, it shores up the prestige and social status of the family. Second, it provides an economic anchor to the family, often protecting families from the frequent cyclical nature of essential consumer commodity shortages in the country. Third, it provides families with access to capital assistance programs designed to facilitate the free flow of goods and services in the global economic market. Fourth, as more and more Ghanaians become connected to the global economic system through international migration and human capital exchange, broader internal social changes are occurring in virtually every aspect of the social fabric of the society. An example is the revamping of both public and private educational institutions in the country to prepare secondary school students to take college entrance exams such as the SAT and ACT. Here again, families join their resources to ensure that some of their children will have the support of relatives abroad to register them to take these exams. Upon passing the exams, the prospective students stand a good chance of securing admission to study in the USA. Some families will then raise the money needed to pay for the tuition.

Within the nexus of family decision-making regarding who to sponsor for international migration, gender is not often seen as a constraining factor. Ghanaian men and women have become equal partners in the westward drift of Ghana's citizens. Women of all ages, educational attainment, class, and marital status are involved in this drift. Previously, Ghanaian migration (internal and international) could be considered a male-dominated activity. The men most often were the ones who first left the rural areas for the urban centers in search of paid employment. The women would join them later. With time, the women migrants have carved their own niche in the urban economy as self-employed traders (wholesalers and retailers). In Ghana, women frequently migrate to mining and marketing centers to trade or sell consumer wares. Ghanaian women are, therefore, not newcomers to the migration scene. The difficulties they encounter as they assume new roles, test new values, and adapt to unfamiliar expectations serve as guideposts in facilitating international migration among Ghanaian women. Today, Ghanaian women travel to all corners of the globe as retailers engaged in the import–export trade, often bringing to Ghana international consumer goods and exporting agricultural goods abroad for the Ghanaian immigrant communities worldwide. The encouragement given by the government of Ghana to private retail and wholesale entrepreneurs in the form of liberal tax incentives and letters of credit has made this sector of the economy the most financially lucrative. This has encouraged Ghanaian families to harness their resources to travel abroad, work, secure capital, and return home to start business ventures. Although encouraging entrepreneurship, the government has been unable to provide the leadership and infrastructure necessary for promoting and supporting an entrepreneurial and manufacturing-based economy, thus necessitating the need for individuals and, at times, groups of families to step in and fill this void.

The time-tested and often proven way to gain a foothold in the ever-expanding entrepreneurial sector of the country's burgeoning economy is for individuals and families to look beyond the shores of Ghana for capital and resources. Ghanaians, therefore, cast their horizons beyond the borders and take steps to ensure that emigration to the United States, Canada, or Great Britain is feasible. Once abroad, they identify segments of the Ghanaian economy in dire need of capital investment and economic improvement. After they have saved enough money to invest, they come home and form business and manufacturing enterprises ranging from real estate development to food processing. The majority of Ghanaians at home and abroad are convinced that the economic and social development of the country have to be undertaken by Ghanaians themselves and that foreign aid, while critical, is not the panacea for achieving self-sufficiency and economic independence. For those Ghanaians who go abroad and return home to set up businesses, the payoff is often very lucrative; access to foreign currency is a major boost to a business's success in Ghana.

Education as a Determinant of Migration to the United States

Prior to World War I, the number of Ghanaians who immigrated to the USA was negligible. It is estimated that fewer than a thousand Ghanaians immigrated to North America between 1910 and the commencement of World War I in 1914. The end of the war in 1918 saw a slight increase in the number of Ghanaians who arrived in the United States. The majority of those who came to this country from the then Gold Coast were mainly civil servants who were sponsored for training by the colonial administration. Many of them returned home and served alongside their British colonial administrators. A few Ghanaians working with subsidiaries of foreign institutions and international aid associations were also sponsored to go abroad, mainly to England, to pursue further training. Intergovernmental sponsorship was also very common. Bilateral and multilateral assistance from the West provided opportunities for Ghanaians to travel abroad to sharpen their skills. These select individuals were the pioneers who blazed the migration trail to the West. When World War II ended in 1945, several Ghanaians traveled to the West as students, civil servants, and business persons. Under Nkrumah's government, thousands of Ghanaians were given the opportunity to travel abroad to England, Canada, the United

States, and more particularly, to the former satellite states of the Soviet Union. They trained in fields of study such as medicine, agriculture, engineering, political science, and education. These Ghanaians formed the cadre of skilled workers who replaced foreign expatriates under the policy of Africanization whose goal was to staff key positions in both public and private organizations with indigenous citizens.

The migration of Ghanaians to the United States is closely linked to the proliferation of secondary and postsecondary institutions in Ghana after independence. Embarked upon by the British colonial administration and followed by Nkrumah, secondary and tertiary institutions were set up in all the administrative and regional capitals of the country. Access to these schools, including primary education, was facilitated by the government's push to increase the literacy rate of Ghanaians. Modeled after the British system of education, Ghana's institutions of learning have ranked at the top of all those in Africa. By 1975, the country had produced a cadre of educated men and women at all education levels; however, the inability of the economy to absorb professional and skilled graduates created underemployment and unemployment among school graduates.

Unemployment of the educated continues to be a major problem in the country. Today, the unemployment rate of university graduates is over 20 per cent. For those who complete secondary school, the unemployment rate is even higher, about 27 per cent. The rate of unemployment is generally higher among the educated than among those who have little or no education. Educated men and women often search for employment in the formal sectors of the economy where jobs can be hard to come by. With their education, most of the country's graduates are reluctant to look for work in the informal sector which is dominated by trading and hawking of consumer goods usually on street pavements in the large cities. Their education has exposed them to a lifestyle and aspiration that cannot be fulfilled by Ghana's economic and industrial labor and employment markets.

The unemployment and underemployment situation of the educated in Ghana and elsewhere in Africa is further exacerbated by the fact that labor markets in Africa cannot expand rapidly enough to incorporate newly trained skilled labor into the work force. The inability of the labor market to absorb the excess labor is directly linked to the stagnation of capital ventures and to the absence of a sustained push on the part of African governments to expand the industrial and manufacturing base of their economies. In turn, this has resulted in the mass migration of Ghanaian talent abroad where their skills are needed and the pay is much better. When graduates are able to find employment in Ghana, it is generally in the civil service sector where salaries are low and opportunities for advancement and promotion are limited. These government jobs come with very few or no benefits at all except for the senior ranks. The costs associated with urban travel, the commute to work, food, and housing, leave the civil servants with little or no money left at the end of the month. Additionally, several Ghanaian graduates find government work unchallenging and fraught with bureaucratic hurdles. Jobs in the service are considered dead end and filled with cronyism, nepotism, and tribal discrimination. Graduates in the system often have to find other employment in the private sector to augment their paltry salary. Others use their private cars as a taxi to make extra money to boost their pay.

Tens of thousands of Ghanaians educated by the country's secondary and tertiary institutions of learning have no choice but to leave the country. Nurses, doctors, pharmacists, and engineers are leaving the country in droves. According to the Registrar of the Ghana Pharmacy Council F. Awuku-Kwatia, 58 of the 96 pharmacists who were licensed by the Ghana Pharmaceutical Society in 2002 have left the country to practice their profession in other countries. He noted that altogether, 250 out of 800 of pharmacists in the country have left the country to seek opportunities abroad. Additionally, lecturers and professors at the country's universities are also leaving due to poor working conditions and recently, the ranks of the scientists with the Council for Science and Industrial Research have fled the country to the West to find employment elsewhere. International recruiters have also decimated the rank and file of the nurses at the country's major teaching hospitals and clinics in Accra, Tema, Kumasi, and Sekondi-Takoradi. Most of them have been recruited for more lucrative jobs in the United States and Great Britain. The country is hemorrhaging from the loss of skilled citizens. Foreign consulates have eased visa restrictions for Ghanaians with skills in nursing and allied health whose services are in high demand in the United Kingdom and in the United States. Only a skeletal cadre of nurses and allied health personnel are left behind to meet the healthcare needs of Ghanaians. A Ghanaian computer engineer and scientist employed in Silicon Valley, the heart of the United States microcomputer industry, was succinct in his remark that "the universities, teacher, and nursing training colleges in Ghana are merely producing graduates for the West." Coupled with this mass exodus of professional and skilled workers is the mass exodus of unskilled workers who are also feeling the economic pinch and have had to migrate outside the country to find ways to survive economically.

Perilous Crossings to the European Union: Ghanaian Farm Migrants in Southern Italy

The level of frustration associated with the economic conditions of Ghana is very high, often necessitating a drastic response. In a bid to escape from the economic doldrums, some Ghanaians have resorted to taking jobs that sometimes expose them to inhuman working conditions. For example, encouraged by the availability of work in the Mediterranean countries, particularly Italy, Greece, Spain and Portugal, some Ghanaians head north and attempt to cross the perilous arid Sahel Desert, enduring bandits and the cold nights to enter North Africa and the Mediterranean. Once in Europe, arrangements are often made to migrate to America or other destinations in Western Europe, but this process is usually arduous and time consuming. Some pay huge sums of money to "migrant mules" who promise their clients safe haven anywhere in that region. Traveling mostly at night, usually in a company of three or more, including women and children, some Ghanaians traverse the desert, bribing their way and paying exorbitant fees to secure protection. For those who make it through this dangerous journey, life begins anew in Spain, Portugal, or Morocco with an application for political asylum. While there, the Ghanaians join thousands of other undocumented immigrants from Africa, the Middle-East, and

Eastern Europe competing for menial jobs. In addition, they also have to endure the xenophobic feelings about the growing number of people who are entering into Spain and Portugal. Some of the Ghanaians who make it move on to other European destinations like Italy, Malta, and Greece. Others continue their immigrant journeys to Eastern Europe. In a growing number of instances, prospective migrants to the Mediterranean pool their resources and send an advance team to scout the path, identify potential problems, and report home. Once the report is substantiated, teams are formed to prepare for the long arduous journey. Some of the migrants travel with camel caravans for safe protection. However, there is no guarantee that the journey across the sand dunes with temperatures averaging over 100 degrees (during the day and possible encounters with poisonous snakes) will be successful for all who undertake the trip. Some make it all the way to the southern tip of Europe only to be repatriated home to Ghana. For those who persevere and survive the journey, the possibility of coming to the West to live and work is very high.

The current stream is the wave of unskilled Ghanaians who are heading to Italy, Spain, Greece, and Portugal. The majority of the Ghanaians working as migrant farm workers have arrived in Italy since the middle of 1980. One-third of the respondents had made the journey to Italy from the Canary Islands, Tunisia, Nigeria, Morocco, Libya, the Middle-East, Ethiopia, or Eastern Europe. A common trend among this group of unskilled workers is chain or stepwise migration. Almost all of them in this group had left Ghana for Nigeria during the economic and political crisis of the 1970s and 1980s. Of this group, 65 per cent emigrated to Italy and Greece from Nigeria after the expulsion of Ghanaians from Nigeria. The migration of Ghanaians to the Mediterranean to seek employment as agricultural migrants has been limited because the journey to the Mediterranean requires unconventional methods of travel such as walking across parts of the Sahara Desert, and depending on lorry drivers for lifts or fishermen to ferry them across the sea. Despite the risks of death from the weather and dehydration, many young Ghanaian males still undertake the perilous journey in search of their economic dreams. Widespread unemployment of Ghanaian youth, coupled with deteriorating standards of living in the slums of Accra for thousands of rural and urban school dropouts certainly encouraging young people to seek greener pastures in Southern Europe. In addition, many Ghanaians who embark upon the journey to the Mediterranean countries often do not possess professional skills or credentials that are in high demand in the West. Several of them have barely completed secondary school and are unskilled. Their lack of marketable and professional skills makes it difficult for them to qualify for a traveling visa to enter Europe legally.

Social, political, and economic factors converge to make Southern Italy a preferred destination for Ghanaian migrant farm workers. First, due to demographic factors associated with an aging Italian population and the reluctance of young Italians to work as agricultural farm laborers, there is a greater need among Italy's agri-business establishments for a reliable work force. Second, recent provisions in Italian immigration law allow for undocumented workers to be hired to fill jobs in the agricultural production sector. Under Silvio Berlusconi's immigration policy which was opposed by the right-wing political groups in Italy, private sector businesses, including agricultural production establishments, can hire illegal workers and subsequently petition the government to legalize the status of the workers. Third, the political influence of the business and private sectors and their need to maintain a steady and cheap supply of labor pave the way for thousands of agricultural farm workers to come to Italy to find work in the labor-intensive agri-business economy of Southern Italy.

A common trend among the migrant farm workers is to work for a short duration (usually five to ten years), save the bulk of their income, and repatriate to Ghana to build a home and start a small business such as hardware store or a mini-bus transportation service. Monies are wired to Ghana every month for safe keeping in case their luck runs out and they are discovered by immigration authorities. The impermanence and seasonality of their jobs mean that they have to live frugally, save the bulk of their incomes, and be ready to move to another farm or employment site with short notification. Some of the migrant farm workers rotate the sites of their employment, sometimes working in Italy for two years followed by another migration to Greece or Portugal. There they are beginning to carve a labor niche for themselves as economic in the agricultural sector and food processing plants. As they acquire more experience, some of the Ghanaians are sponsored by the agricultural produce companies they work for to obtain a legal status. But generally, most of the farm workers never gain legal status in Italy. The application process is cumbersome for some of the migrant workers due to language difficulties and the high fees charged by attorneys to process legal resident work permits. Some of the Ghanaians do not apply for legal status even when they become qualified to apply because of apprehension that they will be deported by immigration authorities for working without valid papers.

In the agricultural fields of Southern Italy, it is not uncommon to find Ghanaians who have multiple relatives working on the same farm. These relatives live together and share the cost of maintaining a home. Some of them made the long journey from Ghana to Italy and Greece together. Upon arriving in Greece or Portugal, the Ghanaian economic migrants find themselves working alongside émigrés from Albania, Turkey, Romania, and the former Yugoslavia. The family of Kofi, comprising a cousin and nephew, made the daunting journey to Italy after finding their way to Tunis where all three worked for a year as cleaners at a local market in Tunisia's capital city. Here they saved the $2,000 to pay an agent who brought them in a boat to Italy. Kofi described the journey as the most frightening experience in his life. Food was scarce and the risk of being apprehended was very high. But the family was resolute, determined to make it to Italy to escape the poverty and economic deprivation that characterized their lives in Accra where they were street peddlers selling batteries and handkerchiefs at the Accra to Kumasi bus terminal. According to Kofi, several of the boys and girls who sold merchandise with him in Accra had no place to call home in Ghana. Most slept near the train tracks or if they were fortunate found shelter in the market stalls at night.

Kofi chose Italy because some of his associates had managed to make it there successfully. Word of their financial success reached Kofi along with news that jobs were plentiful and the pay was good (averaging the equivalent of $650 a month) if one did not mind working as a farm migrant picking agricultural produce. Some Ghanaians Kofi knew had also made it successfully to Spain and Greece to work as farm operatives earning in one month more than what the average Ghanaian earned in a whole year. The potential to earn such an amount motivated Kofi to undertake the journey. On a good business day peddling batteries and handkerchiefs in Accra, he only earned the equivalent of seventy-five cents. The journey from Accra to Tunisia first took them through Burkina Faso, Mali, Algeria and finally to Tunisia, the beach head from where they crossed the Mediterranean Sea to reach Italy. Kofi, the leader of the group had lived in Togo as a child and speaks fluent French which gave the group a sense of security as they made their way through the Francophone countries often bribing lorry drivers to take them to the next commercial center.

From his account, the family spent many nights sleeping in the desert and if fortunate in abandoned makeshift tents which other migrants on similar trips had left in haste. The food and water provisions that they carried with them had to be rationed and nothing went to waste. Purchasing or begging for food from the caravans that traversed the desert was considered economically unwise since the cost was prohibitive. By all accounts, carrying their supplies with them, including batteries and heavy blankets to weather the cold desert nights also made the desert crossing challenging . From Kofi's account, the perilous crossing requires physical endurance, patience, the ability to live on less, creativity, and luck. Traveling with others afforded collective security even though fear of the unknown loomed large at the back of their minds. Once in Southern Italy, the process of finding farm work was very easy, according to Kofi who showed up on a farm in rural Southern Italy looking to be employed. Initially, Kofi and his two relatives secured employment cleaning a meat processing factory. But this was short-lived once the Ghanaians learned from the manager of the meat processing factory that he also owned a tomato farm where several Ghanaians, Somalis, Malians, and Sudanese were employed. Kofi and his two relatives decided to work alongside his fellow Ghanaians and African workers. Securing this job made a significant difference in Kofi's economic situation. Earning about $700 monthly, Kofi sends more than one-half of his monthly wages home to Ghana where his parents save and manage a savings account for him. His goal is to save enough money to buy land in Accra and start building a home. He also intends to use some of his savings to start a trading store in Accra, including operating a transportation business. The work is tedious and back-breaking, and he often works more than fifty hours a week to make extra money. But having to work longer hours is no different from what he experienced as a street hawker in Accra.

The Ghanaians who work alongside Kofi on the farm are united by the same economic goals: to work as long as the Italian agro-business industries will allow them considering their undocumented status, save the bulk of their wages, and be prepared to leave Italy before Italian immigration officials start cracking down on illegal farm migrants. The Ghanaians are apprehensive about the Italian public intolerance of waves of immigrants from Africa and elsewhere coming to the shores of the country to seek work. Eventually, they anticipate that the pipeline of illegal farm migrants who make it to Italy will be curtailed. However, the immigrants believe the agricultural industry is a buoyant sector of the rural economy in Italy, and the ability to attract cheap labor enables this vital sector to maintain its competitive edge in supplying agricultural produce to the European Union. A balanced approach to the continued flow of farm migrant workers to the agricultural communities of Southern

Italy recognizes that a guest worker program and the subsequent documentation of foreign workers in the region will ensure that the migrant workers are not exploited by the growers and that they are paid fair compensation in line with European Union standards of employment.

For the small but growing number of Ghanaians in Southern Italy who have been successful in securing valid work and resident documents, alternate employment may be found in the manufacturing or business sectors where wages are relatively higher than in the agricultural sector. However, language difficulties pose a major problem for most of the Ghanaians as only a few of them speak and understand Italian. Those who want to work in the formal sector usually take classes to hone their language skills. But for the vast majority of the Ghanaians in Southern Italy, the principal form of labor participation is in the agricultural sector where several of the Ghanaians have been successful in carving an occupational niche. Some of the immigrants with legal status are able to travel freely throughout the European Union, often resettling in the UK and the Netherlands. Others migrate to Malta and Cyprus on a temporary basis primarily to work in the agricultural fields and in the hotel and restaurant establishments.

The Ghanaian diaspora community in Southern Italy is being strengthened by the continuous stream of legal and illegal migration of workers from Ghana. Like their counterparts in other parts of the European Union or the USA, the immigrants have formed Ghana immigrant associations to cater to the needs of the immigrant community as they strive to build a thriving community whose eventual goal is to integrate the Ghanaians into Italian society and at the same time create the institutional structures to promote a transnational linkage with the country of origination. At the present moment, the diaspora community of Ghanaians in Southern Italy can be described as an amorphous and loosely organized migrant community that is currently creating an organizational infrastructure to meet the needs of a growing immigrant community.

Economic and social problems at home in Ghana will continue to push out Ghana's skilled and unskilled to the West. Secondary and tertiary school graduate unemployment and underemployment will continue to exacerbate the economic problems of the country. The inability of the central government to mitigate the problem of low wages and the growing discontentment on the part of average Ghanaians to make ends meet will compel more and more Ghanaians to pursue economic opportunities abroad. Hyper-inflation, continued erosion of the national currency, stymied growth in exportable agricultural and mineral resources, the lack of access to basic economic necessities, and a crumbling infrastructural network means that economic and industrial growth is at best anemic. Austerity measures in the form of privatization of public utilities (water and electricity), massive layoffs and redeployments in the civil service, and removal of subsidies on petrol and kerosene have further aggravated the plight of many Ghanaians.

The inability of the private sector to create jobs and absorb the surplus educated population means that skilled and unskilled laborers will continue to look to the expanding economies of the West for gainful employment. The inability of the government to abate the drift of rural dwellers to the urban centers aggravates the problem of delivering adequate social services to the urban areas causing unsanitary and unhealthy slums and squatter settlements in the capital districts. When moderate progress has been made to boost economic and industrial productions, such gains have been ephemeral and fleeting. The burgeoning economic development gains are frequently choked and threatened by the massive structural imbalances such as low economic and industrial capacity that currently pervades the system of production. The result is the inability of the country to maintain and sustain a high economic growth rate over a protracted period of time.

For the prospective Ghanaian immigrants who desire to come to the United States, an awareness of the changing nature of public sentiment regarding immigration is warranted. For those who do not possess skills and requisite credentials that can be transferred to the America labor sector, the short and long-term prospects for gainful and legal employment upon arrival in the United States are very dim. Employment in the underground economy for those who are undocumented and the use of fake social security numbers and identification cards to secure employment has become a risky proposition. On their part, private sector employers are leery of federal immigration authorities who have started clamping down on the use of fictitious documents to secure employment. The tightening of immigration laws in the United States and other countries in the West will therefore continue to test the motivation of prospective Ghanaians who want to emigrate. However countries in the West recognize how labor and occupational niches from Ghana could improve their own internal labor conditions and economies. In the American labor economy, there is always a place for migrant labor from Africa, Mexico and other parts of Central America in vital sectors of economic activities, particularly in housing construction, animal husbandry, and food processing. The continued cultural and economic incorporation of the developing countries into the world's economic system will continue to affect every aspect of the social structure of emerging countries like Ghana. For Ghana, international migration of its citizens to the West to seek better economic opportunities for themselves has become one of the mechanisms whereby Ghanaians seek to forge global incorporation. For the skilled Ghanaians and those who have relatives living abroad, the pressure to leave Ghana and join their relations abroad is forever mounting. For those without any marketable skills and family networks in the West, there is still a continuous search for ways to undertake the journey westward. Lacking the resources to form policies to stem the tide of Ghanaian emigration, the central government can only sit back and watch as this momentous shift and transfer of labor to the West occurs. In the end, Ghanaians who have the resources will ultimately leave the country, usually traveling by conventional modes of transportation. But for some, the journey may involve human trekking across desolate terrains; in these cases the risks are huge and life threatening but the end results are rewarding if they finally escape the harsh economic conditions of Ghana. The Ghanaian caravan to *ablotsi* and *mansɛ* is a well-oiled machine that is constantly on the move to familiar and unfamiliar territories and domains seeking to find and carve newer economic and cultural identities that transcends the social polity of Ghana.

Chapter 4

Structure and Composition of Ghanaian Immigrant Families in the United States

Among Ghanaians, the institution of family is highly revered. The family is viewed as an agency of social, cultural, and economic production. Ghanaians tend to emphasize the extended kin group who are related by blood, marriage, and/or adoption. In this institution, socialization and social control are exercised by an extended network of relatives. Family relationships center around children and women as cultural producers and nurturers. Matriarchs feature predominantly in the lives of both young and old, women feature prominently in the economic production of goods and services. Spirituality and religion, and reverence for ancestors and those who have departed this life permeate the entire fabric of family life.

Family life depends on group goals and mutual assistance, including a human capital dimension which treats every household member as a contributing member. The result is that even though some of the Ghanaian immigrants view themselves as poor in terms of material goods, their strength and vitality as a unit can be found in their cooperative approach to family life. This is the human capital that they have brought with them from the Continent to sustain them in adapting to life in the United States. As Foner (1997) points out, for most immigrants coming to the United States, the cultural understandings, meanings, and symbols that immigrants bring with them from their home societies are critical in understanding immigrant family life. In viewing their family as a cultural and economic production unit, the immigrants are able to minimize the impact of economic deprivation. More notably and when viewed from the contexts of Ghanaian cultural values, poverty and deprivation do not convey the same derogatory meaning as they do in the American context. Whether structured upon matrilineal or patrilineal relationships, the vitality of the Ghanaian immigrant family in America can be found in its social placement function. The pattern of family formation exhibited among the immigrants provides the nexus within which social hierarchies and the collective mobilization of resources are utilized to meet the economic, social, and psychological needs of the immigrants.

Core to the Ghanaian immigrant families is the special place given to parents as cultural nurturers of the young. Ghanaian immigrant families recognize that fathers and mothers as well as other adult figures in the kin group are also responsible for the upbringing of children. Thus, the circle of nurturers and resources available for children as well as other family members is, indeed, very extensive. Families emphasize interdependence and cooperation, and children are expected to conform to age and gender-graded expectations and not to question or challenge parental authority. Children are rarely consulted in matters affecting the family. Discipline and the social control of the behavior of children are exercised to ensure that children remain grounded in societal norms and regulations. When boys reach puberty, they begin to take on major responsibilities at home, especially taking care of and serving as role models to their younger siblings. Female children are socialized into more traditional roles, trained to be non-assertive, and often cast into expectations about their future roles as wives and mothers. Female children are usually assigned chores such as cooking or helping their mothers with doing laundry and house cleaning. Boys tend to associate and interact with their fathers and are often socialized to be independent and assertive.

Parental control, especially the father's, is considered absolute; challenges to the paternal authority are not tolerated. However, the use of physical punishment to discipline children is not tolerated. The role of mothers consists in teaching children about cultural and normative expectations, particularly the standards that children must follow to become good citizens of the community. In some of the upwardly mobile immigrant homes, children have a lot of autonomy and independence. Expectations regarding education and school performance are rigidly enforced and in this matter, children have no voice. Child socialization practices put a strong emphasis on high scholastic achievement and, at times, the parental pressure can become too overwhelming for children, particularly when parents are not able to teach their children how to maintain a balance between academic and extracurricular activities. Success-oriented activities such as intense reading and arithmetic are emphasized, and parents view these subjects as the pathway to a successful career in science and business. Fathers are closely involved with the education of their children, and they spend a lot of time modeling the educational paths of their children.

Despite the powerful influence of fathers on their children, immigrant children also benefit from their interactions with other adults. The boundaries that distinguish the parental rights of fathers and mothers over their children from the parental rights of other family members are nebulous and not fixed. Community parenting structured along consanguine, kinship, and affinal network where other immigrant families assume a collective responsibility for child-rearing is the norm in most of the immigrant families. In general, mothers and fathers in the Ghanaian immigrant community serve as parents for all the children with whom they come into contact. Parental employment outside the home has not diminished the quality of supervision that the immigrant children receive. A network of 'other parents' or 'social parents' supervise and monitor children after school hours. The system of shared care, trans-residential socialization and social control of children has minimized the problem of delinquency among immigrant teenagers. In several of the immigrant households where grandparents do not reside, parents usually designate other immigrant households where children go when they leave school rather than letting them roam the streets or be idle and home alone.

Frequently, multiple families take responsibility for paying for a part-time instructor to assist children with their school work. The teachers who are hired to teach the immigrant children usually come from the same ethnic or tribal background as the children. The immigrant families living and raising their children in larger metropolitan communities often tap into a collective parenting network where multiple families take turns often providing baby-sitting to each other's children. The same collective parenting networks enable the immigrant families to shelter their children from some of the pitfalls of inner city life such as drugs, gangs, and crime in America. The collective responsibility and task of shielding their children from urban problems dominate the lives and thoughts of immigrant parents. In the words of one urban immigrant family, "We cannot afford to make any errors with our children. We have to be strict, vigilant, and keep an eagle's eyes on them. Otherwise, they would be recruited into the dead end urban youth culture of early motherhood and fatherhood, drugs, crime, and early death."

Organizational Features of the Immigrant Families

The internal composition of the Ghanaian immigrant household in the United States reveals that there are variations in the demographic characteristics of the households. As a group, Ghanaian immigrant households tend to be young. The largest group consists of those aged between 25 and 35 years old. They comprise nearly 40 per cent of all households. They are followed by those in the 36 to 45 age group who form nearly 33 per cent of immigrant households. The next group consists of those aged between 46 and 55 years old. They form 20 per cent of all the immigrants who were studied. Those aged 56 years old and above form seven per cent of all households. Of this, four per cent are elderly aged 65 years old and above. The majority of the elderly immigrants arrived in the United States during the past 15 years. Elderly Ghanaian immigrants are less likely to be heads of their household as they tend to live with their children. Since some of them arrived in the United States toward the end of their working careers, they prefer to live with their children to ease the transition of living in a new culture.

The majority of households have children who live at home. The largest group consists of households with children under ten years old. These form nearly 60 per cent of all the immigrants. Households with children who are between 11 and 17 years old constitute 30 per cent. Immigrant households whose members are aged 18 years old and above forms nearly eight per cent. Two percent of households have no children living at home.

The gender composition of the Ghanaian immigrant household is 65 per cent male and 35 per cent female. The gender composition of the immigrant population is a reflection of the historical selectivity of migration by gender where, in the past, male outmigration was encouraged over female outmigration. Social norms now favor the migration of single women to the United States to attend school or to seek employment. The percentage of all households headed by women with no husband present is 25 per cent. Male-headed households with no wife present are 15 per cent of immigrant households. The ratio of elderly male to elderly female is two to one. Immigrant households with grandmothers or grandfathers living in them are almost 20 per cent. These grandparents make significant contributions to the economic well-being of the family. As caretakers of children, the elderly free up time so that the wife and or husband can work a second shift and thereby increase the family's total income. In Ghanaian family life, the elderly are revered for their wisdom and accorded high status at home and in the community. For the elderly Ghanaian immigrant in the United States, the migratory experience has brought new roles and expectations. These roles include cooking, sewing, walking children to school, and taking adult continuing education classes to improve their spoken English. While family members are at work, the elderly immigrants spend their time shopping for food, clothing, and other household items at discount or thrift stores. The elderly immigrants are an important cog in the management of the household economy of the immigrant family. As cultural mediators, the elderly serve as the link between children and their parents. Immigrant children often go to them to share their concerns about adverse parental decisions expecting that elderly grandparents will intervene on their behalf. In their interactions with immigrant household members, the elderly immigrants emphasize cultural continuity, traditionalism, and family heritage, often teaching children about Ghanaian and African culture through story-telling.

Ghanaian immigrant families in the United States tend to be larger than American-born families. The average number of children per immigrant household is four. Generally, the fertility rate and family size of the immigrants have yet to conform to that of the host society. This is higher than the average of two children found in native American-born households. For the Ghanaian immigrant households that were examined in this study, the data showed that in households where at least one partner holds a postgraduate degree, the average number of children is the same as that of native American-born households. Among the immigrant women with a college education, the number of children is three. For those with less than college education, the average number of children is four. Some of the immigrant households reported having five children. The cultural expectation to have many children has not diminished with migration. The desire to have many children has not thwarted the strong motivation on the part of the majority of the immigrants to achieve economic mobility and become successful in America.

The reasons cited for having many children are varied. The economic motivation to have fewer children is offset by the fact that the immigrant families rely on extended family members to assist them in the task of child-rearing. Child-rearing responsibilities and socialization are sometimes entrusted to family matriarchs who are sponsored by immigrant relatives to come to the United States to assist in raising children. In some of the immigrant households where economic conditions do not allow for the sponsorship of a maternal relative to come and assist in child-rearing, arrangements are made to send children home to Ghana where they stay with maternal or paternal relatives. This is a way for families to alleviate the economic burdens associated with child-rearing in the United States. By sending children home, the immigrants are tapping into a culturally-rich heritage of extended family members, especially elderly parents and relatives who are available to assist in raising their grand-or-great-grandchildren. The length of stay in Ghana varies depending upon the age of the children. Immigrant children who are citizens of the United States are usually sent home for the duration of their primary and middle school years, and then brought to the United States to start their high school education. Some of the families keep their children in Ghana and bring them back when they are ready to start college or university. In Ghana, the immigrant children attend elite international preparatory schools usually patronized by the expatriate community. The curriculum is rigorous and international in content. The cost associated with providing for the educational expenditures of the children is very low due to the favorable exchange rate between the American dollar and the Ghanaian cedi.

The relatively higher number of children in the Ghanaian immigrant family household is a reflection of high fertility rates among Ghanaian families in general. Cultural norms associated with fertility behavior such as the reluctance on the part of men to use contraceptive devices or to encourage their spouse(s) to use the same promote pronatal attitudes. In Ghana, large families, especially ones with many sons, are considered desirable. In traditional Ghanaian society, children are viewed as economic resources due to the services that they provide for the family. Such services include hawking or selling consumer items at street corners, assisting family members on the farms, and taking care of the elderly. In the absence of well developed social security systems in Ghana, children become an investment and are expected to contribute to the economic sustenance of the family unit at an early age. Despite the fact that a majority of African governments, including Ghana, have mandated compulsory primary and elementary school education for children, these mandates are usually unenforceable and children are frequently made to work independently or alongside their parents. It is not unusual for child labor to begin as early as age ten.

Furthermore, the economic cost associated with raising children is not typically borne by one person or one's immediate family. Extended relatives frequently contribute to the material and psychological well-being of children. Children often stay with extended family members who are relatively well-off while attending school. School fees, clothing, and healthcare expenses are borne by the extended family members. It is therefore not uncommon in a typical Ghanaian family household to find first, second, and third cousins all being raised by a single family member. The economic strain that otherwise would be put on the biological parents is minimized and in some cases averted. Shared parenting where more mature adults in the extended family unit all contribute to the economical and emotional well-being of children has become a hallmark of Ghanaian immigrant family structure in the United States. These "social fathers and mothers" provide nurturing, serve as role models, and demonstrate honesty and citizenship in the lives of the immigrant children. The absence of the biological father or mother therefore does not deprive children of adult role models.

The Trunk and Sub-Families

Family structure is based upon a strong value and normative system that the immigrants brought with them from Ghana. The Ghanaian immigrant family is deeply rooted in the values of group cohesion, solidarity, and a strong commitment to the use of collective resource mobilization for the attainment of economic and cultural goals; the family unit is the principal determinant of achieved mobility and status among the immigrants. An important feature of the immigrants' family structure is the trunk families. These are multiple families that come together to serve as the center of the immigrant family unit. The trunk families usually consist of well established family members who were the first to arrive in the United States.

They tend to cluster in the same housing sub-divisions located on the outskirts of larger urban areas. It is not uncommon to find multiple families from the same class who are related by blood, marriage, and/or adoption living together in the same household. Some of the members who form the trunk families may live further away from the main trunk households. Despite living in a separate locale, they continue to maintain contacts with every member of the family. Most of the immigrants who form the core of the trunk families are above 60 years old, often well educated, retired, and tend to be economically very successful. The majority of the households where the trunk family members reside are naturalized citizens. Part of their function includes keeping a record of all family members who arrive in the United States. The trunk families are broadly defined to include those family members who live outside the United States, particularly in Canada, Britain, Holland, and Germany.

The trunk families may also comprise young adult family members who are attending school, and in some cases, have completed their education and are working and contributing money to household budget. The trunk families usually host new immigrants for a short or long-term duration. These families allocate resources and make decisions regarding financial assistance to other immigrants from the same family background. Decisions about who to sponsor from Ghana to come to the United States are usually made by the trunk families. Among a fairly large number of the immigrant households (nearly 42 per cent), trunk families play a role in the coordination of remittances to Ghana, the education of young family members in Ghana, and the formulation of the protocols to follow relating to family issues such as marriages, births, and deaths. They assist the newly arrived immigrants to acquire the necessary papers to establish legal status in the United States. This would include paying tuition if enrolled in college or university, applying for a social security card, or a driver's license. Even when they are enrolled in school full-time, student members of the family have an obligation to work to contribute to household expenditures. Upon completion of their studies, the new immigrants often apply for work permits, which enable them to live and work in the United States while waiting for the permanent residency application to be approved. Once permanent residence is established, the process begins all over again with the sponsorship of another family member. Migration to the United States thus becomes a poverty-alleviating strategy and a process whereby Ghanaian immigrant families in the United States minimize economic burdens at home in Ghana and at the same time create resources and opportunities to strengthen the economic fortunes of the family for decades to come.

Additionally, there are subfamilies which also form along matrilineal and patrilineal lines, and are linked directly to the trunk families. They have equal access to the collective resources of the trunk families and sometimes participate in its decision-making. Their members are predominantly recent immigrants who have settled far away from the trunk families. Upon arriving in the United States, some of the sub-families locate in university and college towns where they pursue various programs of study. Upon the completion of their education, they often engage in secondary migration by relocating closer to the trunk families to search for employment. When feasible, trunk families encourage sub-families to relocate near other family members. Trunk families assist those who are willing to relocate to find housing, schools for the children, and employment. In moving closer to the trunk families, the sub-families are able to contribute also to the overall economic well-being of the entire family.

The maximization of the family's economic security is paramount because it determines the intergenerational economic well-being of the family unit. This economic security is achieved by the sponsorship of family members in Ghana to come to the United States. When new family members arrive, they add to the social and economic capital of the entire family. New members assist in creating family wealth and thereby enhance the social mobility of the entire family. Immigrant families that sponsor family members from Ghana to come to the United States often regard the sponsorship as an investment which eventually will pay-off handsomely. After they have completed their education and acquired legal status, family members collectively provide economic support for elderly immigrants who have earlier sponsored them to come to the United States. Elderly members of the family who are retired have a choice of living in the United States or repatriating to Ghana. Irrespective of where they decide to live, the elderly are guaranteed economic support, housing, and healthcare. Though most choose to stay in America, they do make frequent visits to Ghana to attend funerals, oversee supervision of family property or inheritance, and sometimes to recruit young family members for future sponsorship to the United States.

Within the Ghanaian immigrant households, the principal means by which social relationships are nurtured is through the acknowledgement and the accordance of prestige and status to family members who make financial contributions to the newly arrived to become settled. Toward this end, family members are encouraged to adopt a cooperative and altruistic philosophy rather than an individualistic approach in marshaling common resources for the common good. The propensity of the Ghanaian family unit to absorb extended kin group members by incorporating them into the household unit is, perhaps, one reason to account for the resiliency of the immigrant family unit in America. Among Ghanaian immigrants, extended family units live in separate households but share economic and cultural roles. In household units, wives, husbands, the youth, and sometimes in-laws are all expected to contribute to the economic and cultural sustenance of the family unit. Among these families, one finds a work history that is highly stable with minimal interruptions. The inclusion of extended family members in the economic affairs of the family has meant that any opportunity to offer sponsorship to other family members currently not living in the United States is approached with extreme care. After they have lived in America for a lengthy time, secured their green cards, or become naturalized citizens, the opportunity to sponsor the migration of other family members is undertaken with one goal in mind: to enhance the economic viability of the whole family unit.

Case Study of Family-Sponsored Migration: The Awotwi Family

The processes involved in family-sponsored migration among Ghanaian immigrants residing in the United States reveal an interesting sociological facet of family social organization in contemporary society. At the theoretical level, an examination of the internal structure of the Ghanaian immigrant household reveals that these households form with one principal goal in mind: to use collective resources to minimize the fears and apprehensions associated with living in a new culture. Immigrant family adaptation to the larger social and cultural polity of the United States is affected, in part, by the complex processes that immigrants use in facilitating entry to the host society. The vertical and horizontal relationships that are nurtured in these households form the basis for intergenerational migration of kin groups to the United States.

The Awotwi family illustrates the role of the Ghanaian extended family in the sponsorship of relatives to immigrate to the United States. As a case study, it highlights the decision-making processes that Ghanaian families make to ensure the short and long-term economic viability of the family. An aspect of family sponsored migration to the United States is the willingness of family members to engage in circular or stepwise migration by initially migrating to destinations in Asia and the Middle-East before eventually settling in the United States.

The Awotwi family hails from Cape Coast in the Central Region of Ghana. The formation of the Awotwi family's branch in the United States started in 1975 with the arrival of Kwame to pursue graduate education in science. In Ghana, Kwame had attended a local secondary school where he excelled in the General Certificate of Education (GCE) at the ordinary and advanced levels. Though he was able to secure admission to the university in Ghana, his relatives wanted him to travel abroad and pursue advanced education. The family raised the necessary funds from extended relatives living in the Middle-East and Nigeria to sponsor him to migrate to the United States. Kwame relied on family members to register him to take the Test of English as a Foreign Language (TOEFL), which is required by several tertiary institutions of higher learning for prospective international graduate students for whom English is a second language. Based on Kwame's performance in the GCE and TOEFL scores, he was accepted by a university in the United States. When the letter of admission arrived, the entire family was elated. The challenge was how to raise enough money to pay for his tuition. His extended family in Ghana and abroad contributed money to assist Kwame pay part of the tuition for his graduate education in the United States. With part of the tuition paid, Kwame was able to secure a student's visa at the American Consular Office in Accra. At his send-off party, he was admonished by his parents, aunts, and uncles to work hard and never forget the rest of the family who have made it possible for him to travel abroad. To meet his daily expenses, Kwame was allowed by his institution to work twenty hours a week on campus while attending school full-time.

During the summers when he was not taking classes, Kwame worked full time off campus where he made enough money to pay for the tuition and also remit home. Upon the completion of a graduate program in chemistry in the United States, Kwame obtained practical training at a major polymers company in the American Midwest. After the practical training, the company successfully petitioned immigration authorities to change Kwame's non-immigrant visa to that of permanent resident based on the third preference visa category, which allows non-immigrants with skills in short supply to become legal residents of the United States. The polymers company offered him a salary of $60,000 a year. By the end of his first year of work, he had managed to save about $12,000 which was to be used in sponsoring another family member. Kwame contacted his uncle in Ghana who called a family meeting.

At this meeting, a decision was made about who to sponsor to join Kwame in the United States.

Takyi, a first cousin of Kwame who had left Ghana to teach secondary school in Nigeria, was the family's choice. He had already completed Winneba Teacher's Training College in Ghana prior to leaving for Nigeria. Kwame found a school for him in the United States and used the money he had saved to pay his tuition for one academic year. With this, Takyi was able to secure a student visa from the American consulate office in Lagos. Takyi's choice of specialty in college was computer science. While pursuing his studies in the United States, Takyi stayed with Kwame and his wife and often assisted in every aspect of day-to-day household functions.

Takyi completed the two-year associate degree in computer science and was able to obtain employment before the completion of his studies. He then enrolled at a university where he successfully completed a bachelor's program in computer and electrical engineering. Within eighteen months of completing his studies, Takyi had become a permanent resident of the United States. Like Kwame, Takyi was able to find an employer that sponsored him for permanent residency; five years later he became a naturalized citizen. After he got married, Takyi continued to live with Kwame's family. The two families combined their resources and shared in all the household expenditures. They took turns providing baby-sitting, cooking, washing, cleaning, and assisting the children with their school work. Upon becoming a naturalized citizen, Kwame sponsored two nieces from Ghana to come to the United States and attend school. When the two nieces graduated from college, they too landed jobs and with their income were able to sponsor more family members to immigrate to the United States. With the arrival and settlement of the two nieces, the nerve center of the first wave of the Awotwi family to immigrate to the United States had formed.

The second wave started with the sponsorship of the parents of both Kwame and Takyi under the family reunification provision in American immigration law. Not long after their arrival, they in turn petitioned the immigration authorities to reunite in the United States with their unmarried children living in Ghana. The second wave of relatives set up a household in close proximity to Kwame and Takyi. The household comprised of two parent couples (Kwame's parents and Takyi's parents), three unmarried children, and another relative. To assist the members of the second wave settle in the United States, financial contributions came from other Awotwi relatives living as far away as Germany, Spain, and the Middle-East. Immediate expenses included purchasing a home, payment of their children's education, and providing adequate healthcare for the parents. Upon becoming self sufficient, the second wave of family members will start contributing funds to enable other family members in Ghana to come to the United States.

The economic relationship between the first and second wave households is symmetrical. The immigrant household is both a welfare agency and a corporation. The norm is self sufficiency and independence. Household members contribute to the continued economic well-being of the family unit and group rather than promoting individual well-being. Every member is viewed as a resource and asset in harnessing the collective potential of the members in two main areas: education and labor force participation. Shared expenditures are common and very frequently, members of the two households meet and make decisions about household welfare. The household units also maintain a savings fund out of which they send regular remittances to Ghana. Additionally, every effort is made to promote the education of the younger members of the household. After all, this is how the Awotwi family has managed to enhance its human capital potential in the United States. Family members who are reluctant to play according to the prescribed rules are often sanctioned. For example, when one of the newly arrived children started skipping school and not doing their homework, a family meeting of the two households was called and using a combination of cajoling and threats, the young lad was straightened out.

The first wave of relatives stays in the same geographic region. As more family members immigrate to the United States, new subsidiaries or branches of the original family are formed. Lateral mobilization of resources from all new families is undertaken with the goal of raising capital for more sponsorship, or to help family members meet their economic and educational needs. As indicated, the first-wave of families usually serve as the trunk families and are often called upon to make decisions about monetary appropriations, and social control of household members who have violated family norms and expectations. Though rare, some households apply a wide range of sanctions in the form of ostracism, avoidance, and outright withholding of family resources to family members who stray from family traditions. This happens when the collective wisdom of the family is able to establish abuse, neglect, failure to work, having children out of wedlock, alcoholism, and law violation of some of its members.

The Ghanaian immigrant family is not a passive, isolated unit that is separate from the surrounding community. Rather, the immigrant families shape, and in turn, are shaped by the communities in which the immigrants reside. Always a dynamic unit, the Ghanaian immigrant families are connected, in varying degrees, to the political, cultural, economic, and social vitality of their new communities. In the immigrant community, the family unit is regarded as a site for cultural and economic production. As a cultural production unit, the Ghanaian immigrant family in the United States has the responsibility of transmitting the cultural and normative beliefs of Ghana to its members. Family cohesiveness and ties are fostered by kin-group bonds that are structured on feelings of loyalty, obligation, responsibility, and philanthropy. Among the immigrants residing in predominantly immigrant and African ethnic enclave communities, family life is seen as an extension of community life. Demarcations of where family life begins and community organization starts is very thin as family life is interwoven into community organization. The community is viewed as a resource organization with the means to assist families in meeting such critical needs as education, healthcare, and social defense. Understanding the community contexts of social relations and participation in its activities is *sine qua non* for the attainment of community integration.

Due to their immigrant and "foreign" status, Ghanaian immigrant families carefully construct their community and civic engagements with four goals in mind: the accentuation and affirmation of values that promote family cohesion, recognition of the special place of children in family life, reverence for the elderly, and frugal living with an eye toward future economic security. Like other immigrants living in the United States, Ghanaian immigrants also believe that community transcends a fixed spatial location. The sense of community as a shared space is defined in terms of a symbiotic relationship. This relationship rests on the notion that communities provide the form and structure within which collective goals become attainable. For the Ghanaian immigrants in the United States, the very idea of family expands to include both close and distant relatives living in other parts of the world. This world view of the family unit defined across international borders is significant because it provides the family a wide array of economic resources to tap into to meet collectively defined goals. Again, this strengthens the hand of the family unit as an agency of economic production.

In spite of its remarkable internal resiliency, the Ghanaian immigrant family unit is also a site for conflicts and schisms. Strains caused by intergenerational differences between young and old are evident in several domains of immigrant family life. There are second and in some cases third generation Ghanaian immigrants who are forging identities quite different from the ones formed by their predecessors in the United States. The second and third generation immigrants and their children have experienced almost complete assimilation and possess characteristics that are common to the generalized society of middle-class America. These families no longer stress the imperative of traditional African social values and normative expectations. Young men and women are adopting the American cultural ideal of marriage, dating, and gender roles. The shifts to egalitarian marital relationships have empowered Ghanaian immigrant women to seek better opportunities for themselves and their children.

Redefining Gender Roles and New Economic Realities

The nexus of gender and marital roles offers another glimpse into the web of the Ghanaian immigrant family life and how it is organized in the United States. The distribution of tasks between husbands and wives has usually followed traditional Ghanaian expectations regarding the role of men and women in Ghanaian society. Primarily, the task of child-rearing in Ghanaian society is entrusted to women or matriarchs. But this major responsibility has not in any way hindered the full participation of women in the labor force. In three key sectors of the Ghanaian economy (agricultural production, marketing, and distribution), women have carved a professional niche for themselves. For example, Ghanaian women control the bulk of retailing and distribution of essential economic commodities in the country. Though not very large or capital intensive, many of the retailing and distribution activities provide Ghanaian women with incomes, employment, and an opportunity to meet the economic needs of their households. The opportunity to work in the retail and distribution sectors of the economy has also influenced the social status of Ghanaian women.

Upon migrating to the United States, Ghanaian immigrant women have continued in the tradition of maintaining gainful employment outside the home. Like their male counterparts, the immigrant women have been able to find and maintain successful employment in all sectors of the American economy. Their ability to find jobs has been enhanced by the fact that over 93 per cent of the women had completed secondary, technical, vocational, or teacher training education prior to their immigration. A few completed their university education in Ghana. Having secondary or tertiary educational credentials has opened up many options for employment for the women outside the home. In addition, a tertiary degree also makes it highly possible that prospective immigrants who want to pursue further education in the United States would be granted visas.

The shared breadwinner role of Ghanaian immigrant fathers and mothers has not undergone major transitions following the migration to the United States. Indeed, it has rather been strengthened because the majority of the immigrant men and women recognize that the path to a successful economic future does not rest solely on the shoulders of one person. Instead, a family's financial security is directly associated with the existence of a household where both spouses are active in the labor force and make regular contributions to the family's income. The emphasis on egalitarian notions in their domestic arrangements have proven financially rewarding for the Ghanaian immigrants. In households where both spouses worked for at least 35 hours a week, average total family income is as high as $82,000 per year. In several instances, many immigrant husbands and wives hold multiple jobs to supplement family income. Using a network of immigrant families who provide baby-sitting assistance and sometimes cook for each other or take turns eating at each others' homes, immigrant husbands and wives are able to free up time to hold additional jobs or improve upon their income earning potential by going back to school.

As these families pursue economic and cultural opportunities offered in America, they have blurred the traditional distinctions between men and women's roles that they had left behind in Ghana. The need to harmonize their collective resources to meet economic goals in the United States has promoted greater gender equality between immigrant husbands and wives. To cope with chronic unemployment, families will often relocate to more favorable employment centers in the United States. The cost of moving is usually shared by extended family members. Relocation is embarked upon only to destinations where other extended family members have already settled. Often times, it is these families that will provide initial economic support until the unemployed migrant is able to secure employment.

The identities of some of the Ghanaian immigrant women have undergone significant transformations due to migration, education, and labor force participation in the United States. The employment of the immigrant women outside the home has given them the economic resources they need to better negotiate more egalitarian terms of marital relations with their husbands. The case of Afi, a Ghanaian immigrant woman illustrates the importance that the immigrant women attach to the importance of having paid employment outside the home. For three years, Afi did not work and depended on the husband for economic support. According to Afi, "getting my husband to pay for all the household expenses diminished me in his presence. I lost his respect, particularly when he insisted as he did often that I account for every cent he gave me to buy food and clothing for the children. I always had to ask him for money to buy personal things, even including money to send home to my aging parents." Eventually, Afi decided to look for employment and put her licensed nursing practitioner training to use. She found work at a nearby senior citizen center where she made a little under $2,000 a month with benefits included. This changed the dynamics of her relationship with the husband. With this income, Afi stopped depending on her husband for financial support. She started operating a personal savings account independent of the joint account she shared with her husband. From her point of view, the conflicts that she was having with her husband over financial matters ceased only because her husband came to recognize her as an equal partner in economic terms. Earning an income outside of the home environment means that several of the women will not have to depend on their husbands for total financial support. And even though the Ghanaian immigrant woman's employment outside the home has yet to lead to an increase in the share of household and domestic work performed by their husbands, work outside the home is an affirmation of the autonomy and growing gender equalization in terms of household power dynamics.

Although migration and the opportunity to work outside the home have increased the economic power and status of Ghanaian immigrant women, in some cases there is still a strong attachment to the patriarchal style of marital relationships because of the protection and security they offer to women. For some of the women, work outside the home combined with having to perform the bulk of household work does not symbolize an acknowledgment of having a lower status relative to their husbands. Instead, combining employment outside the home and taking care of family needs at the same time is seen as an affirmation of a woman's commitment to her children and not the embracing of patriarchal structures that traditionally dominated women. According to one immigrant woman who manages a large department store in a suburban county near Houston, "the cooking, cleaning, and nurturing of my children after I return home from work, having worked eight hours, is not intended to demonstrate to my husband that I have a subordinate status. It is instead an affirmation of my natural role to work to ensure the economic security of my children. It is therefore not about my husband's power over me. It is about my children who happen to be the future." Another immigrant woman echoed this sentiment. She stated that while work and family life have become inseparable domains for immigrant women, the multiple tasks involved in managing a home is not intended to cast them into a subordinate role relative to their husbands. Having control over how their household functions is a way for the women to ensure the future security and stability of their home while at the same time embracing the notion that the continuity of the family unit does not rest solely with whether or not the husband performs his obligations to the family. "Several of the women I know from Ghana who are here have been very successful in meeting the economic and psychological needs of their children without the tacit support of their husbands. They (referring to the men) can hold on to their patriarchal roles if it makes them feel powerful. We will hold on to our children," she proclaimed.

The Immigrant Women's Circles: Bounded Trust and Economic Survival

Women are active participants in the shaping of the Ghanaian diaspora in the United States. The roles and statuses occupied by Ghanaian immigrant women are important to the understanding of gender relationships and household dynamics. As a result of migration, the women have managed to empower themselves and have gained an equal voice in family decision making. Some of the immigrant women have formed social groups that bring together immigrant women from different households and families who regularly interact and exchange information about strategies to effectively manage the day-to-day functions of their households. In communities where there are several of them, Ghanaian immigrant women usually form a social circle or networks. These networks often serve as a form of voluntary association designed to enable the women meet the day-to-day economic and social (parenting) needs of their individual households. The women in these circles are from different immigrant families who live in the same community. The inner relationships that are fostered in these circles are intended to collect and mobilize the resources of the members to meet the economic, cultural, and psychological needs of the entire family. The goal here is not to overtly challenge male dominance and the patriarchal system of power. Rather, it is intended to enlist the assistance of their husbands in the rearing of children and the provision of economic sustenance for the family. Through the immigrant women's circles, some of the women have been able to forge compromises with their husbands over a wide range of issues related to gender expectations.

Membership in the women's circles is opened to any immigrant woman who wishes to join. One does not have to come from Ghana or even from the same ethnic or tribal community to join. In cases where there are not enough women from the same ethnic community in Ghana, efforts are made to expand the boundaries of family to include any immigrant women of the black African-Caribbean and American black diaspora currently in the United States. This is what some of the women immigrants referred to as distant kin. In extending the definition of kin, the immigrant women are able to widen the circle of their support network and at the same time mobilize resources for dealing with the uncertainties of living abroad. Kibria (1993) and Koltyk (1998) reported of similar kin group extensions and the formation of collective groups among Hmong and Vietnamese immigrants in the United States. And as Oxfeld (1993) pointed out, immigrants are not passive actors who are influenced by external forces all the time. Most immigrants in the United States are active creators of culture, often reconstructing and redefining their culture to ensure its survival

Each circle is made up of ten to fifteen members. The groups vary in their membership and structure. The women's circles can be divided into two groups according to the age of the members. There are circles of young women who are aged between 25 and 40 years old and the circles of women who are been 41 and 55 years old. All the women in the two age cohorts hail from different class and ethnic groups. They are drawn from professions ranging from school teachers, engineers, and pharmacists to hairdressers, maids, parking ramp attendants, and grocers. The women meet regularly, sharing information and resources about jobs, healthcare, children's education, and childcare. They exchange used clothing, food, housewares and appliances. Tips on how to handle social service agencies, law enforcement, school authorities, and abusive husbands are also discussed.

In Ghana, the kinship ties and friendship networks that women form are primarily with their husbands' extended family relations. The patriarchal structure limits the opportunities that women have to form their own networks to find a common expression of their dreams, hopes, and aspirations. This diminishes the collective power of women in family and community decision making. Decisions regarding economic and political concerns frequently are made by men with little or no input from women. However, in instances where women operate their own businesses, they contribute substantial income to the household budget, but despite the equal contributions that they make to household maintenance, women in Ghana still remain marginalized and powerless at the community and national level. Historically, men have abrogated to themselves this right.

Coming to America has altered the gender roles among the Ghanaian immigrant men and women. While the immigrant women have maintained their role as cultural producers and nurturers, it is in their relationship with their husbands that significant gender relations have undergone transformation. Equal partnership and collective decision making is now the norm. While husbands still have the prerogatives to pursue their patriarchal interests, the expectation on the part of the immigrant women is that these prerogatives should not conflict or be at odds with the overall interests of the family, especially that of the children. However, though the immigrant women reject the rigid patriarchal structure of family relationships in Ghana, they are nonetheless willing to work within a similar structure, no matter how unequal it is, to ensure that the interests of children or dependents are not economically jeopardized. For most of the immigrant women, the balancing of the husband's traditional and patriarchal rights against the rights of the children is premised on the belief that children are entitled to be nurtured in an environment that is not only safe, but also one in which couples join their resources to ensure the economic security of the family. The immigrant women's circles have been able to recreate and negotiate new roles and obligations by expanding kinship groups to include non-relatives who are also adapting to the challenges of international migration. By having fewer in-laws to deal with in the United States, many of the women indicated that they have managed to have a voice in family decision making. When elderly parents are sponsored to come to the United States, it is usually the husband's parents who are the first to arrive. For some of the immigrant women, having to live with in-laws have come to mean conflicts with their mother in-laws which often centers on child rearing issues, particularly the appropriateness and forms of child disciplinary approaches to use when children disobey parents or violate family rules. The conflicts or misunderstandings become more volatile when the husband takes the side of the mother over a spouse. In the case of one immigrant family, this rift resulted in the in-laws having to relocate elsewhere. Even so, the relocation did not bring about a cessation to the tension between the wife and her mother in-law. The conflicts ended only when the mother in-law voluntarily repatriated to Ghana.

Generally, the immigrant women indicated that they are supportive of their husbands often when some of them had to cope with job-related issues and how to maintain a balance between the expectations of fatherhood in the United States as well as in Ghana. In some instances, as a result of migration, immigrant men have experienced downward mobility due to unemployment, lack of job skills, education, and nontransferability of educational credentials. This downward mobility has had a deleterious impact on family relationships. Immigrant men suffering from downward mobility resent having lost their economic support role; this loss is often accompanied by shame, guilt, and loss of self-esteem. Some of the families in the women's circles have dealt with this problem by drawing on their close-knit bonds and economic cooperation to ensure that these men are not negatively affected. Strong kinship bonds and the economic integration of these men into household management and family decision making has meant that for the most part, they have been able to retain their status even though their breadwinner role has been jeopardized or diminished. Still, perceptions of males who lost their status and earning power have been a major impetus of domestic violence, and child abuse. Reluctant to call the police or alert child welfare agencies about abuse, some women silently endure violent victimization at the hands of their husbands. Informal arbitration and reconciliation using extended family networks have often failed to alleviate the problem. Some of the women have been able to leave their husbands and set up new residences elsewhere. Some immigrant men who are confronted with drastic downward mobility choose to abandon the family unit and relocate to a new community away from external family members.

Intervention in family disputes and arbitration is common to the women's circles. The circles rely on informal social control to resolve pressing intra and inter-family disputes. Using a combination of gossip, shaming, and ostracism, the women's circles often succeed in nudging wayward family members (especially husbands) to comply and fulfill family expectations. The case of the ex-husband of one of the immigrant women illustrates the use of informal social control to obtain compliance and conformity. The estranged husband had abandoned his children and for a while was not providing financial support; therefore, his family depended on community support from other immigrants. Some of the women openly chided the estranged husband for shirking his familial responsibilities. When word spread in the immigrant community about this man, he felt that the only way he could avoid the shame, disrepute, and anger of the other immigrants was to resume his financial obligations to his family. The risk of being completely ostracized is costly. His access to community economic resources would diminish. He would also risk not having the psychological and emotional support of family members which could also dim prospects for employment if he suffered a job loss.

A sense of collectively held values and sentiments prevail among the women's circles participants as to how to garner their resources to obtain egalitarian relationships with their husbands. United in their common experience of migration, the women in the circles rely on the support of the circle members to define and construct meanings unique to their individual and collective circumstances in the United States. Through these circles, some of the women have been able to gain power in their relationships without destroying the fundamental cultural ethos of family life. In fact, the existence of these circles has strengthened ties within the family unit and provided informal outlets for the mediation of conflicts. The women have succeeded in using the informal structure of the circles to gain and wield influence over the young. While husbands maintain their patriarchal authority regime over children, the women have been able to gradually chip away the absolute power of the men in their households. In doing so, they have managed to alter the economic and cultural balance of power in their favor. Combined with their high rate of labor force participation and financial contributions to household consumption, many of the women in the circles have managed to maintain an egalitarian pattern in their relationship with their husbands, and at the same time recast their womanhood in ways that protect equal status in family relations.

For women in the immigrant circles who do not have to depend on their husbands to obtain their permanent resident status (or green card), the degree of personal autonomy and independence diminishes the husband's ability to exercise control and enforce patriarchal norms. The women viewed the possession of legal status as essential for minimizing and warding off intra family schisms particularly when their husbands insist on following patriarchal traditions. The protection and security that comes from having an immigration status that is not dependent on the husband's status is perceived as liberating and empowering. The immigrant women who have a legal status that is independent of their spouse are usually able to sponsor relatives from Ghana to join her family in the United States. This sponsorship has the potential to further enhance the economic security of the women and increase their bargaining power in their relationship with their husbands. Having an immigration status independent of the spouse ensures egalitarian family relationships at home. When the women have to depend on their husbands to obtain legal status, the husband's hegemony over the household is increased, making the wife more dependent and unequal in household decision making.

Finding suitable male partners is proving difficult for a growing number of Ghanaian women, especially the well-educated professional class. The marriage squeeze is due, in part, to an imbalance in the ratio of marriage-age women to marriage-age men. The median age at first marriage is approximately 36 years old for immigrant women. This is certainly higher than the age of first marriage among Ghanaian women at home where the median age of marriage is about 24 years old for women with secondary or postsecondary education. For Ghanaian women with secondary school education or less, the median age at marriage is 22 years old.

The preference among the immigrant women with postsecondary credentials is to marry men with similar or higher credentials and socioeconomic status. The majority of these women had completed their university education in Ghana prior to immigrating to the United States. Some of the women have pursued postgraduate degrees in the arts and sciences and are gainfully employed in professional and managerial roles. This group of immigrant women indicated that they would be married had they not immigrated to the United States. The absence of a suitable male partner does not mean that these women do not intend to create a family of their own. Adoption of Ghanaian children is commonplace among immigrant women who are single. Some of the women have tried to adopt American children but reported that the process was too cumbersome and costly. In addition, immigrant women with legal status often sponsor male spouses from Ghana to immigrate to the United States. Immigration laws give preference to legal immigrants to petition the immigration office for permission to reunite with spouses who are nonimmigrants or do not have legal status in the United States.

Family-arranged marriage is becoming a common experience among single immigrant women. Frequent visits are made to Ghana to find suitable marital partners. Sometimes, when extended family members find a suitable mate, they pass word to relatives in the United States. For those women seeking to find future partners, visits are regularly made to Ghana to find or meet a potential spouse. Romantic love is not the sole basis for mate selection among the women. Compatibility, ethnicity, education, and transferability of skills from Ghana to the United States weigh in the decision of whether or not to sponsor a spouse.

Another strategy of adapting to the marriage squeeze among the Ghanaian immigrant women is to marry into the black diasporic immigrant population in the United States, particularly those from the Caribbean and other parts of Africa. Ethnic mixing is becoming very common among the immigrants in terms of choosing a marriage partner. The women are not obliged to marry someone from home even though that option is considered. The cultural norms and family pressures that previously encouraged endogamy have been weakened by the changes that accompany migration and the gravitation toward a common value orientation. Several of the women feel free to choose who their partners are going to be based on homogamy and shared beliefs. Romantic love forms the basis for the selection of partners although a few of the immigrant women prefer to marry someone from the same ethnic or clan background.

Migration and the Status of Ghanaian Immigrant Women

Women and migration in contemporary African society have not received a lot of attention among social scientists. Studies on African migration have focused on male out-migration. Males have dominated the migratory process largely because of the division of labor and gender specialization. Throughout Africa, young men are expected to migrate to look for employment in the urban sector. The economic, social, and political advantages that stem from male migration are numerous. Males migrate as a way to acquire status and community prestige. Returning migrants become agents of social change, bringing with them the innovations in culture that they have been exposed to in the urban social system. Male migrants use the economic benefits reaped from their migratory undertaking to start businesses or run for political office. For young men, the migration experience tends to boost the prospects for finding a wife.

While there were no social rules that prevented women from migrating, most did not because the system of domestic relations and economic production cast women in household and agricultural roles which thwarted their movement away from the family on a short or long term basis. When women have migrated to urban centers, they have done so on a temporary basis: either to buy consumer goods in the urban areas to sell in the rural areas, or very infrequently, to accompany a husband who is working in a mine or factory located in an urban or remote setting, or to attend school. Even when they have migrated, sometimes the objective is simply to assist family members living in urban areas with household chores and childcare, fulfilling a domestic role.

The proliferation of primary and secondary school education in Ghana opened up opportunities for women beyond the rural or village environment. Following independence, women from Ghana's rural areas started flocking to the commercial and urban centers after leaving school to work in the formal and informal sectors of the economy. A number of women have been very successful in establishing their own trade businesses and stores where they hawk local and imported merchandise. With time, some of the women have been able to expand their horizons beyond the borders of Ghana by engaging in inter-regional retailing (for instance traveling to and from Accra and Aflao, or Accra to Lagos). As they became more seasoned travelers, women began to cast their eyes to more distant lands, often to pursue economic and cultural goals in destinations such as the United States.

Ghanaian immigrant women are seasoned migrants. Some had engaged in circular migration when they left Ghana and went to Nigeria, Liberia, or Zimbabwe to teach or work as nurses during the reign of General Acheampong. During the 1970s and 1980s, Ghanaian women started looking at the Eastern European countries as possible destinations because of the relative ease of securing visas. The lessons learned from engaging in regional migration in Africa certainly enhanced their subsequent migration to Europe and later to the United States. Initially, the migration of Ghanaian women was highly selective by education. The majority of the migrants tended to be those who had at least completed secondary school education or possessed postsecondary credentials. But as the economic benefits bestowed upon women who migrated to other destinations for work or education began to be felt, women with poor educational backgrounds started to follow in suit.

Many of the Ghanaian immigrant women describe their immigrant experience in the United States as a "positive one." Among those who came to the United States to pursue education, the most important influences on their lives since arriving in America have come from the new contacts, values, choices, and lifestyles that they perceive to be available to them. These changes have enhanced the status of the women by opening up opportunities for schooling, entrepreneurship, and family life. New aspirations are being formed even as old values regarding women's roles in African cultural life are also affirmed.

For Ghanaian women who migrated to the United States independent of any sponsorship from their extended family or spouse, the immigration experience is perceived to be very beneficial in enhancing the status of women. Speaking often in economic terms, the women noted the material improvement in the quality of their lives following their migration to this country. For these women, the opportunities to work, earn their own income, and become economically independent have proven beneficial as well as liberating. These women describe the limiting effects of Ghanaian culture on their lives, where their identity was shaped largely by fathers, husbands, and entrenched patriarchal relations that deprived them of their full potential. Their high rates of labor force participation has meant that Ghanaian immigrant women are able to support themselves economically and at the same time contribute to the financial well-being of their families. Immigrant women's enhanced economic and cultural roles have also led to their increased decision-making power in marital and household affairs. Cohorts of Ghanaian immigrant women are defining and living their own formulations of family life in America with or without the support of their male partners.

An analysis of immigrant household or family structure, gender roles, and kin networks and composition are very important for the understanding of Ghanaian migration to the United States. The adaptation of the Ghanaian immigrant households to the realities of life in America has been facilitated, in part, by the loose definition of family membership to include both kin and fictive relations. In defining the family in broad terms, the immigrant households are able to preserve the traditional underpinnings of the Ghanaian family and at the same time alter it to meet the new expectations arising from the migratory experience. Migration to the United States has definitely had an impact on family life and gender relations in the Ghanaian immigrant household. The women are relying on the new status that they have managed to forge in this country to renegotiate more equalitarian relationships with their spouses. Many of the women use the power that they derive from the immigrant women's associations to minimize the strong patriarchal norms that dominate their lives. The continued increase in the Ghanaian immigrant population in the United States is going to test the limits of immigrant familial relationships and possibly redefine the contextual dynamics and future direction of the Ghanaian-American immigrant household in the United States.

The Ghanaian immigrant family in the United States is still evolving. The future of the immigrant family is going to be shaped by the forces of immigration, labor market conditions, gender relations, and the ability of the immigrant families to adapt or blend their cultures to an ever-changing social, political, and economic landscape in the United States. The Ghanaian-American family in the United States is very diverse in structure, size, socioeconomic status, and kinship networks. In spite of its internal differences and diversity, the immigrant family is the centerpiece of the creation of the Ghanaian-American diaspora in this country. Strong networks of kinship that bond individuals who are related by blood, marriage, or friendship have been pivotal to the adaptation of immigrant families in the United States. These bonds have facilitated acculturation and entry into the larger society. Family interactions are designed to promote the economic interests of the family and to ensure that resources are organized to achieve familial cooperation and ultimately, economic independence. For a majority of the Ghanaian immigrant families in the United States, continued migration of extended family members has become the dominant strategy for economic and cultural survival. To a large degree, the bonds that are fostered in the immigrant families are meant to continue and maintain the culture that the immigrants had at home before their migration. The new bonds that they establish here are not intended to replace the old bonds. The embracement of the new bonds in the United States does not symbolize complete assimilation into American life. Rather, the new bonds are selectively chosen to affirm beliefs and values the immigrants already subscribe to. This form of segmented assimilation as Portes and Zhou (1993); and Portes (1995) have affirmed are carefully chosen to augment Ghanaian beliefs, not to replace those beliefs with American beliefs.

Chapter 5

Identity Matters: Carving Patterns of Racial, Ethnic, and Class Niches

Immigrants and the Construction of Identities in the United States

As part of the new transnational migration of people from predominantly non-European ancestries to the United States, Ghanaian immigrants have become part of the continuously evolving racial and ethnic mosaic of America. Their subjective expressions and manifestations of racial, ethnic, and class identities become part of the collective experiences that newcomers to America must forge with the members and institutions of the majority society. From a sociological point of view, the manifestations of these identities, as complex as they might be, are critical in defining the relationships among minority and majority groups. The processes involved in defining and expressing notions of race, ethnic, and class identity formations become significant in determining access to opportunities and resources in the host society. These processes help define the forms and styles of adaptation, and community integration that immigrants who come from Ghana, and elsewhere in the world to the United States establish with their new home.

When people migrate from one country to another either, for a temporary or permanent settlement, they become part of a minority group and must adapt to the social structure or culture of the host society. The multidimensional processes involved in learning the expectations of a new culture are challenging. Adaptation requires that immigrants undergo a socialization process to learn the values, norms, and culture of the dominant society. The relationship between the dominant culture and the minority culture usually becomes a contested terrain as both members of the superordinate and subordinate groups become embroiled in interethnic schisms and rivalry over the allocation of power, status, and the distribution of scarce resources.

The system of ethnic stratification and the exercise of power by the dominant cultures over new settlers have often resulted in genocide, expulsion, discrimination (*de jure* and *de facto*), enslavement, segregation, incorporation, or assimilation into the body polity of the dominant society. At the core of this inter-ethnic tension between the majority and minority societies is the perceived or real threat on the part of the majority society that their values, culture, and normative identity and heritage will be diluted or even lost forever. The fear and uncertainty held by the majority group toward the minority ethnic group lie at the heart of institutionalized and legal discrimination in a highly diverse society like the United States.

Ethnic and racial categorization and distinction in the United States are intense, entrenched, and have been sustained over a long period of time. Skin color and place of national origin are two poignant factors that have shaped the inclusion or exclusion of immigrants and minorities into the body polity of American society. Throughout American immigration history, various ethnic and racial groups have tried to replicate their cultures and identities as newcomers in America. Many a time, this negotiation and entrance-seeking inclusion into the majority society have proved very contentious. While some immigrant groups are able to gain acceptance and hence inclusion, especially those from Western European backgrounds, others, such as people of black African ancestry struggle to gain inclusion due to racism, discrimination, and having the status of "visible other."

Theories explaining ethnic relations are diverse yet not encompassing enough to explain the varied aspects of ethnic relationships. These theories emphasize assimilation, pluralism, and power-stratification. Assimilation theories stress that minority groups conform to the norms and values of the dominant group, exhibiting unqualified acceptance of their ways of life. The pluralist perspective maintains the imperative of multiple cultures coexisting and preserving each other's cultures within a framework of tolerance, respect, and mutual harmony rather than hostility, prejudice, discrimination, and violence. The power-stratification theories stress the mobilization of power by the superordinate ethnic groups to create and control an ethnic caste system in which those who are subordinates would be cast to positions of low socioeconomic roles and statuses.

Racial and Ethnic Identity Expressions of Ghanaian Immigrants

The construction of racial and ethnic identity among Ghanaian immigrants in the United States is a confluence of two interrelated factors. The first consists of the immigrants' own assumptions about black America that they brought with them from Ghana upon their arrival in the host society. The second is the immigrants' subjective and objective experiences of how groups with unequal power and status in American society express racial and ethnic identity. Ghanaian immigrant cultural images of native born black Americans are filtered through communication outlets in Ghana. The Ghanaian immigrant is cognizant of the historical discrimination that black Americans have had to encounter over the centuries and denounce the poor treatment of blacks in America. Often cast in subservient, disparaging roles, and negative stereotypes in American society, the cultural images Ghanaian immigrants form about black Americans suggest that they are second class subordinate citizens in their own country, often having to live with the vicissitudes of deeply entrenched institutionalized racism and discrimination. Even after the end of slavery, the integration of blacks into the core of American society was seen as half-hearted and woefully inadequate. The image that is etched in the minds of Ghanaian immigrants is that black Americans have to fight the white establishment for everything that many white Americans take for granted: equal opportunity, access to education, employment, and quality housing. In this regard, Ghanaians in America see a paradox in the predicament of black Americans: they are permanent outsiders, living in America but not yet part of it, excluded from full participation and integration through conscious and deliberative denigration by the white majority society. This denigration extends to people of color irrespective of their immigration status. For blacks in general, there is a strong sense that they are stigmatized negatively by the white society. This stigma creates a heightened sense of consciousness among blacks that they are a minority group enclosed within a world of very powerful whites (Sutton and Makiesky, 1975).

In spite of the immigrants' perceptions about the poor treatment of blacks in America, most of the immigrants believe that American-born blacks are relatively better off on all measures of economic and social well-being compared to their counterparts in Africa. They note the progress, albeit slow, that blacks have made in education, home ownership, labor force, and political participation; they find this advancement inspiring and use it as a frame of reference to be optimistic about their own life chances in the United States. To most Ghanaian-Americans, being an American citizen has intrinsic worth because of the economic and cultural opportunities America offers.

Stereotypes in the wider culture associated with people of black African ancestry in America no doubt have had an impact on how Ghanaian immigrants construct and express racial and ethnic identity. The immigrants are conscious of the sub-cultural images and perceptions associated with criminal behavior and gang lifestyles of male urban black youth. Antiblack sentiments usually form the basis for rationalizing the low social and economic conditions of blacks in America. To most Ghanaian immigrants who have settled in the United States, these antiblack and African sentiments are illustrative of the insidious racism in America. The immigrants perceive that these sentiments affect the life chances and opportunities for blacks in general to advance and achieve social mobility in America. While a few of the immigrants perceive that racism is on the decline in the country, the majority of the émigrés perceive that the deleterious impact of racism is firmly entrenched in American society and that its abatement will require significant policy shifts at the national level to incorporate racial minorities into the body polity of American society. For those who perceive that race relations have improved significantly, there is a tendency to emphasize class, income, and occupational membership rather than race (Wilson, 1980).

Leery of the pervasiveness of white institutionalized racism and political monopoly, the majority of Ghanaian immigrants believe that the development of strong pro-black, positive images anchored in enterprise, motivation, personal ambition, and the belief that anything is attainable are proven ways to defeat antiblack sentiments in the United States. From the perspective of the immigrants, Ghana is still home and the identities of the immigrants, who they are, their self image and character have all been formed prior to their migration to the United States. The Ghanaian immigrant identity is based upon positive images of black self-worth, strong traditional and moral anchors, and role models who affirm collective social norms based on respect for individuals and the community-at-large. This identity is based on affirmation of blacks who are successful in all walks of life, and who hold important community and national positions of leadership. Thus, the cultural images and identities the immigrants bring with them to the United States coupled with the commitment to maintain those identities upon arrival are what shields them from the stultifying effects of generalized antiblack sentiments that are pervasive in the United States. The continuity of that identity in America is premised on the belief that ultimately, what matters is how they are seen by their fellow Ghanaians at home, and not how they are defined racially or ethnically while living in the United States. Images of racial and ethnic identity are therefore constructed in consonance with the immigrants' ideals about who they are first as Ghanaians, and second as black Africans. In defining identity emphasis is placed on achievement, mobility, and a strong reliance on Ghanaian traditional institutions, such as the network of family and friends who work tirelessly to provide for, and cater to each other's needs.

To ward off the effects of racism and discrimination in the United States, Ghanaian immigrants tend to stress Ghanaian nationalism, which they celebrate through the various Ghanaian National Immigrant Associations (GNIA) and their local chapters formed all across America. This nationalism provides the immigrants with a sense of belonging and a prism through which to filter the constant negative race and class biases and pressures that peoples of African descent in the United States must contend with. When they celebrate with pomp and pageantry the national independence day of Ghana and other Ghanaian holidays, the goal is to accentuate their separateness in a foreign land while at the same time negotiating an identity with the rest of America that is based upon their citizenship, identity, and place in Ghana. This sense of belonging is an invaluable affirmation of their individual and collective identities, which is often mediated through language, music, carnivals, dress patterns, foods, and fads that define what it means to be Ghanaian. In spite of the fact that they are not monolithic in terms of how they express their Ghanaian identities, and indeed are often divided along tribal and class lines, the Ghanaians are nonetheless united in their resolve to nurture and preserve aspects of their culture that they are able to replicate in the United States to ensure their survival. Always looking towards home for the continuity of their identities has meant that ties and bonds with home are not severed. The cultural cleavage nurtured by spontaneous affiliations and identification with anyone who hails from Ghana has served to widen the circle of Ghanaian nationalism among the immigrants. When they gather in each other's homes to discuss matters affecting Ghana as they often do, the immigrants affirm their minority and outsider status in America. At the same time they reorient themselves to the notion that while their full incorporation into the core of American society is impossible, experiences with being excluded are not sufficient reason to thwart or impede their motivation to become successful both in the United States and Ghana.

An appendage of Ghanaian immigrant nationalism sometimes finds expression in Pan-African ideas and ideals as a way to maintain immigrant identity. The identity that is emerging among Ghanaians in America is a Pan-African ethnicity based on the history, culture, and experiences of peoples of the black African diaspora and descent. This identity enables the Ghanaian immigrant to define and maintain a cultural manifestation or identity that intersects with other minority and ethnic cultures that span international boundaries. It has also enabled the immigrants to portray an identity of the "black international outsider" who holds a fierce and loyal attachment to African cultural heritage and values. The self-applied label of "black international outsider" enables the Ghanaian immigrant to minimize the problem of having a marginalized status in a skin color conscious society and at the same time to find a medium for the expression of Ghanaian nationalism and Pan-Africanism.

What shapes the contents of this ethnicity is kinship. This identity is ideologically centered and based on self and collective identification with African values, cultural artifacts and symbols. This Continental identification serves a functional purpose for the immigrants. First, it provides the immigrants with a cultural prism from which to explain issues that confront Africa from their individual and collective experiences. From the Ghanaian immigrants' point of view, this self-identification rests on the belief that Africans and only Africans are naturally equipped to define and interpret the contents of their shared cultural experiences and future destiny. It is a nationalistic-cum-continental consciousness that prizes and cherishes everything African. Second, the expression of this identity is based on an African worldview that champions the political, economic, and social emancipation of Africa from all forms of colonial, neo-colonial, economic, and political entrapments and exploitations. In focusing on their blackness and Ghanaian or African cultural identities, the immigrants are able to minimize the deleterious effects of racism in the United States. As one immigrant expressed it, "You have to feel comfortable in your skin and feel good about who you are. If you allow white society to define your identity as to who you should be in America, you are not going to like the image of blackness that they might apply to you. White America's image of what it means to be black is not pretty."

In embracing a Continental African identity and suffrage with other African immigrants in the North American diaspora, the Ghanaian immigrants are affirming a deeply entrenched anti-colonial identity whose goal it is to develop an African-centered approach to solving the myriad of problems confronting the Continent of Africa. The quest for Ghanaian immigrant identity in America is underpinned by the ethos that the social and cultural processes involved in defining and maintaining identity transcends physical attributes such as skin color. The immigrants perceive that identity finds expression and is illuminated by one's role and contribution to community goals. Identity connotes membership, belongingness, and commitment to the principles and goals for which the entire community strives to attain. In this regard, identity is the organic whole of an individual's character, status, and place in the social system. The attributes of the individual (education, status, family background, gender, age, language, tribe, place of origin, and even skin color) all find convergence in shaping identity. The consensus among the immigrants is that when black American identity is denigrated and marginalized while white American identity is elevated, the America cultural panoply is greatly diminished.

The conscious or unconscious translation of this denigration and marginality into public policy and institutionalized forms is the subtext which influences the attitudes and opinions that the Ghanaian immigrants hold about racial and ethnic identity relations in the United States. The immigrants rationalize that a community, and by extension a nation that celebrates everyone in its midst, irrespective of skin color, is one that is fulfilled and truly inclusive. In the words of one immigrant, "The privilege of being white should not be continually maintained at the expense of America's minority populations, especially Blacks, Hispanics, and Native American Indians." A majority of the Ghanaian immigrants from the study (67 per cent) agreed that remnants of white privilege which began in the days of slavery have persisted to contemporary times, and that the enduring legacy of discrimination and racism leads to the privileging of white Americans. A third of the immigrants indicated that they have faced racist and discriminatory encounters in the form of racial harassment, derogatory slurs, or physical threats, on account of their skin color. The immigrants made references to the structural assimilation of blacks into mainstream American society and decried the fact that in core sectors of American life (politics, economy, housing, health, and education), African-Americans have been left behind and have yet to become fully integrated into the dominant culture. The views of the Ghanaian immigrants on race and ethnic relations in the United States is that access to equal opportunity is limited to many blacks in America irrespective of whether they have been born in Africa or the United States. To the majority of the immigrants, skin color is a major determinant of access to resources in America even though most Americans continue to believe in the saliency of the American dream and the notion that there is equal opportunity and fairness for all.

Ghanaian-Americans believe that the continuing barriers to structural integration of blacks of the African diaspora in the United States have persisted because of the perception held by whites Americans that as a group, blacks have yet to take full advantage of the economic and cultural opportunities that the country has to offer. The immigrants believe that often times, white Americans have tended to blame the slow economic incorporation and social mobility of blacks to a subculture of poverty and a troubled black underclass whose values are the antithesis of white values. This perspective often denies the continuity and lingering effects of institutional and entrenched racism and discrimination in the United States. As one immigrant eloquently stated, white attribution of the problems confronting blacks in the diaspora in the United States stems from white America's view that, "If only black people would assimilate to values espoused by white America, embrace the culture of responsibility, perseverance, hard work, and stop complaining about racism and discrimination, they too, like the Jews, Irish, Italians, and some Asiatic groups, can attain high social mobility and economic power." In contesting America's race and skin-color based society, very few of the immigrants ever see an accelerated improvement in the social, cultural, political, and economic conditions that perpetuate racism and discrimination in the United States. There exists a racial hierarchical order in the United States with entrenched interests whose vestiges do not recognize the inherent rights of blacks (and those of African ancestry) to compete with whites at all levels of American society.

As they affirm their identities and express their values, the immigrants have had to cope with negative stereotypes and prejudices associated with immigrants and ethnic minorities, especially black Americans. These negative stereotypes have had a significant impact on the structural adaptation of Ghanaians as well as other immigrants from Africa currently living in the United States (Holtzman, 2000). As a subordinate and powerless group, many Ghanaians feel that their chance of surviving in a polarized and race conscious United States will be determined by how well they are able to preserve their identity, cultural heritage and the Ghanaian social institutions that they have recreated in the United States. Indeed, identifiability and structural adaptability are both independent and dependent variables that shape how Ghanaians in America confront issues dealing with their visible minority status. Knowing that their complete integration into mainstream American society is not feasible, Ghanaians in America have had to rely on the construction of symbolic manifestations of their culture to distinctively demarcate themselves from American society. In pursuing a form of instrumental adaptation, Ghanaians in the United States have carefully selected the aspects of American culture that they would structurally engage. Education and economic participation are two aspects of American society that have been critical for the immigrants' advancement and social mobility. The returns that many Ghanaians in the United States have derived from pursuing advanced education in this country have proved very significant in their efforts to carve a niche in the labor force. Therefore, these aspects of their lives are seamlessly integrated into the dominant educational opportunity systems in this country. Education is highly prized and valued. It is seen by the immigrants as a conduit for achieving social mobility and self-improvement. In spheres of social, cultural, and political participation, the immigrants recognize that there are barriers to full inclusion and integration into American society, and have come to accept the fact that it is only those who are in power who can change this situation by granting greater access to economic opportunities for blacks. The Ghanaian immigrant consensus is that, historically, the white American power structure has never liked blacks whether they hail from Africa, the Caribbean, or the United States. This, the immigrants perceive, is the reason behind the slow incorporation of blacks into the core of American society.

For the Ghanaian immigrants, a coping strategy for dealing with this persistent exclusion and antipathy toward blacks is guardedness coupled with voluntary alienation and marginalization. Dominant in the psyche of the Ghanaian immigrant is the notion of impermanence as it relates to their migratory experience in the United States. The temporary status of the immigrants in the United States is often used as a frame of reference to explain away problems such as racism and discrimination that the immigrants encounter. Even though they are confronted with prejudice and discrimination, the Ghanaian immigrants view these encounters as tolerable as long as such practices do not hamper the attainment of the long term goal: repatriation to Ghana when economic conditions improve. Having a view that American culture is antagonistic when it comes to race and ethnic relations, the immigrants often resist assimilation by clinging to their African heritage and culture even if it means that they have to isolate and alienate themselves from the dominant culture. A coping strategy in response to the harmful effects of racism and discrimination among the immigrants entails the development of a supportive cultural environment in which positive self-image and a sense of independence can be nurtured. As one immigrant stated, "Being black and a foreigner in America is an anathema, a heavy burden and a drag, sometimes a liability that can have damaging consequences in America's undeclared racial wars. To survive, one would have to have an awareness of the various forms of racism, and then develop mechanisms for minimizing its impact." From another immigrant's perspective, "those who inhale racism and give it a place in their psyche are bound to be filled with rage, low self-esteem and denigration. Eventually, they are destroyed by it."

In America, cultural notions of black Africa conjure up stereotypical and negative images of economic dependency, failed aspirations, and proclivities toward criminality. The perception of Ghanaian immigrants is that while these labels or definitions are very powerful and stultifying, they can also engender competition, hard work, and an unfettered ambition and drive to overcome all the subtleties of overt and covert discrimination. From the perspectives of the immigrants, the prevailing sentiment is that the racial tension in American society should not become a source of disillusionment to prevent the immigrants from achieving their goals Having a more realistic expectation of the racial divide in America has enabled immigrants, then and now to confront the problem and find solutions to it (Thomas-Hope, 1975).

In the world view of Ghanaian immigrants, race and ethnic identification should not serve as barriers to full citizenship and social participation in any society. Coming from a Ghanaian society where class or tribal affiliation rather than skin color determines access to opportunity, a majority of the Ghanaian immigrants find themselves being pigeon-holed into assuming a black racial identity which sometimes makes it difficult to affirm their culture and heritage. But as they find strength in numbers due to the growth of the African-born black immigrant population settling in the United States, and as many of their children grow up affirming African values and identity, many Ghanaian immigrants perceive that the fears and threats associated with being black and foreign may begin to diminish. As a group, the immigrants remain undaunted by the negative connotations associated with blackness in the United States. They do not see their blackness as a liability, and they have rejected the popular misconceptions in American popular culture that link black culture and black Americans in general with various kinds of social and cultural pathologies. Relying on their strong cultural traditions and heritage, education, and cooperative and indomitable spirit, many of the immigrants work hard to dispel the myths, stereotypes, and misconceptions associated with black culture in the United States. To achieve this goal, the majority of the immigrants teach their children the value of education, family life, African history, and folklore. The continued influence of African culture on the lives of the immigrants serves as the rallying point among the immigrants for coping with the negative stereotypes and racism in the United States. To build the self-esteem of children and foster in them a sense of identity, families inculcate age-graded expectations in their children and engage in rituals that emphasize social conformity, citizenship, personal responsibility, and reverence for adults and authority figures. The construction of identity among the immigrants does not find sole expression in symbols of attire and cultural artifacts. Instead, as one immigrant stated, the expression of identity and cultural manifestation, "Starts with the nurturing of oneness with the spirit, a sense of common destiny, spirituality, cooperative bonds, and community and self-improvement."

A majority of Ghanaian immigrants stressed the cultural heritage and affinity that they share with black America and tend to register their disapproval against the stereotypes whites associate with blacks. From the above immigrant's perspective, "Most of the black immigrants in the United States do not buy into the stereotypical labels regarding crime, violence, and welfare that are often linked with blacks in America." Another immigrant highlighted the fact that the destinies of black immigrants are tied together with that of their American-born counterparts; that black immigrants owe a debt of gratitude to the black Americans who were and still are at the vanguard of racial and civil rights equality for blacks and minorities in America. In the words of this immigrant, "I would not be here had it not been for the black civil rights activists who cleared a pathway for blacks in America by standing up against racial and ethnic discrimination and inequality. We stand tall, shoulder to shoulder, and very grateful to black Americans for their resilience and endurance in forging an identity for themselves in white America against all odds." In the end, what emerges for some of the immigrants is an attempt by white society to get African immigrants to separate themselves from American-born blacks by forging a different identity; but this idea is counterintuitive to the beliefs and principles of afrocentrism and African-centered values. Core to immigrants' beliefs is the cultural view that wherever they meet and come together, as a group, the peoples of the African diaspora are united by a common legacy and heritage that they need to guard and preserve, a tradition that is steeped in altruism and anchored in group centeredness as opposed to individual centeredness.

Different strains of racism and discrimination confront Ghanaian immigrants in the United States. The immigrants who have advanced university degrees and live in predominantly white suburban and affluent communities spoke often about the feelings of rejection and alienation that they and their children encounter. Despite their professional status, education, and income, some of the immigrants felt that when the racial hierarchy of their suburban communities is constructed, they are still placed at the bottom of the ladder, and thus considered less desirable by the neighbors and friends that they interact with at neighborhood tennis clubs and swimming pools. "If anything has been very difficult for me to explain to my children, it is to tell them to be proud of who they are, and always appreciate their black African heritage because it will be questioned and derided," one immigrant stated. "Being successful does not preclude being black; inequality is framed largely in racial terminologies and white ethnocentric beliefs that denigrate people of non-European stock," another immigrant living in suburbia stated.

The ethnic diversity that some of the immigrants are bringing to their homogeneously white communities and other sites of social life have been contested by whites who sense that the presence of Ghanaians and other immigrants are having an overwhelming impact on their way of life; whites feel powerless regarding the future direction of immigration. In predominantly white suburban communities where some Ghanaians have settled, the tensions brought about by their presence have, in some respects, galvanized white anti-immigration fervor which blames the immigrants for the social problems in communities and states where there are high populations of immigrants. Even when they work and pay taxes, the Ghanaian immigrants feel powerless to contain the angst of whites support conservative political candidates that advocate for policies that tend to be against welfare, immigration, affirmative action, public education, and in favor of law enforcement and the social control of cultural dissension. The recession and the anemic economic growth which started in the waning months of the Clinton presidency and continued to persist even more than three years into the Bush presidency also intensified public consternation about the imperative of controlling legal and illegal immigration. Immigrants, old and new, become scapegoats during periods of social and economic uncertainties. Nativistic fervor has increased as immigrants are singled out and blamed for increases in crime and welfare and human service expenditures. These anti-immigrant sentiments usually culminate in public calls for tighter border control, restrictions of legal immigration, and possibly the deportation of any immigrant who commits a felony crime.

From the Ghanaian immigrant's perspective, there is a seamless linkage of racism and discrimination and the day-to-day lives of many minority groups in the United States. In their encounters with the general public, mainly white America, Ghanaians, like the rest of black America, feel that they are socially constructed and viewed as "other," less deserving, and at times, less able. Of equal consternation to the immigrants is the simplistic racial categorization and paradigm that pitches black versus white in the United States. In this racial paradigm, antipathy toward blacks (whether they are American-born or foreign-born), is commonplace. This racial and ethnic inequality is perceived by the immigrants as core to their exclusion from mainstream society and as the cause of the discriminatory practices that they are sometimes subjected to from police, labor recruitment agencies, educational institutions, and public and private housing authorities. The Ghanaian immigrants realize the futility of challenging America's institutionalized racist polices and discriminatory practices. In the words of one immigrant, "Fighting the institutionally embedded advantages of being white and privileged in America is like trying to collect water into a container from a pond using a basket. You can get the basket wet, but the basket will still be empty."

In the Ghanaian immigrant's psyche, the effervescence of American cultural identity is framed in terms of ideals associated with freedom, liberty, equality, and rationality in economic production and organization. This cultural ethos, in a sense, is also embraced by the immigrants who posit similar ideals for Ghana. However, there is consternation among the immigrants that the distribution and practice of these ideals are exclusionary, leading to the affirmation of some groups, especially Americans of Western European extraction, to the exclusion of others. Blacks and people of color are generally excluded from this affirmation. Irrespective of how long they have lived in the United States, the majority of the immigrants believe that blacks will always be a despised minority, outsiders who have the status of second or third class citizenship.

It is the view of the immigrants that as a country, the United States must embrace the multiple cultural and ethnic manifestations that exist in the country, and that immigrants and minorities should not be pressured to adopt the culture of the powerful and dominant ethnic groups as this will violate freedom of cultural expression. While they identify with the core institutions of American society (especially the educational and economic systems), the majority of the immigrants manifest a cultural representation that is based on the mixing of multiple international ethnicities and the cultural lifestyles, symbols, and images associated with the mix and remixing of cultures. Even as more and more Ghanaians in United States acquire citizenship, they still remain leery of the chasm between white and black America. Citizenship has not offered Ghanaian immigrants full protection from discrimination in housing, education, healthcare, and employment. The perception held by some of the immigrants is that issues that affect blacks and Hispanics as well as other minorities in the United States is of no great concern to the political establishment and power brokers. The status of the Ghanaian immigrants in America's system of racial hierarchy relative to the status of whites serves as a barrier preventing full and total integration. From their immigrant perspective, white America has defined certain expectations for immigrants and ethnic minorities in terms of how far they can go. The notion of egalitarianism and equal opportunity for all, which supposedly characterizes the American cultural ethos, varies depending on the legal status of the Ghanaian immigrant. For those Ghanaian immigrants who have attained a legal status, there is always a sense of hope that eventually, America will deliver and make good on its ideals of justice and equality for all. An egalitarian culture might eventually be established, but for the many immigrants of non-white ancestral backgrounds who are classified as undocumented, the individual and collective sense of the future is dim. Fear is rampant that they will be deported if apprehended by the Immigration and Custom Enforcement agents or by local law enforcement authorities for minor traffic violations. And when subjected to abuses by unscrupulous employers, many of the undocumented immigrants do not pursue any claims they might make against the employer for fear of being reported to immigrant officials or fired from their jobs. Even for those who qualify for welfare and public assistance, several of them do not come forward for fear that the authorities might raise questions about their status and report them to the immigration office.

Roles, Statuses, and Identity Transformation

To many Ghanaian-Americans, the tendency of the host society to mark them as members of a racial group rather than as individuals with varying degrees of cultural nuances has a deleterious effect on majority–minority group relations in the United States. The intricacies of race relations in the United States dominate the public and private lives, as well as the discourses of Ghanaian Americans. The immigrants use terms like marginality, alienation, third class citizen, and exclusion to describe how they are perceived by American society.

The growing number of Ghanaian immigrant entrepreneurs serving Ghanaian, other African, and Caribbean immigrant enclaves in the major metropolitan areas of the country has generated some hostilities from disenchanted and antagonistic whites as well as some urban minority youths. The climate of antagonism and prejudice has been caused by the erroneous perception that Ghanaian immigrant entrepreneurs do not hire non-Ghanaians and do not contribute significantly to the economic improvement of the communities in which they operate their businesses. Criticisms have highlighted the fact that the Ghanaian immigrant and ethnic stores only hire extended family members or other immigrants from Africa and the Caribbean. Native-born African Americans feel left out even though they patronize these ethnic enterprises. The result is an uneasy tension, edginess, and consternation on both sides. Unprovoked harassments have resulted from these exchanges in major American cities. In spite of these acts and other subtleties of discriminatory practices, the Ghanaian entrepreneurial class have yet to mount any visible and sustained protest against those who harass and discriminate against them on account of their national origin and ethnicity. Even when they have responded to acts of antagonism and harassment, their response has been a low-key protest in order to avoid calling undue public attention to their plight. The decision not to openly contest and confront those who harass them is not hard to trace. As a group, Ghanaian immigrants in the United States, unlike their Asian or Hispanic counterparts, have yet to mount an effective political organization and mobilization to confront and deal with the discrimination and prejudice they face. Lacking the critical mass of the major immigrant groups, Ghanaian immigrants continue to respond to discrimination and prejudice by relying on the law enforcement agencies for security and protection.

In constructing images of race, ethnicity, class, and gender identity in the host societies, immigrants have followed different pathways. Over a protracted period of time, racial, ethnic, class, and gender statuses that have been negotiated by majority and minority status groups have become sites for inter and intra group conflict, genocide, or accommodation. In many respects, the negotiations of the pathways to these identities have largely been determined by the nature or the form of the initial contact between minority and majority groups, the degree of inclusiveness or exclusiveness prevailing in the host society, and the existence of laws in the host society designed to promote integration and assimilation of the foreign-born population or immigrants.

Identity connotes an individual's sense of belonging. It is the product of self, the social environment, culture, race, genetics, physical characteristics, and kinship connections. While Ghanaians in America may view themselves as a common group from the same national origin, there is no single factor that has been pivotal in shaping the self-identity of the immigrants. Cultural and ethnic pluralism or the co-existence of multiple identities is what describes most Ghanaian immigrants. Self-references and ethnic identification stress first a Ghanaian national cultural heritage, and second, an African-centered continental heritage. In addition, cultural and ethnic identity among Ghanaians is also expressed in terms of ethnic descent. Here, cultural identities are expressed in terms of place of origin in Ghana and linguistic background. Descent-based associations are formed along the lines of matrilineal and patrilineal descent. Examples are the Akan and Twi-speaking immigrant groups from Ghana living in Atlanta and Toronto. These immigrants celebrate all the traditional festivals of the Akans such as the *Odwira* festival. Similarly, among the Ga-Adangbe-speaking immigrant groups in America, an ethnic and cultural marker is symbolized by the celebration of *Homowo* festivities. Among the Fanti-speaking immigrants from Ghana, the ethnic and cultural marker is the celebration of *fasheye.* The Ghanaian immigrants bring to the United States their varied ethnic experiences and these traditions serve as the medium whereby the immigrants are able to connect with their past, present, and future heritage. In celebrating these annual festivals, the immigrants maintain and affirm the social and religious bonds that define their cultural heritage and identity.

The expression of ethnicity and cultural heritage finds saliency and articulation in group membership, possession of common language, and a cultural frame of reference unique only to the members of that ethnic and cultural group. In addition, the experiences that arise out of common ethnicity and cultural heritage are meaningful, and while there are noticeable cultural differences among the various Ghanaian immigrant ethnicities, these lines are seldom sharp enough to limit inter-ethnic crossings. A unifying denominator among the Ghanaians is a common national heritage. Immigrant ethnic and cultural identification markers are very fluid and not fixed in time and space, thus allowing the Ghanaians to enter and exit numerous cultural or ethnic sites, and voluntarily share in social and cultural rituals.

Immigrant Notions of Class Identity and Internal Differentiation

The importance of class membership and the privileges that come with class formations have long been recognized by social scientists. Class membership matters because it affects life chances. Life chances associated with access to healthcare, income, education, housing, law, and employment are all influenced by class. Max Weber, a German sociologist, used class to refer to groups who share similar levels of wealth, income, power, and prestige. Class distinctions alongside racial distinctions are pivotal in determining social mobility and stratification.

Two approaches can be used to investigate class formation. These are the subjective and objective approaches. The subjective approach emphasizes a self-reported format where individuals are asked which class they think they belong. The objective measure uses the income, occupation, and education of people and uses that as a basis for determining a person's socioeconomic status. While Ghanaian immigrants in the United States have shown a strong orientation for group solidarity and a Ghanaian pan-ethnicity based on cultural pluralism, the immigrants are by no means monolithic in terms of their attitudes about class formation. Social classes and internal differences are sometimes ignored and overlooked when the objective of social exchange is rationalized in terms of cultural expression and celebration of everything that is Ghanaian. At other times, class differences become poignant and are stressed to remind the key participants in social action that class lines are real and therefore ought to be recognized and celebrated.

There are differences in the class formation and structure of the Ghanaian immigrants. Class differences among the immigrants are largely influenced by educational level attained in Ghana prior to emigration, post-migration educational attainment completed in the United States, prestige of secondary school attended in Ghana, employment, occupation, income status in the United States, and tribal or clan affiliation in Ghana. Approximately 40 per cent of the immigrants from the study identified themselves as lower class. Most of the immigrants in this class came to the United States with middle school or secondary school education and have not been able to pursue college or university education. The majority of them tend to work as cooks, car wash attendants, waiters, supermarket store clerks, convenience store clerk, janitors, gas station and parking ramp attendants, and as farm laborers. Combined household income for this group is about $34,500 for those who are married compared with approximately $20,000 for those who are single. Most of them work full-time but lack any fringe benefits, healthcare, and retirement. As renters, some of them live in public housing with three or more children at home. They tend to depend on strong kinship ties and social networks to trade services like baby sitting, car pooling, and cooking. Female-headed households are very common among this group. On average, most have been living in the United States since the 1990s and had originally arrived in the United States to reunite with family members or had won the immigration lottery. A few are undocumented and entered the United States from the Middle-East, Asia, and Eastern Europe where they had sojourned and worked low-paying menial jobs. Considered part of the American urban working poor and underclass, many are confronted with persistent unemployment. Upward mobility in this group has been very difficult as these immigrants lack the educational credentials and the skills necessary for them to advance.

Many of the immigrants in this group are pursuing adult continuing education programs at technical institutes and colleges to enhance their job prospects and improve upon their earnings. Social mobility to the ranks of the middle class is becoming common, especially among those in this class who have relocated to suburban districts to take advantage of more favorable employment opportunities. The 1996 Welfare Reform Bill which was signed into law by President Bill Clinton clearly had an impact on some of the immigrants in this group. Under this law, the federal government either scaled back government support or made eligibility rules more stringent for housing, childcare, and healthcare. For young female immigrants in this class who have become mothers at an early age and who are raising their children by themselves, there are identifiable structural barriers to economic and occupational participation. Lack of access to affordable daycare, transportation, and housing constrain the ability to retrain for higher paying jobs. Confined to minimum wage jobs or jobs not offering any fringe benefits, these Ghanaian immigrant women have accumulated little wealth, often living from paycheck to paycheck.

The meaning of having a lower class membership is very fluid among this group of Ghanaian immigrants. Most of them do not see themselves as economically deprived because they compare their living standards in the United States to the standard of living they were accustomed to at home in Ghana. Considering their current class status, a majority of them perceive that they are living an economic dream in the United States. One of the immigrants captured the full range of sentiments reflected by a majority of the immigrants in this class group. He stated, "I could not afford a car, television, or even a one-bedroom to lay my head at night when I was in Ghana. I drive a good used car, able to educate my children, and I have some money left to remit home. I do not make much but even in this status, I earn more than what over 70 per cent of Ghanaians at home earn. This is my American dream." An immigrant woman echoed this sentiment: "I did not attend any of the prestigious preparatory schools in Ghana; neither did I attend any of the top notch schools in Ghana like Achimota School, Wesley Girls, Adisadel, or Prempeh College. I went to one of the trade schools and later completed the General Certificate of Education at the Ordinary Level. But look at me in America. Thousands, if not millions of Ghanaians will trade places with me here in the United States. I feel good, great and very fortunate. Class is in the psyche." To a large degree, then, many of these immigrants have experienced intergenerational mobility because their current standard of living in the United States is much higher than the class position attained by their parents, grandparents, or school mates now living in Ghana.

About 50 per cent of the Ghanaians who were studied identified their socioeconomic status as middle class. With incomes ranging between $40,000 to upwards of $60,000 per year, many of the immigrants in this class status arrived in the United States with college or university degrees, and have since pursued advanced professional and non-professional degrees in the United States. In two income family households with both the husband and wife working, total incomes remain very high, averaging over $80,000 a year. Included in this category are immigrants who had graduated from prestigious secondary schools like Wesley Girls High School, Achimota, St. Augustine, or Prempeh College. Some attended Accra, Kumasi, and Takoradi Polytechnic, teacher training colleges, and universities in Ghana. The transferability of degrees and diplomas from Ghana to the United States has aided the structural integration of these immigrants into the American labor force. Conscious of their educational class backgrounds, the immigrants who attended these schools have formed alumni branches of their respective schools in the large metropolitan communities in the United States. This facilitates the formation of alliances, networks of economic and psychological support. These middle-class immigrants have a sense of financial security, living in suburban homes and driving new cars, and they are very conscious of their middle class status. While the majority of them have pursued advanced degrees since emigrating to the United States, a few of them have relied on the educational credentials they brought with them to the United States to negotiate entrance into semi-professional and professional occupational status.

In terms of occupation, the immigrants in this class group are public school teachers, nurses and other allied healthcare workers, computer technicians and analysts, social workers, community college instructors, university faculty, county employees, bankers, and accountants. Upward mobility has been facilitated by the completion of advanced degrees in the United States. For this professionally skilled class, the benefits of post-secondary credentials have been phenomenal, and due to their educational backgrounds, most of them are able to secure employment even following periods of economic downturn and lay offs. As indicated previously, education is highly valued; children are expected to attend college and pursue advanced degrees, often following; in the footsteps of their parents. Some of the families pay for private tutors to supplement the instruction that their children receive in the public or private school systems. Even though they earn more than their counterparts in the lower class, the immigrants in the middle class also tend to pursue continuing education to enhance future employability. The perception is that the opportunity to retool and enhance one's professional credentials is perhaps the best policy against having to swim against the structural tide of economic changes that is taking place in the global labor market.

A majority of the immigrants in this group are able to afford the trip back home to Ghana every year or two to visit relatives and check up on the homes that they have built in preparation for their future repatriation. Many of them have benefited from amnesty and from the IRCA of 1986, and have managed to secure employment authorization and permanent resident status. Many have since become naturalized citizens and frequently do sponsor relatives from home to come to the United States to join them. Some have benefited from membership in professional associations and unions, and unlike the immigrants in the lower tier of socioeconomic status they have fair to excellent fringe benefits. In these households, both husbands and wives work, and are able to send their children to private as well public schools. A growing trend in these households is to send children home to be educated at the prestigious international preparatory schools in Accra, Tema or Kumasi, usually attended by the children of expatriates, the upper hierarchy of civil servants, and corporate officials, where they prepare for the Scholastic Aptitude Test (SAT) or other college entrance exams, and then return to the United States to attend prestigious colleges and universities. Most of the families have the resources to pay tuition of over $300 a month in Ghana (about the yearly wages of the average Ghanaian). They tend to support charitable and civic organizations in their communities such as the Boys and Girls Club of America, the Young Men's Christian Association (YMCA) and the Young Women's Christian Association (YWCA). Some of them identified themselves as Protestants, and indicated that they often vote for conservative candidates. A few have been successful in local government participation and are using this access to influence local political decision-making. The majority of them left Ghana in search of greener pastures abroad because they could not endure the frustrations emanating from the political instability and economic stagnation that has confronted the country since the attainment of political independence in 1957.

The upper class makes up about ten per cent of the Ghanaian immigrant community. They are drawn from the ranks of professionals and managers working for major corporations. Most of them constitute the first wave of Ghanaian immigrants who settled in the United States. While in Ghana, some held senior civil service or military jobs, or management positions in the private sector; others operated their own businesses, or were lecturers in the country's universities. A few had transferred a significant portion of their assets to the United States. Incomes in the group range between $85,000 and $120,000 per year for a family of four. Many of these immigrants had previously lived in Great Britain, Australia, or Canada before immigrating to the United States. They tend to maintain a sojourner status in the United States and shuttle between the United States, Ghana, and the United Kingdom. Eventually, most of them intend to repatriate to Ghana where they already have built their dream homes for retirement.

Irrespective of their subjective class membership, the prevailing attitude among a majority of the immigrants is that their standards of living have improved significantly due to the benefits of migration. Cultural pride, and a rich tradition and heritage have also made it possible for them to systematically negotiate entry into the core society, albeit very guardedly. As they forge ahead in American society, they remain cognizant of the fact that their culture and heritage will serve as a main sustaining factor that will aid their incorporation and integration into the affairs of American society.

In sum, as immigrants of the African diaspora in the United States, Ghanaian Americans can be classified as an ethnic minority group as well as a racial minority group. Culturally, they are distinguishable by their languages and second, by their physical characteristics. Ghanaian immigrants often cast their racial and ethnic identities in terms of the outsider-looking-inside role, a foreigner. This role is premised on the belief held by the immigrants that they can never become full members and achieve complete integration into the affairs of the host society. Even when they become naturalized citizens, they still define their racial and ethnic identities in terms of being foreigners, and reject wholesale identification and inclusion into the affairs of the host society. The Ghanaians become acculturated but hardly assimilate completely, and should they assimilate, the pattern of assimilation is not designed to ensure full engagement and participation in the affairs of American society. What is striking is that the degree of assimilation is often limited to participation in the material realm as opposed to the nonmaterial cultural and social realms. In essence, while assimilation may occur, it is often defined to include the acquisition of physical products of American society that the immigrants find necessary to ensure their survival in the United States. Cultural and ethnic affiliation and identification with other groups is an important aspect of immigrant adaptation in the American immigrant and ethnic quilt. To the members of the dominant group, which has the power to impose labels on subordinate groups, African immigrants as a whole are part of the black experience in America because of the physical characteristics and assumed cultural traits and similarities that Ghanaian immigrants share with native-born blacks. Rejecting the notion of being monolithic, Ghanaian immigrants are largely dependent upon the ethnic institutions they have created in order to gain access and entrance to the native society. To preserve their ethnicity and foster collective security, the immigrants often cluster in enclaves near kinfolk and friends where they share the same language and institutional affiliation. In this regard, the Ghanaians are following a proven path to warding off racism that black immigrants from the Caribbean follow: to stress a different form of blackness unlike the one associated with native-born black Americans (Cashmore and Troyna, 1982; Sutcliffe, 1982).

Among Ghanaian immigrants in the United States, the formation of racial and ethnic identity takes on many varied forms. Like immigrants from other parts of Africa and the Caribbean, Ghanaians in America generally acknowledge their subordinate status as blacks living in a predominantly white society. Their physical and cultural characteristics separate them from the dominant group. Most of them are predisposed to view themselves as having a subordinate and minority status and therefore likely to be confined by white society to a low social stratification in virtually all aspects of social endeavor. A coping strategy to offset the racism and discrimination that they experience in American society is to affirm an identity that is purely African, Ghanaian, and at times transglobal. For a majority of the Ghanaian immigrants, the system of racial and ethnic inequality that prevails in the host society is seen as a major stumbling block to full social participation and citizenship among the immigrants. This system of racial and ethnic inequality assigns status, based in part, on racial and ethnic preferences. In this system, according to a majority of the immigrants, being black, foreign-born, and African ranks very low in terms of white notions of racial and ethnic superiority. The reinforcement of the system of racial superiority and the advantages that come with it has meant that for the Ghanaian immigrant, the formation of racial and ethnic identity is carefully negotiated to ensure the continuity of Ghanaian culture in the United States and to carefully pursue limited integration and inclusion in the affairs of the host society. In the end, identity formation becomes purposive for the Ghanaian immigrant and is designed to achieve a clearly defined objective: to give meaning to their immigrant experiences and to coalescing Ghanaian and American belief systems to ensure adaptability in the West.

Chapter 6

Immigrant Institutions – Building Communities and Forging Integration

The majority of Ghanaian immigrants in the United States attribute their success to education, strong religious values, and a strong extended family system anchored in hard work, motivation, and deferred gratification. The continuity of their diaspora is facilitated by the institutions they establish or import from Ghana. Two such immigrant institutions and organizational structures are the immigrant mutual benevolent societies and the churches or houses of worship. These institutions form the bedrock of the Ghanaian immigrant diaspora in the United States. They provide the infrastructure as well as the building blocks of the Ghanaian immigrant communities across America. They link individuals, groups, and organizations to the core traditional values of Ghanaian society: individual and community self improvement, collective empowerment for goal attainment, and a firm belief in religious worship and service to others. In addition, these institutions serve as a link between the Ghanaian immigrants and the socio-cultural and political structures that operate in the host society.

When they meet to discuss how to aid newly arriving Ghanaian immigrants, as they do frequently, or when they meet on weekends to worship and observe religious rituals, the immigrants are not only affirming cultural identity, but are also building from the ground up sustainable immigrant communities to preserve their Ghanaian traditions and normative systems. Their considerable distance away from home, the stress they often encounter from their immigrant journeys to the United States, the daunting task of providing financial support to relatives at home to alleviate grinding poverty, coupled with the pressure to achieve economic mobility means that they have to rely on these institutions to help them stay on course toward the goal of fulfilling their individual and collective immigrant dreams. When Ghanaians seek to become naturalized citizens of the United States, they are affirming a sense of belonging to the host society by becoming part of the normative system of beliefs, values, culture, and political governance. In essence, their political and cultural assimilation via naturalization is intended to signify a convergence of the attitudes they share with Americans. Their naturalization also affirms their identificational assimilation with the United States. This form of structural assimilation is important because it provides a lens through which to gain an understanding of how the Ghanaian immigrants' lives are constituted and how the ethnic infrastructures they create work to preserve their cultural heritage. Naturalization as a form of institutional affiliation assists the immigrants in defining a group-centered shared essence and the pathways they follow in their quest to achieve self sufficiency and ultimately integration and incorporation into American society.

Immigrant patterns of adaptation provide insight into the extent of the affiliations newcomers establish in order to celebrate and preserve their cultures and identities in a foreign land. The adaptation patterns also provide a gauge of the contextual forces that shape how immigrants negotiate inclusion in the affairs of the host society. To better grapple with the processes whereby newcomers in any society seek to build institutions and create communities, a structural paradigm that stresses the contents of community integration and the functionality of units in the social system for the survival of the whole system is warranted. This approach, for example, compels one to examine structures of immigrant community and institutional processes, the interdependency of immigrant institutions, and the roles, norms, and statuses that undergird immigrant community and institutional polity. More importantly, a systemic approach to community inclusion, as it relates to the social construction of identity highlights, the imperative of conflict as groups with varying degrees of social, cultural, political, and economic powers vie for access to scarce commodities and resources. In setting up immigrant institutions such as the mutual aid benevolent societies, seeking naturalization, and establishing their religious institutions, the Ghanaian immigrant diaspora in the United States are fostering social organizational structures that will link and integrate them to their adopted country.

Building Ghanaian Immigrant Communities in the United States: The Mutual Aid Societies

The structure of the Ghanaian immigrant community is a major determinant of immigrant adaptation and integration. Institutionally, the Ghanaian immigrant community is not a self-sufficient or institutionally complete community. In matters of education, economics, housing, and healthcare to name a few, the immigrants rely on the existing structural components and social organization of American society to meet their routine needs. Though fewer in numbers compared to other immigrant groups such as Asians or Hispanics, the Ghanaian immigrants are leaving their marks in those communities across America where they live in large numbers. Like other immigrants in America, Ghanaians also create their own institutions to meet the challenges posed by migration to a foreign land. In essence, they create their own community to enable the newcomers to adapt to a new country and fulfill their immigrant aspirations.

Internal differentiation in the structure of the Ghanaian immigrant community and the extent to which it shares common values with the host society have been pivotal in defining the contents of adaptation experienced by Ghanaians living in the United States. Formal and informal institutions that the Ghanaians have created include churches, mutual aid and benevolent organizations, business and entrepreneurial organizations, and media structures. Collectively, these organizations and institutions organize community events such as Ghana Day celebrations, child-naming ceremonies, funerals, marriages, youth rites of passage rituals, group sporting events, lectureships and symposia, and classes on naturalization. These events and organizations serve as links between the immigrants and the members of the host society.

The majority of Ghanaian immigrant newcomers use the voluntary mutual aid and benevolent societies to affirm the cultural continuity and bonds of cohesiveness that they share with other Ghanaians who come from the same clan, class background, or ethnic and tribal areas. The informal friendships and networks formed in these organizations sometimes function as surrogate kin group organizations, offering emotional, economic, and practical support to immigrants with or without family. The types of assistance offered by these societies include grants to assist newcomers to put down a deposit on an apartment or house, paying for the airfare of bereaved immediate and extended family members in the United States and at home, donating used clothing and household utensils, paying attorney fees for immigrants with immigration problems, and directing newcomers to sources of employment. The Ghanaian immigrant in the United States is nested in a complex system of social relationships and networks derived from African social structure. Within these complex and self-sustaining networks of exchanges can be found shared norms, meshed institutionalized roles, and a system of lore designed to maintain social equilibrium and help protect the sanctity of the community and its members.

Explicit formulations of norms appear to guide how these associations operate in the United States. The activities of these organizations tend to be guided by one major consideration: to promote norms and ideals that link the immigrant to the heritage and culture of Ghanaian society while assisting the immigrant to focus on "home affairs." Ultimately, as these associations attempt to educate their members, the success of the immigration experience is going to be judged by how well Ghanaian immigrants are able to maintain a connection with their relatives back home and how they have managed to use their migration experience in the United States to alleviate the economic plight of relatives still in Ghana.

The underlying social cohesion that is promoted by these groups is maintained by a system of checks and balances, including using the apparatus of informal social control to promote conformity to the ideals of the immigrant, ethnic, class, or professional groups. The pressure to conform to group ideals has been paramount in ensuring the stability of the Ghanaian immigrant associations. In some instances, these associations (for example, the Ga-Adangbe Association) expect their members to maintain the utmost respect for the laws of the host society, refrain from engaging in behaviors that would tarnish the name of the tribe as a collective, and be guided by probity and moral transparency in all undertakings. In this connection, immigrants from Ghana from all walks of life who hail from Ga Mashie, whether they are from Jamestown, La, Bukom, Chorkor, or Teshie, share ascribed bonds of tribal kinship which form the basis of social interactions and exchanges. Collectively, the members of the Ga-Adangbe Mutual Aid Society constitute a "home boy" and "home girl" club. The nurturing of these home associations is core in forming a sociological understanding of the rituals associated with social exchange, mutuality, and norms of reciprocity. Groups of home buddies form a clique, usually to serve as economic, psychological, and social anchors for the members. A high degree of social and cultural affinity coupled with a strong sense of shared ethnicity permeates the fabric of the immigrant associations. Given the minority and invisible status of Ghanaians in America, the formation of bonds of kinship among the immigrants serve to provide a voice and content to the relationships that the immigrants forge with the members of the host society. Through cooperative action (such as doing voluntary work for community projects like building homes for Habitat for Humanity) these groups have been successful in negotiating an inclusion into the civic culture of American society. Negotiations for inclusion into the body polity of American civic culture have promoted adaptation and incorporation but have yet to facilitate wholesale assimilation of American culture and ethos.

In Ghana, the mutual aid and benevolent society is a major reference group. Formed along ethnic, tribal, religious, and professional lines, these secondary social groups foster a link between the individual and the larger society. They assist in the social integration of people of diverse social experiences and backgrounds into the public domain, minimizing the apprehensions associated with group dynamics and relationships. They confer status to the members and help in bridging the gap between social alienation and social participation within a defined territory or community setting. These associations bring together individuals and groups who attended the same schools, worship at the same churches, speak the same language, or are bonded by a common kinship and tribal affiliation. These kinship and social bonds have a broader social and political extension with the establishment of Pan-Ghanaian immigrant associations.

The immigrant mutual aid societies have a long history in Ghana. They were initially started by migrants who left the rural areas and came to urban metropolises in search of better economic opportunities. Tribal members from the same ethnic group would form these associations to provide assistance to their ethnic and tribal group members who migrated to the urban areas. Over time, as rural–urban migration increased, these groups proliferated; they often broadened their functions and services to include economic, social, cultural, and psychological support. These networks enable the migrants to cope with the isolation and alienation that some of them feel having left their relatives and friends behind. In essence, these associations enable migrants, who leave the rural areas of Africa to look for better economic opportunities in the cities, the opportunity to re-create in the urban milieux the village life that they are familiar with. The networks of bonds fostered by these associations enable the migrants to pool their resources in order to better cope with problems of adjustment to the alienation and fast-paced living of urban life.

As informal organizations, the Ghanaian national immigrant associations in the United States serve as the fulcrum for the propagation of Ghanaian culture and identity in America. Though social activities such as the celebration of Ghana's Independence Day on March 6 preoccupy the national associations, they have, from time immemorial served as political watchdog organizations with the political clout and leverage to influence political decision-making at home. Over time, the continuing deterioration of the country's economic system and the crumbling of state institutions in Ghana have transformed the Ghanaian national immigrant associations into a political action group, lobbying for social, political, and economic reforms while at the same time supporting political candidates and parties that embrace, in part or in full, their agenda. Broad classification of the national associations as political power brokers serves to fulfill two central goals: to protect and promote the economic survival of the immigrant newcomers, and to serve as the principal source for sustaining their cultural ethos. In this respect, these organizations are the cords that have tied the newcomers to their respective places of birth while at the same assisting them in defining the contents of their culture in America.

The heterogeneous character of Ghanaian immigrants in the United States, reflecting people from different socioeconomic levels, language, and cultural backgrounds, has not thwarted the need to forge a framework for national unity among the immigrants. Differences in class, gender, education, ethnicity, and religion that would otherwise divide the immigrants back home have become secondary. Variations in internal stratification are acknowledged among the immigrants but national identity has superseded these differences. There is a collective sense of national heritage and a fierce sense of Ghanaian identity. The Ghanaian national immigrant associations provide the immigrants with the institutional mechanisms of collective self-expression and an outlet for the immigrants to express their Ghanaian-ness, as well as a medium for expressing their autonomy, asserting their cultural awareness, and seeking remedies to their common migrant problems.

When they have traveled and lived in communities other than their own, Ghanaians have always utilized these mutual aid societies and national immigrant associations to define their identity, and foster group solidarity. The individual and group interconnections engendered by these organizations enable the migrant who is far away from home to connect with like-minded individuals who are confronted with similar experiences in the "new" home or locale. The multiplexity of roles that form within these organizations serves as anchorage to minimize apprehension and make the migrant experience more predictable and salient. In short, these associations form in order to finesse the uncertainties and sometimes alienating forces associated with the migratory process. Ghanaian immigrants make a conscious effort to rely on the immigrant associations as a medium for definitions of not only who they are but also to express their immigrant aspirations, hopes, and dreams.

The vicissitudes associated with employment, education, healthcare issues, child-rearing, births and deaths, and legal matters are often ironed out and discussed within the social framework of the mutual aid and immigrant groups. To provide economic support and ensure a meaningful outcome from the immigrants' experiences, the associations often establish a credit rotation scheme or *susu* expressly for the purpose of helping immigrants save money and provide financial support to their relatives in Ghana. The *susu* is organized in such a way that every two weeks or so, members contribute a set some of money to an appointed treasurer. At the end of every three months, a member of the group is chosen to receive all the money collected. Then the process begins again until every member of the group has had the chance to collect the money accumulated during the quarter. With a lump sum of money in hand, some of the immigrants may buy land, start a business in Ghana, or help pay for the tuition of a family member to come to the United States. Some of the immigrant associations often use the savings to help their home towns refurbish school buildings or build new ones, dig wells to supply water, or establish scholarship schemes for students. The ties that are fostered among the home associations based on the town of origin or ethnic affiliation form the centerpiece for the cultural production and expression of clan identity, racial and ethnic sentiment, class relations, and national and transnational heritage. The fluidity of the ties and bonds that are nurtured among the associations gives rise to a culturally-sustaining ethos that is based upon the preservation of time-tested Ghanaian values such as the nurturing of family members, good citizenship, assiduousness, spirituality, and the protection of Ghanaian values and heritage.

Seeking Naturalization and Citizenship

Ghanaian immigrants in the United States can be placed on a continuum regarding their naturalization status. There are those who have applied for and have already received their certificate of naturalization. Another group consists of those who have completed all the paperwork and are waiting for official processing of their documents to commence. Others are in the process of applying after completing the naturalization and citizenship classes. The last group consists of those who have no intention of applying or are ambivalent about the process of naturalization even though they have not ruled out the possibility of applying. Slightly more than one half (53 per cent) of the Ghanaian immigrants who were studied have become naturalized citizens of the United States. Another 16 per cent have completed all the formalities of naturalization and are waiting for the official swearing-in ceremony, while 11 per cent have embarked upon the first stages of preparation (taking citizenship classes) toward naturalization. The remaining immigrants indicated no intentions of seeking naturalization or remain ambivalent about the process.

Acquiring citizenship in another country is a major change in one's cultural and political identity and orientation. The naturalization process constitutes a formal identification and affiliation with the host society. It represents a change and redefinition in status, roles, normative orientation, and psychological affiliation. Core to the acquisition of citizenship is the notion that the process of naturalization is conditioned by the degree of inclusiveness, assimilation, and openness of the immigrants' host society to accommodate and integrate the newcomers into their body polity. The transformation that this change in legal status entails is illuminating because it highlights the immigrants' perceptions about their country of origin and their expectations regarding the new country they have adopted as home. The aim of this section is to delineate the contextual factors (structural and individual characteristics) that account for the acquisition of American naturalization and citizenship among Ghanaian émigrés in the United States. I highlight the meanings and attitudes that the immigrants attach to the acquisition of American citizenship, particularly the perceived incentives and disincentives the immigrants associate with naturalization and citizenship. Despite the fact that a majority of the immigrants maintain a strong attachment to Ghanaian and African identity, and have intentions of repatriation, they nonetheless perceive that the acquisition of American citizenship through naturalization is a crucial aspect of the transnational ethnicities and identities they are creating through the process of international migration. Naturalization is a form of incorporation into this transnational identity that the immigrants seek to forge.

Economic factors dominate the reasons for seeking American citizenship. Nearly 80 per cent of the Ghanaian immigrants cited economic security as the main reason for applying for citizenship. The immigrants perceive that acquiring citizenship offers them access to well-paying jobs, some degree of employment security, and should they need it, the chance to collect unemployment, welfare, and disability benefits. From their perspective, citizenship offers another layer of welfare protection for themselves and their families. For certain jobs requiring security clearance at state and federal levels, having the status of citizenship is considered an added advantage. The security that is offered to immigrants who naturalize forms a significant aspect of political and cultural integration among immigrants in general. Writing about Latinos, Pachon and DeSipio (1994) noted that for a growing number of Latinos, citizenship has become the vehicle used by immigrants to seek full membership and integration into American life. Even where structural barriers such as language difficulties and discrimination hamper their integration, majority of Latinos perceive that gaining citizenship is a mark of status and inclusion (Portes and Curtis, 1987; Cardenas and Flores 1977).

The economic status of the immigrants was found to be a motivating factor in the propensity to seek naturalization. Ghanaian immigrants who own a home, a business, or have received postgraduate education tend to stress economic factors as the motivating factors in the decision to acquire citizenship. The results indicate that naturalization is also influenced by occupational and labor force attributes of immigrants. Generally, skilled Ghanaian immigrants who hold managerial, professional, technical, and administrative jobs are more likely than their unskilled counterparts to apply for citizenship. Among those who listed occupational and labor force participation as the primary motivation for seeking naturalization, there is a perception that career advancements in their professional life are enhanced with naturalization. The rate of citizenship and naturalization is higher among Ghanaians who hold postsecondary credentials. Within this group, significant variations in the level of naturalization can be discerned. Though postsecondary education influenced who became citizens, those immigrants with higher education credentials in professional disciplines such as engineering, mathematics, computer science, and business administration tended to naturalize more than those with two-year associate degrees. From their perspective, citizenship is a prerequisite if one is to achieve successful economic integration into the affairs of American society. This is particularly the case among the immigrants who operate small scale business enterprises. This group cited access to bank loans and credits, business management advice from banks, and access to whole markets for their goods as one of the benefits of naturalization.

The results from this study show that a number of individual immigrant traits influence naturalization. These include an immigrant's age, year and timing of immigration, education, income, occupation and labor force participation, prestige of occupation, length of stay in the United States, and gender. Other traits include repatriation plans and age of children living at home. Ghanaians who apply for naturalization tend to be young (average age about 40), and the majority of them immigrated to the USA in their twenties. When rates of naturalization are compared across various age groups, the highest rate of naturalization is among the 40–45 age group. This is followed by those in the 50–55 age category. The age group with the lowest rate of naturalization is the 20–30 age group though several of them are eligible for citizenship. The low rates of citizenship among the relatively young (those in the 20–25 age group) can be attributed to length of stay in the United States.

Timing and year of emigration correlates with naturalization. In general, the majority of Ghanaians who have become naturalized citizens immigrated to the United States during the early to mid-1980s. This period was characterized by favorable immigration policies, notably the IRCA of 1986, which was an attempt to deal with illegal immigration. As part of this legislation, those immigrants who had been residing in the country continuously since 1982 were allowed to have their status adjusted to become permanent residents. IRCA also include a provision that would impose a penalty on employers who knowingly hire illegal immigrants. Over three million undocumented aliens benefited from IRCA (United States Immigration and Naturalization Service, 1993: 17). Closely related to the timing of immigration is immigrants' length of stay in the United States as a determinant of naturalization. Even when they have met the residency requirements, some Ghanaian immigrants prefer to wait until they have lived and worked in the United States for a long time before applying for naturalization. In a few instances, some of the immigrants wait until they become eligible to apply for social security benefits before putting in their application to naturalize. The only exception is when they perceive that they stand to benefit educationally and economically if they apply for naturalization while they are in school or when they are about to enter the labor force.

The decision to naturalize is also influenced by income earnings. The rate of naturalization tends to increase with income level. Ghanaian immigrants earning $35,000 and above tend to apply for citizenship more than their counterparts who earn less. At relatively higher incomes ($50,000 and above), the rate of citizenship is about 70 per cent compared with 30 per cent for those who earn below $20,000. Among immigrants reporting no income, naturalization is the lowest. In addition, significant differences in the rate of naturalization were found among those immigrants who indicated that they receive retirement and health benefits from their employers and those who do not receive benefits. The rate of naturalization is higher by a ratio of two to one among the immigrants who receive benefits compared to those who do not receive benefits.

Overall, Ghanaian female immigrants tend to seek naturalization at a higher rate than their male counterparts. The ratio is three to one in favor of the female immigrants. For the women who came to the United States independent of a spouse or family member, and who have pursued tertiary education, the tendency is to apply for naturalization once eligibility requirements have been met. For these single women, early naturalization means they can visit home and find a husband to join them in the United States. For those women who came to reunite with a male spouse, naturalization is sought immediately after the residency requirements have been met. Because some of the women migrate to the United States to join a husband, the legal right they have to stay in the United States is determined by the migration status of their spouse. If the husband has already acquired citizenship, the wife can file immediately after she becomes eligible. This way, if the marriage breaks down, ends in separation or divorce, the woman would have already secured citizenship, and thus her right to stay in the United States. Additionally, filing for naturalization upon becoming eligible safeguards the woman's inheritance rights should something happen to end the marriage. That is why some of the women who were sponsored by a male partner reported that their husbands have kept their green cards and passports from them, because they are afraid the women will sever marital ties with them once they acquire their residency documents. The Ghanaian immigrant women's circles reported instances where some Ghanaian women who either came to the United States to look for husbands or were sponsored by male partners to enter the United States have been subjected to physical and psychological abuse, sometimes by being locked up at home, forbidden to have visitors, or go out to socialize with other women. In situations like this, immigrant associations may intervene, otherwise the information is passed to social service agents who will then investigate.

The presence of minors in the immigrants' household contributes to the propensity to seek naturalization. One-third of the immigrants indicated that a major consideration in applying for naturalization is the perception that it brings security and protection to their children, offering the children the opportunity to become American citizens as well. This means the children can stay in the United States permanently, and have access to cultural and economic benefits such as education and social welfare services. In general, the rate of naturalization is higher by a ratio of two to one in those households with children under 10 years old versus households with children older than ten. The reason given for applying for naturalization while children are young is that the naturalization of children at an early age avoids the possibility that the children will have to go through the process upon reaching adulthood. Secondly, it makes traveling with children overseas much easier if they have the same immigration status as their parents. Thirdly, a majority of the immigrants expect that their second-generation children are more likely than their parents or grandparents to identify as Americans and perhaps stay permanently in the United States, unlike the parents who intend to repatriate in the future.

Immigrants' perceptions about structural conditions in Ghana were identified as a major reason for seeking naturalization. Ghana's perennial social and economic problems weigh in the minds of the immigrants when they seek naturalization. The general perception among the immigrants is that becoming a naturalized citizen serves as a buffer against the deteriorating economic and social conditions in Ghana. The immigrants' unfavorable perception of their country of origin spurs naturalization because of the opportunity that it offers to immigrants to sponsor their relatives to reunite with them in the United States. The acquisition of citizenship is used as a strategy to assist extended family members back home by improving the economic standards. Politically, having the status of American citizenship enables the immigrants who repatriate to Ghana to take part in the task of national reconstruction by engaging in politics and by providing another layer of insulation and protection against political violence, abuse by government officials and political opponents. According to one immigrant, "being a Ghanaian American facilitates entrance to the political process for those returning immigrants who want to be at the vanguard of political change by unearthing political problems and taking a stand against entrenched vestiges of corruption and political cronyism."

The analyses of the data collected from the immigrants show a link between naturalization, repatriation, and remittances. While the majority of the immigrants intend to repatriate to Ghana, this decision does not hamper their naturalization. This finding is consistent with the opinions expressed by a majority of the immigrants that while their preference is to repatriate, it is imperative for them to naturalize because of the perceived political security that comes with naturalization and being an American citizen. In this regard, the decision to seek naturalization is made against the backdrop that conditions in Ghana may worsen to necessitate moving back to the United States.

Once they become naturalized, the immigrants anticipate that they will be offered services in Ghana by the American embassy upon repatriation. These services include the opportunity to receive social security payments and medical assistance, to participate in the American political process, and also to sponsor relatives to come to the United States on a temporary or permanent basis. From the perspective of Osei, a Ghanaian immigrant who naturalized, "the push to naturalize was made in close consultation with extended family members in Ghana. The collective wisdom of the family was that the economic status and mobility of the family in Ghana will be improved if I become a citizen." For Osei, the decision to seek naturalization is a manifestation of the security obligations he owes to his extended family. This sense of altruism is buttressed by the belief held by many immigrants that as with every step in their immigrant journeys and lives, the pressure to balance their needs as immigrants or sojourners in a foreign land and the expectations of their extended family at home become a paramount consideration in the decision whether to naturalize or not. Osei linked his decision to naturalize to his family's economic well-being. He expressed the sentiment that naturalization confers on his family a transnational identity and a heritage that ultimately will assure his family a place in the new global economy through international migration.

To several of the immigrants who have naturalized and intend to repatriate, obtaining citizenship is seen as beneficial when they travel to Europe, Canada, and Asia for pleasure or for business. Having an American passport facilitates safe passage through major ports of entry throughout the world, usually without the need to apply for a visa. The same cannot be said of immigrants who are resident aliens or hold permanent resident status in the United States. Immigrants in this category cannot apply for and receive an American passport. They can only use the passport issued by the Government of Ghana, and will have to apply for a tourist or business visa every time they travel abroad.

The social networks that Ghanaian immigrants establish facilitate naturalization. Information about the pros and cons of naturalization are disseminated by the immigrant ethnic associations, the immigrant women's circles and the religious organizations that Ghanaian immigrants have established in the United States. While these groups help their members to assimilate or acculturate in America, they also provide a forum for the exchange and processing of information regarding naturalization and the perceived benefits associated with citizenship. These groups share information and procedures about immigration regulations, provide access to financial assistance for members who need to consult with immigration attorneys, and organize naturalization and citizenship classes for their members.

Reasons for Not Seeking Naturalization

For Ghanaian immigrants who choose not to seek naturalization, the primary reason given is the perception that naturalization will lead to the loss of their Ghanaian identity and the eventual erosion of cultural heritage. Some of these immigrants expressed cynicism toward the American political and social order, particularly their lack of confidence and trust in key institutions such as the judiciary and the political system. From their perspectives, these institutions do not offer minorities in America sufficient protection from racism and discrimination. These immigrants remain skeptical of the American system of jurisprudence, especially in law enforcement, and the way that it relates to minority and immigrant communities across America. There is a strong feeling among those who decide not to naturalize that being black will hamper and negatively affect their chances of securing citizenship, despite the protection accorded to immigrants by the Immigration and Naturalization Act of 1952 which established the right of persons to become naturalized citizens irrespective or race or sex (Fong, 1971). Despite this legal protection, some of the immigrants still remain skeptical. According to Asare, a Ghanaian immigrant who is not considering naturalization, "Having a naturalized status and being black does not insulate one from negative police stereotypical and prejudicial attitudes towards people with my skin color." Furthermore, according to another immigrant who has chosen not to seek naturalization, "political apathy and negative experiences that I associate with the American system of politics is such that I do not feel comfortable seeking participation in this institution by becoming a citizen. I can still be political and mobilize people to vote without having to participate in the electoral process myself."

In addition, some of the immigrants do not apply for naturalization because of the perception that with the exception of the right to vote and carry an American passport, citizenship does not provide them any benefits beyond what they already have as legal residents of the United States. Non-citizens who have a permanent legal status in the United States are able to travel around the world but usually have to apply for a visa to the places to be visited. As Frimpong, an immigrant who is eligible to naturalize but has yet to do so indicated, "I do not mind applying for a visa to visit Europe and Asia where I usually travel to. If you plan ahead, you can always apply for a visa to any country online. In addition, being screened by immigration and custom officials upon re-entry to the United States as a non-citizen is not as cumbersome as some have implied." For other Ghanaian immigrants, the reason not to seek naturalization was attributed to a perception that even if they become naturalized, the status of being a "foreigner" and an "outsider" will continue to persist, especially in matters related to race and ethnic relations in the United States and the subtle marginalization that confronts many people of color in America. "Naturalization does not provide one with a passport for full acceptance and inclusion into American society. Several of my friends have naturalized, but they show a greater willingness to think of themselves as Africans rather than as Americans; you are never a first-class citizen if you are black," according to Tawiah.

Currently, there are no severe restrictions on employment eligibility for permanent residents who have been legally admitted into the United States. As long as they are able to find employment in sectors of the United States economy in which citizenship status is not a prerequisite for employment, some of the Ghanaian immigrants will continue to be non-citizens. However, etched in the minds of the immigrants who choose not to become naturalized is the possibility of forced deportation should they commit a petty or serious crime, denial of welfare benefits and social services in case of job loss, and inability to hold elective office or serve on a jury. These are costs that most non-citizens who have permanent legal status are able to live with. The key for many immigrants is the opportunity to be able to participate in the labor force, to educate themselves and their children, and to be free of any statutory provisions that exclude them from employment opportunities by virtue of not being citizens of the United States. Once the economic (opportunity to work) and cultural (pursuit of educational goals) aspects of their stay in the United States are fulfilled under the provisions of their permanent residency status in the United States, the benefits of naturalization become less enticing.

In some of the immigrant households, it is not uncommon to find that only the male or female head of the household is naturalized even though the rest of the household members meet all the prerequisites for naturalization. Usually the main breadwinners in the household tend to be older immigrants (average age 60 years old) who have domiciled in the United States for more than 20 years, and have sponsored several extended family members to migrate to the United States. In such households, a common reason cited for not seeking naturalization is the perception that there are no incentives and tangible payoffs to obtain naturalization beyond the benefits provided by having a "green card" or permanent residency status. In addition, information about naturalization and the processes involved in seeking this status is sketchy among this group of immigrants. Moreover, the lack of a strong bonding to the United States, a weak political integration, low levels of efficacy and trust for the government, apathy, and a low civic obligation are also linked to the reasons why immigrants in this group do not seek naturalization. This finding confirms support to studies on naturalization and citizenship among Mexicans which found that the low levels of citizenship and naturalization among some Mexicans can be traced to negative political orientation, ethnic persistency, and weak integration into society (DiPalma, 1970; Hirsch and Gutierrez, 1973; Buzan, 1980; Garcia, 1973). In essence, the adaptation process of this group in terms of their civic and political orientation, attitudinal dispositions, apathy, or negative sentiments towards the host society, including the immigrants' knowledge and access to information about citizenship and naturalization will continue to define and affect the decision whether to affiliate with the United States via naturalization.

Role of Religious Practices and the Making of the Ghanaian Immigrant Diaspora

New immigrants to the United States never shed their religious beliefs (Herberg, 1960). Historically, they have integrated or replicated their religious rituals in the new locale (Warner, 1993). As a group, Africans are deeply religious people. Religion permeates the entire fabric of African societies and communities. When they come to North America, Africans bring their religious institutions with them to their sojourn. Through these religious institutions, the Africans anchor themselves in their heritage and at the same time forge cultural and ethnic ties to their homelands. Through the churches or religious organizations, new identities are formed and new ones strengthened and given meaning in a different context (Nuako, 2006; Addai, 1999; 2000). Young and old immigrants find and establish mutual bonds within the framework of organized worship, often relying on the churches not only to affirm their cultural beliefs but also to foster attachments to secondary groups (Ebaugh and Chafetz, 2002).

For the Ghanaian immigrant, the churches and places of worship that they have set up in the United States are not only places to affirm one's spiritual faith. Churches and places of worship also serve as social and cultural nerve centers of the immigrant community, where people from all walks of life meet other immigrants from Ghana and have secular or non-secular fellowship and at the same time affirm their traditional ethos. The organization of religion, and the beliefs and practices associated with it are central to the understanding of a society's social structure. Religiosity is very strong in Ghana, and most Ghanaians belong to a religious faith. The dominant religious groups are Protestantism, Catholicism, Islam, Animism (traditional Ghanaian worship), and Fundamentalism. Coming from a country where religious tolerance is practiced, the immigrants have imported their religious beliefs with them to the United States and in the process have created complex religious institutions to capture the full meaning and essence of their individual and collective religious beliefs.

The majority of Ghanaian immigrants who were studied indicated that they regularly attend church or a house of worship to observe religious practices. Seventy per cent of them attend a church or house of worship that is predominantly Ghanaian. These churches have been modeled after their parent churches in Ghana, with the entire leadership comprised of Ghanaians, some of whom have come from Ghana to help set up these churches and organize parish activities for the immigrants. The order of service follows the model of religious worship in Ghana with occasional modifications and blending to accommodate non-Ghanaian worshippers. Occasionally, the preacher leads the service in English accompanied by translation into local Ghanaian languages, particularly Twi, Fante, or Ga. During the service, announcements are made about how family members are coping in Ghana, births and deaths that have occurred, and any illnesses in the extended family. Sometimes, donations are taken and sent to family members on behalf of the entire congregation to help pay for hospital fees for members whose family members are ill or bereaved. Donations are also solicited to help fund capital improvement projects such as school refurbishments, providing pipe-borne water, and the construction of health clinics in villages across Ghana.

Child-naming ceremonies and funerals are major aspects of the church's role in the immigrant community. During child-naming ceremonies, libation is poured on the ground to protect the spirit of the newborn child, and blessings are sought from the ancestors to protect the welfare of the child. This ceremony is often accompanied by festive activities like singing, drumming, and eating. Everyone dresses in traditional Ghanaian attire, and the ceremony is video taped to be sent home to relatives. When there is death in the congregation, funeral services and all night wake ceremonies are held to honor the deceased. Typically, the deceased are buried in the United States, and the entire ceremony is also video taped to be sent home to relatives in Ghana. After the burial rituals have been performed, a piece of the earth immediately surrounding the burial site is scooped and sent home to be spread in the ancestral village. This is to symbolize the arrival of the spirit of the deceased to Ghana and the spirit's reconnection with other extended family members who have departed this life. As one of the immigrants who is leader of a Ghanaian immigrant church near Chicago stated, "Without this ceremony, the spirit of the deceased is said to wander abroad restlessly trying to find a place of rest and reconnection with ancestral spirits. In spreading the piece of earth in the ancestral home, the spirit of the deceased is reunited with the dead ancestors." The piece of earth that is sent home is often accompanied by the deceased person's personal belongings which are handed over to extended family members.

When members lose a loved one in Ghana, the immigrant churches step in to organize simultaneous funeral rites for the family members in the United States. Announcements about life-changing events (births, deaths, marriages) are usually included in the newsletters that are sent out monthly to members. During bereavements, the preferred practice among the immigrants is for the churches to send a donation to the bereaved family to help defray funeral expenses. However, it is also frequently the case that financial assistance is given to the relatives of the deceased to fly to Ghana to attend the funeral. If the funeral and memorial services are held in the United States, the entire congregation participates in the rituals. A festive mood usually surrounds the atmosphere at these observances. Food, music, and dancing often become part of the ceremonies as the members celebrate the life of the deceased.

As immigrant children reach the age of puberty, elaborate celebrations in the form of age-graded rituals are performed to mark the transition from childhood to adulthood. Though not accompanied by the pomp and pageantry that characterize such celebrations in Ghana, the local churches nonetheless organize activities to celebrate this transition. From their perspective, the observance of these rituals are significant because they anchor young adults to Ghanaian culture; provide those who are initiated with a sense of solidarity, identity, and cohesion to group goals; and promote strong kinship bonds. At these church-sponsored ceremonies, the young adults are informed about the community's expectations and behavioral standards that they must strive to attain. They are also admonished to uphold the family's reputation in the community, be model citizens, and not act in any way to bring shame or disrepute to the entire extended family. For the second generation, defining and maintaining an identity similar or different from that of their parents is a daunting challenge. As their parents struggle to maintain the identity and culture that is exclusively Ghanaian, the second generation children find themselves being pulled into different directions by different forces such as peer group pressure, media influences, and urban hip-hop subcultures and countercultures. The key challenge is how well the children respond to the religious identity and heritage that their parents prefer they adopt. The majority of second generation immigrant youth indicated that it was not until they started participating in the activities of the immigrant associations and attending activities sponsored by the immigrant churches that they began to form an identity about their Ghanaian-ness.

A number of the immigrants (16 per cent) indicated that they do not identify with and are not members of a particular church group or house of worship organization.

The immigrants in this group tend to worship at different churches depending on proximity to the church, composition of church membership, and the denominational beliefs of the church. In general, however, several in this group prefer to worship at predominantly Ghanaian or African-American churches located in their respective communities. Despite this loose affiliation, the immigrants do participate in the social and cultural events organized by the churches for their young children. The purpose is to provide the children with Ghanaian or African-centered religious forms of worship, and at the same time, forge cultural links between their children and other Ghanaian or African immigrant children.

For those immigrants who are Moslems, the practice is to find the nearest mosque even if it involves traveling long distances. A few Moslem families organize their own prayer services on Friday afternoons. They also hold religious classes to teach their children how to read the Koran and celebrate Eid Al Fitr, which marks the end of the fasting period. Most of the Moslems keep a very low profile about their religious activities in order not to draw anti-Islamic sentiments from their communities. Leaders of one of the Moslem groups mentioned the curtailment of fundraising activities for charities in Ghana, particularly charitable contributions given to the Ahmaddiya schools in Nima near Accra for fear of being linked by American authorities with raising funds in the United States to support terrorist groups in Africa and the Middle-East. They have also suspended their intra-faith activities with Islamic groups cited by the American government as having radical or fundamentalist leanings in the United States and Western Europe post 9/11.

In place of providing charitable assistance to Moslem groups in Ghana, the Moslems have extended their intra-faith collaborations with non-Moslem community civic organizations to educate the public about Islam. The Moslems participate regularly in consultations with non-Moslem organizations in the interest of mutual understanding and support of community charitable events. To counteract the growing concern regarding the prevailing negative stance and depiction by media outlets regarding the threats posed to the West by radical Moslems, some of the leadership of the various Moslem centers of worship have instituted round-table discussions to combat discrimination against Moslem children who attend the public schools. There is consternation among the membership of the Islamic group that they are being monitored very closely by United States law enforcement agencies based solely on the practice of their faith. This bias, as one immigrant noted, is rooted in what he termed "Islamphobia," or the belief that Moslems constitute a gathering threat to public safety in America. This fear has even led to some parents withdrawing their children from the public school system and home-schooling them.

An examination of the bonds that are fostered by religion provides yet another insight into the Ghanaian immigrant community. The institution of religion is a major source of cultural representation among Ghanaian immigrants. In serving to meet the spiritual needs of the immigrants, religion in the immigrant community is taken very seriously, often transcending the social, cultural, political, or economic differences that exist among the immigrants. Religious pluralism is what characterizes the Ghana immigrant community as evidenced by the wide subcategories of religion and religious beliefs permeating the fabric of the community.

In the Ghanaian immigrant community, religion serves an integrative social and psychological function. Whether practiced through a church, temple, mosque, or synagogue, religion forms the moral basis of the immigrant community while providing them with a sense of cultural identity and meaning to the myriad of issues that confront and define their diaspora experiences. To the majority of the Ghanaian immigrants, religion is seen as the "heart" of the immigrant community, and the fortunes and success of the members of the community are contingent upon meeting the favorable approval of God. Immigrant houses of worship have come to symbolize a haven where anyone can feel free to retreat to when all else fails.

Often when Ghanaian immigrants move to a new area, one of the first institutions they seek attachment to is the immigrant churches or houses of worship. When Afrifa arrived in Chicago as an immigrant with his family, it was one of the Ghanaian churches on the Southside of the city that assisted his family in finding suitable accommodations, school for their three children, and help with employment and job outlets in the city. Though the family did not possess valid papers for employment, the church was able to find Afrifa and his wife, Sheila, employment at a nearby hotel and restaurant chain. For the education of their children, the church allowed them to enroll at the church-sponsored elementary school. For a three month period, they received social services from the church: free meals, clothing, household appliances, and medical assistance. According to Afrifa, the church helped his family to "have a sense of community and solidarity and gave us a public presence by connecting us to the services that we need to get started in America." These churches serve as the connecting point between the immigrant and the larger community where they reside. In providing material as well as spiritual comfort for their members, these houses of worship serve as mutual aid, benevolent, and philanthropic societies, providing a wide range of social services to its members in times of joy and sadness. Provisions are made for meeting the food, housing, clothing, healthcare, and educational needs of the members as well as non-members. When they meet, as they frequently do, to celebrate the birth of a child or the arrival of a new immigrant who joins the group, or even mourn the death of a member, the goal is to celebrate the continuity of the diasporic experience. At the same time, immigrants seek guidance and assistance from the spirit world to hallow their efforts and continue to provide them with sustenance and protection as sojourners in a foreign land.

The Ghanaian immigrant churches have set aside a portion of their financial resources to assist members who fall on hard times. Often financial assistance is provided to defray the cost for relatives who have to travel to Ghana to mourn a deceased relative. The houses of worship recognize that in alleviating the pressing needs of its members and by assisting its members cope with crisis, the entire immigrant community is strengthened. In meeting the spiritual needs of its members, the houses of worship are able to keep the immigrants connected to their culture and institutions. Philanthropy is core to the mission of the immigrant churches. In the words of one of the leading officers of a Ghanaian immigrant house of worship, "the immigrant community and the church are linked in a common mission: to nurture and promote the well-being of the immigrant population."

Ghanaian immigrant churches in the United States consider their universe of service to include not only the immigrants living in the United States but also all

Ghanaians living at home. They have taken it upon themselves to assist in the development and implementation of programs to alleviate poverty and suffering in Ghana. In the basements of these churches are bags of used clothing, pens, pencils, shoes, computers, exercise books, wheelchairs, and water purification systems ready to be shipped home to meet the needs of various communities in Ghana. This form of institutional transfer of resources has become a major preoccupation of the immigrant churches based in the United States. In participating in these programs, these churches recognize that the task of nation-building is a gigantic one and that raising the standard of living of Ghanaians at home and abroad is not only a governmental responsibility but a collective responsibility that involves organizations like the church and other houses of worship.

The exercise of informal social control underpinned by religious admonishment is another area of service provided by the Ghanaian immigrant worship houses. Social control often takes the form of dispute mediation involving members and non-members of the religious organization; providing counseling services to immigrant families in crisis with the law; and mediating intra-family problems such as abuse, neglect, marital dissolution, and drug addiction (Nuako, 2006). Often when the immigrant churches have been involved in dispute and conflict resolution of their members, the goal is to find an amicable solution that the parties to the conflict can live with. Rather than use the formal social service agencies to resolve their problems, parishners are encouraged to use the more informal dispute resolution councils usually comprising of church elders. The elder male members of the churches usually provide council to young men who are having marital problems. Elderly female members take it upon themselves to counsel and provide mentorship to young girls. Peer group associations are established to provide additional counseling and services to the youth members of the churches, particularly recreation, assistance with school work, church-sponsored field trips, and tips on dating.

The Ghanaian Immigrant Houses of Worship and Political Mobilization

Despite the fact that spiritual issues dominate the religious agenda, the immigrant houses of worship are not isolated from political issues in the United States or political happenings at home in Ghana. The preaching is often mixed with political pronouncements regarding events in Ghana as well as in the United States. Support from the rank and file is often solicited by the hierarchy of religious organizations to support political activities in Ghana. Members are kept abreast about significant political events at home and are encouraged to write letters home to solicit the full participation of relatives in the political process. At times, these organizations have taken a stand on sensitive social, economic and political issues that impact the lives of their members and their relatives back home. A case in point is the recent increase in gasoline prices by almost 100 per cent. A number of the immigrant churches in the United States mobilized their members to send letters of protest to the Ghanaian embassy, and consular representatives in New York and Washington, to decry the impact of the increase on the average Ghanaian and to appeal to the government to find ways to minimize the effects of the removal of subsidies on other utilities, including water and electricity.

The churches also support political activities in the United States, often collecting and sending financial contributions to political parties and candidates whose manifestos and goals align with Ghanaian values. During the 2000 and 2004 political campaigns to elect the American President, Ghanaian immigrant churches in Houston, Atlanta, and Chicago mobilized their members to register voters and distribute political literature to church members and non-members alike. On election days, the churches mobilized transportation to carry its members to polling stations across these cities, including making telephone calls to encourage their eligible members to cast their votes. The political activities of the churches are not limited to national political elections. At the local level, these churches often invite candidates who are seeking political office to come and meet with their members. While they do not openly and publicly declare their support for particular political parties, the churches and their members tend to lean left to center on the political continuum and tend to vote for the democratic, Green Party, and libertarian political candidates.

In sum, the process involved in Ghanaian immigrant institutional integration is not monolithic but rather varied. While some of the immigrants are going to seek integration and incorporation through naturalization, others may prefer to set up their own immigrant networks and associations to reflect their religious, ethnic, class, or national identity. The Ghanaian immigrant community is therefore not a single community. Rather, it is composed of segmented, and sometimes fragmented groups whose values and beliefs intersect often, as well as contradict, depending on the circumstances surrounding their migratory experiences in the United States and situations at home in Ghana. The boundaries of this community in terms of where individual as opposed to group norms and goals intersect are therefore very difficult to delineate. However, in creating their institutions in the United States while embracing the institutions of the host society, the immigrants are positioning themselves to confront the uncertainties associated with relocation to distant and foreign lands.

The complexities of Ghanaian immigrants' transnational lives are such that they complicate notions about the community structures and institutional affiliations that the immigrants themselves attempt to construct. The creation of the Ghanaian immigrant community and its institutional infrastructure in the United States is intended to ensure the continuity and adaptation of the group. And while some of these institutions and organizations are replications of what the immigrants are used to having as Ghanaians, they can also symbolize a representation of new cultural institutions designed to define and give context to the immigrants' new circumstances as members of American society. From their individual and collective perspectives, the immigrants believe that the real greatness of America is the promise and the vision of a better tomorrow that it provides to its citizens as well as to foreigners who are fortunate enough to live in America. As they weave the tapestries of their immigrant institutions and social organizations to create an identity for themselves, the immigrants remain mindful of the fact that their continued success in America is premised on their belief that these institutions and social organizations will be allowed to flourish in an atmosphere where the rule of law prevails, and where foreigners and immigrants are accepted freely by the social polity of America.

Religion has always been an integral and important feature of immigrant groups in America. Worship and attending religious ceremonies are integral aspects of the Ghanaian immigrant community in the United States. The church is the centerpiece of Ghanaian immigrant culture, a visual affirmation of culture and social participation. From these organizations radiate social and economic support systems, programs, and activities that are designed to keep the members connected and committed to their individual and group spiritual and non-spiritual needs and obligations. Many of these churches and worship centers continue to reflect worship traditions imported from Ghana. Church rituals are often adapted to correspond to the needs of the congregation abroad. While some of them attempt to be ecumenical to appeal to a broader congregation membership from differing sociocultural and religious backgrounds, for the most part, the order of church services tends to reflect the religious orthodoxy of the parent church.

The degree of their reliance on strong immigrant group networks has facilitated the integration of the Ghanaians into American society. At the same time, although acculturation has taken place among the émigrés, the form of acculturation is instrumental and is forged by the immigrants only to the extent that it allows them to participate in social and economic activities. There are contradictions regarding how the immigrants relate to the broad social polity of American society. On one hand, the immigrants want access to education for themselves and their children. They want quality housing and delivery of social services for their communities. Access to the labor market is equally important for the immigrants. But on the other hand, they tend to promote their own institutional structures because of the perception that government-based social institutions cannot be relied upon to provide the full range of services that will ensure the inclusion and integration of the immigrants into the mainstream society. As their numbers increase and they continue to establish institutional mechanisms to ensure adaptation, some of the immigrants are beginning to abandon acculturation and integration in favor of separation and the segmentation of their lives as distinct and different from the normative structural systems of American society. The contending views among the immigrants are that the persistence of racism and discrimination in American society makes it imperative for them to pursue separation and institutional isolation even if this approach will eventually lead to social exclusion. Additionally, the evidence from the present study suggests that the increases in Ghanaian immigrant institutions have inhibited the willingness of the Ghanaians to seek inclusion into American society. There are overt appeals among some of the immigrants that they must preserve their traditions and not allow their heritage and culture to be co-opted by mainstream society. The increases in the number of Ghanaian immigrant churches, ethnic markets, newspaper and other media outlets in the USA also suggests that the immigrants are desirous of maintaining and reinforcing their own ethnic stratification independent of the general society. Among those who have sought and obtained naturalization and citizenship, becoming an American has not lead to any significant shifts toward a wholesale adoption of American cultural and political ethos. Naturalization is peripheral to the ethnic associations and the religious institutions that the immigrants have created. While naturalization may facilitate political participation, ensure the right to vote, and ease travels across the world, for many of the Ghanaians who have become citizens, a strong identification with and incorporation into the immigrant associations and networks is seen as offering greater social capital and benefits than naturalization. For these immigrants, the ethnic associations continue to dominate the consciousness of the immigrant community, often helping to form and shape their identities, values, and moral beliefs. The reliance on these homogeneous institutions and the promotion of Ghanaian-based immigrant affiliations may thwart assimilation and the successful integration of the immigrants. The immigrant-based associations are not total or complete institutions that meet and fulfill every aspect of the needs of the immigrants. The inability of these institutions and associations to meet the entire needs of their members imply that a certain degree of acculturation and or assimilation on the part of the immigrants is warranted. In the long-run, the effectiveness of Ghanaian immigrant community building and social participation in the affairs of the host society is going to be contingent upon a number of factors such as immigrant educational attainment, length of residence in the country, residential mobility, and age-cohort effects based on the timing of arrival in the USA and the extent of immigrant fluency in English. The ability of the immigrants to rely on their homogeneous associations to create avenues for employment will be a critical factor in determining the form(s) of integration and community building that the Ghanaians will seek and establish in America.

Chapter 7

The Second Generation Immigrant Youth: Multiple and Shifting Identities

Social scientists have commented on the social construction of youth culture and identity. A majority of studies view youth as in the process of becoming, often emphasizing rites of passage, subcultural tendencies, age defined roles and statuses, and the separateness of youth culture from adult culture. The Birmingham School in England depicted working class youth culture as opposing established middle-class values. Albert Cohen's (1955) working class youth were seen as resisters and protesters engaged in never ending class schisms with established authority figures, mainly parents and school administrators. Sociologist Stanley Cohen emphasized the separateness of youth culture from adult culture via the strong attachments that the youth form with music and the consumption culture. William Whyte (1943) offers an approach that examined youth identity in terms of the street-corner society and cliques that the youth form to express identity. Eminent sociologist Talcott Parson explained youth culture to mean a distinct world that is structured around age and sex roles.

The concept of age and intergenerational differences is a universally acknowledged phenomenon. The cultural expectations, age-graded role definitions and statuses that different societies attach to youth are varied. In most of Africa, youth are expected to conform to culturally predetermined roles, and are often guided to fit into and find their place in the social system. There is no strict demarcation between youth and adult roles within the social world in which both groups operate and exist. It is not uncommon to find youth taking care of younger siblings and elderly parents, assisting parents on the farm, and selling goods in markets and along principal roads. The cultural identities of youth are shaped by the community at large. This collective responsibility is underpinned by the norm that for the youth to find their sense of place and belonging in society, they must be offered practical guidance throughout the period of adolescence even if it means the period of apprenticeship from youth to adulthood is prolonged.

Youth are active agents and propagators of culture. The interpretative abilities of the youth to construct and re-construct identity, and at the same time, bring meaning to these identities are both illuminating and invigorating. As cultural producers, the identities that youth develop and the roles they play in cultural development have become an important aspect of social reality. Their lives are usually seen through the lens of adults. The attributions of their behavior by adults are often explained within the contexts of socialization, age-graded expectations, and more often than not, intergenerational cultural conflicts. A common strand or theme in the socialization of children is the notion that children acquire and construct knowledge from what they interpret from the surrounding society, and the context that they form as a result of their socialization becomes pivotal in the social construction of child or youth identity.

All the youth whose identity experiences are discussed in this chapter have different migration experiences to the United States. Some were born in the United States. Others came with their parents as refugees seeking to reconstitute their shattered lives due to political oppression, wars, civil unrests, and drought. Still others came with parents who had engaged in stepwise or chain migration by first leaving Ghana and going to the Middle East, Eastern Europe, or to Asia before settling permanently in the United States. The majority of their parents can be considered as economic and cultural migrants who are seeking better standards of living for themselves and their families. Irrespective of why and how they got to the United States, one thing remains certain: their attempts to reconstruct their lives in a foreign land and find new meanings and ways to express their collective identities are crucial to the ways that immigrants cope with the voluntary and involuntary separation and sometimes sense of loss and nostalgia that immigrants have to endure when they uproot themselves and their families to foreign places.

Once in the host country, different forms of social structures influence how immigrant youth form their identities. Two themes have guided scholarly inquiries into the issue of adjustment process and the formation of identity among second generation immigrant youth in the United States. The first emanates from the social or human capital perspective which contends that the individual or group traits that immigrants import or bring with them to the intended country of destination is pivotal in shaping how the immigrants define and adapt to their new environment. In this regard, the immigrants' norms, customs, values, and social institutions play a major role in shaping the formation of youth identity. A second perspective examines the interplay of the cultures of the host society and the willingness of the newcomers to assimilate or learn and incorporate the expectations of the new society into their lives. This approach emphasizes the presence or lack thereof of institutional structures that the host and guest collaboratively put in place to facilitate the integration, acculturation, or assimilation of new arrivals into the new society. Also, this approach presupposes that the host society is an open and inclusive society that is tolerant of ethnic diversity and immigration. The confluence of the two approaches is important in unravelling the social construction of identity among second generation Ghanaian immigrant youth in the United States.

As Ghanaian immigrants constitute their families in the United States and define their transnational ethnicities and identities, one of the enduring issues is whether the second-generation children will adopt Ghanaian identities or assume the identities and normative value systems of their parents or grand parents. A second issue is whether they will adopt American identities or opt for identities that span cultural barriers.

The first generation immigrant parents have successfully replicated and preserved the Ghanaian and African cultural values that they brought with them to the United States. In constructing their identities, the first generation parents have incorporated principles of African culture such as self-empowerment, altruism, community-centeredness, extended family and kin group goals, and the orientation of the family as an institution of economic production. From their perspective, drive and ambition, commitment to quality education, and the zeal to succeed in America, are the core principles and values which they expect their children to embrace. These values have served the first generation of Ghanaian émigrés in the United States very well, and a majority of the immigrants credit their success to the Ghanaian based institutions and the ethnic infrastructure that they have built to adapt to life in America. For the first generation parents, a major responsibility is to bring up their children properly and assist them first, to find their place in Ghanaian culture and, second to make them learn to conform to the expectations and mores of living in America.

The pattern of socialization of second generation Ghanaian immigrant children is anchored in Ghanaian mores. In Ghana, children are socialized to participate in every aspect of household chores from a very young age. These include assisting with cooking and washing, accompanying parents to the market and the farm, and cleaning. They perform these tasks in addition to attending to their school work. Children assist their parents in performing those tasks that they will be called upon to perform when they reach adulthood. By the time they reach adolescence, Ghanaian children are expected to undertake most of the responsibilities that adults perform. Boys often learn roles of fatherhood. Young girls are taught the roles of motherhood. But increasingly, the patterns of gender socialization of the young are beginning to reflect the need to expose both boys and girls to the values and learning that they need in order to become responsible adults.

One of the most contentious issues within the Ghanaian immigrant family unit is how the second generation youth react to and live out the expectations of their parents and immigrant elders. On the one hand, the immigrant parents find themselves defending the traditional Ghanaian values that have anchored them in the United States. On the other hand, the second generation children are struggling with how to balance the pressures of conforming to family defined expectations and to those of the larger youth subcultures of America. This, as the adolescents in this study pointed out, is a difficult balancing act. When the children are at home with their parents, the age and gender graded expectation, and values that they have been taught are strictly enforced. The boundaries of what constitutes appropriate versus inappropriate conduct are not blurred. As a matter of cultural principle, children have little or no say in the day to day management of the immigrant households, for adults formulate and define the parameters of conduct and behavioral norms. Hierarchical structures of age and gender roles are such that children are expected, and trained to respect and defer to authority figures in and outside of their household unit. The internal dynamics of immigrant family relationships are such that they allow for the social control of wayward youth to be sanctioned when they violate family held values. The youth are expected to model their behavior after adult role models in the family. Adolescent females are socialized to conform to the mother's expectations regarding womanhood. For boys, the expectations are that they will learn the roles of fatherhood and, in particular, position themselves for leadership responsibilities in the kin group at an early age. The expectations placed on children to conform are not limited to the confines of the household but also include the community at large. Children can be appropriately punished by parents or by adult authority figures in the household even when the locale of their norm infraction is away from the confines of the home environment. The sanctioning of public norm infraction is posited on the belief, held by the first generation immigrants, that children are expected to behave appropriately by showing reverence to any adult male or female that they come into contact with, including when they are outside the family unit.

As children mature and assume adolescent roles in and outside of the immigrant extended family unit, the struggles that arise in defining an identity to reflect the needs of the immigrant youth become very daunting. The parents and elders of the immigrant youth accept that a certain degree of Americanization among their teenage children is inevitable. The question is the degree of Americanization that the parents are willing to tolerate among the youth. The attitudes of the parents are that the children will choose to engage aspects of American cultural life selectively. For example, in aspects of American youth clothing styles and music, the parents give the children a free reign to choose their own preferences as long as children also wear traditional Ghanaian attires during festive occasions and religious functions. However, complete autonomy and the independence to create a distinct American youth identity is frowned upon, especially if that identity alienates the parents from the children. Children are steered in the direction of kin group goals. This stems from the parents' belief that family life is a cooperative and altruistic affair and that solitude, estrangement, and alienation, or the creating of an isolated identity, mar the cohesiveness of family relationships.

The children of the first generation immigrant households are expected to associate with children of immigrant families. Efforts are made by the parents to establish strong bonding among the immigrant youth. Family sponsored activities are organized regularly to provide the youth an environment to bond and learn together. Educational and cultural excursions to theme parks, safaris, soccer events, museums, fairgrounds, and exhibitions are frequently organized by the families, and the youth are expected to participate in these trips. The immigrant families usually take turns transporting the children. When children return home from school, it is expected that an elderly relative will always be at home to welcome them. After they are fed, children are expected to start on their home work and school projects. The children are often not allowed to be idle or spend unproductive time watching television or speaking on the phone. Success in school is highly prized, and the immigrant parents ensure that their children will attain educational credentials higher than that of the parents. Particular emphasis is placed on finding tutors to come to the home and assist the youth with home work, particularly in subjects such as mathematics and the sciences. The expectation is that the youth will achieve high scores on standardized high school aptitude tests, so that they can obtain scholarships to attend selective colleges and universities in the United States.

Fathers are particularly instrumental in directing the choice of where to attend college. The preference is usually for youth to attend private colleges and universities not too far from the family's residence. The majority of the parents prefer that their children live at home while attending college or university. The purpose is to allow parents extended opportunities to continue to shape the character of their children and at the same time derive maximum interactions with them before they leave home.

For the majority of the second generation youth, the reference group relied upon in shaping and defining identity is the urban black youth subculture. The tastes of the immigrant youth in music, dressing, hairstyle, speech patterns, and general outlook reflect the influences of urban black American culture. While the second generation youth recognize that there are significant cultural differences between them and their black American youth counterparts, they nonetheless feel the need to forge a strong affiliation with urban black America. In a sense, the second generation immigrant children rely on the urban black American youth to assist them in making choices regarding music, dress, and haircut styles. Being fluent in English and lacking their parents' accents, these immigrant youth are able to widen their circle of interactions and have a more visible identity. Without an accent, most of them are seen as American youth. The stress that the youth place on defining their ethnicity becomes important in determining the identity they will pursue. So are other sociocultural variables such as education, class, and time of arrival in the host society (for a discussion of the role of intergenerational change in the construction of ethnic identity, see Rogler et. al.).

The difficulties often encountered by the youth in trying to forge their own autonomy and independence away from parental figures are phenomenal. Usually, the youth have not been successful. They have often been annoyed and rebellious when their parents refuse to identify with the choices the immigrant youth make regarding styles of clothing, music, and even food habits. Even when they perceive that their parents do not understand the choices that they make in terms of clothing, food habits, and musical preferences, the immigrant youth still recognize and revere the authority of their parents and will not run away from home, drop out of school, or engage in other delinquent acts. On their part, the immigrant youth impress it upon their parents that they understand American cultural practices far better than their parents and hence can be trusted to make the right decisions that will not end in bringing shame or disrepute to the dignity of the family. The parents perceive the need to protect their children from the influence of the mass media and from the culture of the urban peer group. Regarding the media, the parents feel that it encourages children to become prematurely independent of their parents, often resulting in the child's disregard for the traditions that the immigrant parents are trying to instil in the children: hard work, respect, drive, ambition, and a commitment to education. The images depicted on television are seen as incompatible with the parents' desire that their children channel their energy into productive activities, particularly education. No matter the source of intergenerational conflicts, solutions are always found within the immigrant network of community when youth identity clashes with parental values. Child protective services are usually kept out of intergenerational conflicts that surface when a child leaves home or decides not to attend school. If a child has to leave home (a rare event), they usually go and live with another immigrant parent known to the child's family. Intense negotiations among elderly matriarchs and patriarchs are made to enable the child to return home to their parents. The resolving of intergenerational schisms are facilitated and resolved within the nexus of immigrant family networks. Exceptions are when an immigrant child becomes a victim of violence by adult family members; in this case, school and law enforcement agencies are notified by third parties. Matriarchs and patriarchs who reside in the immigrant households are usually not familiar with

American legal norms regarding how children should be sanctioned if they break family rules. Male elders in the immigrant households tend to be very strict in their disciplinary actions and sometimes will use corporal punishment. Culture conflicts resulting from a strain between traditional Ghanaian culture and American culture are usually resolved in accordance with American values. It is not uncommon for some of the immigrant parents to seek advice from their American friends on matters of youth. For parents who are not American citizens, the resolution of conflicts with their teenage children is approached with caution, as extreme forms of punishment, such as withholding food from minors can lead to arrest and subsequent deportation from the United States.

Frequently, when parents have disagreed with their teenage children about the choice of their friends, acquaintances, and lifestyles, some of the children have responded by going outside their immediate family unit to involve the parents of their American friends that they attend school with. Stepping outside the family unit (another rare occurrence), serves as notice to the immigrant parents that though they exercise biological rights over their children, outside forces determine and sometimes may influence whether or not the parents have the free reign to be arbitrary in their methods of discipline. The parents are aware that the American friends of their children will not hesitate to inform social service agencies if they suspect that there is abuse or neglect or any other conditions at home that may jeopardize the welfare and interest of the child.

For adolescent girls who date or establish a relationship with someone of the opposite sex who is outside of the Ghanaian immigrant community, parents often respond by curtailing such interactions, albeit with mostly unsuccessful results. While they accept the notion of romantic love and reject arranged marriages for their children, the parents tend to intervene when they perceive that their daughters or sons have formed romantic relationships with children whose values and lifestyles they disapprove of. The parents admit that they do not influence the dating choices of their children, or who their children choose as a marital partner. They prefer that their children date or select a marital partner who is from Ghana and preferably shares African values. Conflicts between adolescent girls and their parents are usually over the differences in interpreting values and norms concerning dating. The adolescent girls feel that their parents are too strict and very controlling when it comes to dating. To the girls, making friends with boys who are schoolmates is part of the identity that they have established in the United States. They do not read any sexual connotations into the relationships that they have with their male counterparts at school. To the parents however, it is improper for young girls to associate with male adolescents, even if those relationships are free from sexual involvement.

Work is an important feature of the identity of immigrant youth, who spend an average of fifteen hours a week in a structured work environment. The wages they receive form a significant portion of their spending money. The money is spent on clothing, compact discs, cigarettes, and entertainment. A few save their money to buy a used car. When I met Ayibonte, he was saving the money he received from working at the local Wal-Mart to buy parts for the used Honda Civic he had just bought. Similarly, his sister worked after school at Burger King, and she also spent the bulk of her pay on a deposit for a used car. For the immigrant youth, work outside the home is also a way to meet and make new friends and expand their range of activities. For some, it is a way to leave home for a while to interact with the public. It also provides a forum for meeting opposite sex peers. Girls like Esi, Henrietta, Mavis, and Georgina, whose parents reside in the same housing subdivision, spend Saturday evenings at the local skating rink. For them, getting parental permission to bring their boyfriends home or to stay out late is difficult.

An important aspect of identity that evoked strong emotions from the immigrant youth, irrespective of the form of identity that the youth had constructed, is their general perceptions about the relationship between blacks and the police. They decried the pejorative public and media representations of black youth identity, particularly black male youth. The misperception that black youth are misguided and crime-prone hooligans overshadows the positive identity that the youth try to portray. As a group, the second generation immigrants feel that discrimination and racism still exist in the United States and that the immigrant children often become its victims, particularly the immigrant youth who have difficulty communicating effectively in English. The tendency to be labelled crime-prone and lawless engenders feelings of mistrust on the part of the youth toward the dominant culture. "The stories about police systematic abuse directed toward the black youth are real and not exaggerated. Some of my friends have been victims of these harassments where you are assumed to be guilty of violating the law because you are black," according to this immigrant youth. "My parents warn me not to ride in my friend's BMW because they are afraid the police might label all of us as drug-dealers. A few blacks have given every black person a bad name. But that is no different from the few whites who give whites a bad name. Bad people come in all skin colors. My skin color is always linked to crime by the police, media, and by the majority of Americans. I do not understand it," explains another immigrant youth.

As an immigrant youth, Kobina feels that his Ghanaian accent coupled with his status as a foreigner predisposes him to police racial profiling. "When we go to the mall, the police watch us with an eagle's eyes. They think we are dealing drugs or plotting to commit crime when all we are doing is just killing time milling around; we do not have air conditioning at home. In the summer we go to the mall to stay cool. White and Hispanic kids do that as well. But as black kids, we are always singled out and harassed by the mall security officers. Sometimes our encounter with them is fatal. Remember Ahmadou Diallo, the West African immigrant who was gunned down by New York City police," Kobina said. This mistrust has created a chasm between the black youth and the local agents of law enforcement. Even the female black youth are not immune from this generalized climate of mistrust that the youth associate with the police. Kobina described his sister's encounter with police harassment. "My sister took my dad's Lexus to the mall. She had permission to drive the car. She picked up her friends and they rode together. Right at the entrance to the mall they were stopped by the police and had our car searched for controlled substances. And the reason the police gave was that the car was reported stolen. This was a lie. Even when my dad came to the scene to tell them he owns the car, the police did not believe him. And my dad is an administrator at the local community college." According to this immigrant youth, "Black youth and blacks in general are not completely free to form and express their own chosen identity. Sometimes, your role and identity in society as a black person is already chosen for you. You have no hand in it. And often, this identity is sometimes demeaning."

Blended Identities of the Second Generation Immigrant Youth

Using the information collected from the focus group sessions of second generation Ghanaian immigrant youth, the contemporary cosmopolitan culture of the immigrant youth can be portrayed. This youth culture, seen through the lens of its participants, is rich in its prose and often interlaced with a transnational image that is unique and multifaceted. Their immigrant landscape is constantly struggling to create a voice that resonates and is rooted in three legacies: American cultural ethos, Ghanaian cultural mores, and the reconstituted poly-identities currently being forged by immigrant and diaspora groups in the United States. The arenas in which these landscapes of immigrant youth identities are being depicted and played out are constantly shifting, often between what is contemporary and what is traditional. The individual stories of the second generation immigrant youth provide us with a lens through which to observe the imagination and the values behind the identities that the youth create to express their personalities. For the majority of the youth, a characteristic theme that defines their youth identity is what Wuff described as the notion of agency, the concept that people do form or influence their culture and that identity is mediated by certain key agencies in society (mass media, peer culture, family, religion, schools, and politics). The construction of these identities is being shaped by social and cultural factors that are external to the immigrant youth culture. Cohort attributes, particularly the experiences formed and acquired through interactions with both primary and secondary group relations may also impinge on how these youth identities are created and lived. In the end, identities do not exist in isolation.

Case Studies of Second Generation Immigrant Youth Identities

Adjoah is a 17-year-old Ghanaian American whose parents migrated to the United States from Ghana in 1983. The family's suburban home is located in DuPage near Chicago. Her parents attended a university in Ghana and worked for a few years before leaving the country to go to Nigeria to teach. While in Nigeria, the couple saved money and later came to the United States on a visitor's visa. After the visa expired, the couple went back to Ghana and then re-applied for a long term business visa to enter the United States. They gained permanent residency status through the immigration diversity program and subsequently became citizens of the United States.

To Adjoah, identity is a lived experience that encompasses time and space. As a daughter of first generation immigrants, Adjoah rejects the pressure from her parents to not adopt a black American identity. Her parents' preference is that she will adopt a Ghanaian cultural identity. During our conversation, Adjoah asserted that the recasting and redefinition of her identity is posited on her stance that, sometimes, identity can be ambiguous and blurred. When I asked about whether she considers herself as Ghanaian American or black American, Adjoah reiterated that the parameters of a national identity or what it means to be American are individually and collectively defined. "My parents collectively define their identity as Ghanaian; they totally reject all other identities, including a black American identity. I cannot reject the identity of black America because I move in that culture; I have a place in black America; I belong in black America. I am a product of black American culture." About maintaining a Ghanaian cultural identity as well, she stated, "I cannot have an identity with a place in Africa whose sense of history and culture I know nothing about. How can I be Ghanaian when I barely speak any Ghanaian language or dialect? My only affinity with Ghana is my name and my parents' place of heritage. If you drop me in Accra today, there is nothing there that I can identify with. The customs are strange. The violence, exploitation of children, corruption, poverty all over the place; the image of Africa and Ghana that my parents have is not real. It is just a way for them to cope with being foreign here in America. I was born here. My taste in music, dress, hairstyle, and everything is American. My parents' identity is too stable and fixed, no variety; their circle of friends are all from Ghana; they don't even mingle with other immigrants from the Caribbean. They act as if they are afraid of black Americans. How can that be? My parents are close minded and unwilling to explore and venture out. All their friends are Ghanaians. People from Haiti, Jamaica, Brazil, and India live in our community, and I go to school with them. But my parents don't want me to associate with their children. I do, anyway. That's racism on the part of my parents. These kids are just like me, the kids of first generation immigrants."

From Adjoah's perspective, the image of her identity that she is constructing as a second generation immigrant black youth is one that is fluid, crossing cultural boundaries, and highly contrasting. The vivid and rather eloquent testimonies that she presents about her second generation immigrant youth identity offer a glimpse into how the immigrant youth construct and interpret the roles and statuses in society. The social psychological meanings that the participants bring to this youth culture world are usually difficult for Adjoah's parents to fully understand. In essence, Adjoah is echoing a salient theme in social psychology that identity formations are never stable; that as a process, identity formations are always evolving as actors transform themselves in time and space. As part of the urban teenage culture of America, Adjoah's stance on the negative depiction of black youth culture is that, for adults who live outside and look into this culture, the tendency is to characterize the culture as a hopeless dead end. But to her, this culture is resilient and not an antithesis to Ghanaian immigrant or white culture as her parents often imply. The youth culture that defines her emerging identity, "Marches to a different drum beat, very creative, inclusive, expressive and highly adaptable. We create and share our culture with white teenagers. They like our songs, our clothes; they copy us, we copy them at times, we get along with everyone, though our parents don't. That's their fault. In our school, kids party and are in each other's world, constantly mixing." She went on to say that "The culture of Ghana cannot offer us the future; the culture chains you, puts a noose around your neck, and is too moralistic. If it is such a strong culture in Africa as some of our parents depict it to be, why do they sit back and allow children in Africa to be used as child soldiers? On the telly you see children who should be in school but instead are selling things on urban street pavements. Is that the identity of what I should be part of? The culture has no meaning for me to identify with."

Adjoah dismisses the notion that ultimately she will come to embrace her Ghanaian roots, celebrate that identity, and reflect that identity in all or some aspects of her life. In a sense, her complete adoption of an American youth identity is a form of protest, a cultural resistance to ward off the pressure to conform to her parents' predetermined normative values. "I am part of the contemporary black youth experience in America, nothing more," she added. "I am cognizant of Ghanaian or African culture but that culture is invisible to me. What is visible is what I experience and encounter in urban black America, not what is distant in Africa."

Regarding her identity with black youth culture in America, Adjoah and other immigrant youth see value in accenting an American identity. The choice about identifying as a black American of African descent is only a small aspect of her identity. Her participation in several aspects of the social structure of American society confers on her multiple identities which she has to negotiate and construct in the general body polity. In her own words, "I have an identity as a black female, high school pupil, cheerleader, artist, and designer. I carry all these identities with me wherever I go. I answer to all of these identities and more." From her perspective, her multiple identities are formulated from the wider American cultural context. Individuals and groups become cultural entrepreneurs in embracing these identities, and as an active negotiator of the cultural values dominant in American society, she decides which identifiers or markers to accept and which ones to modify to conform to her value system. In this regard, her identity as a black youth is one that is based upon active engagement in the various cultural frameworks available to her, and a continuous transformation of these identities is imperative. For Adjoah, the ability to express herself fluently in Spanish serves as an identity marker as well. It has given her access to the Hispanic community and made her a partaker of the cultural lore and ethos of the Hispanic immigrant youth. It has given her an opportunity to express another aspect of her complex identity. This ethnic cultural identity has widened her range of role options in the community. For example, she recently joined a Hispanic literary club in her community to immerse herself into Spanish culture. The diverse roles and statuses that emanate from these multi-layered identities can often times be adapted, reproduced, or transformed in accordance with the kind of value and belief system the actors wants to maintain.

Adjoah's circle of black immigrant friends also provides another glimpse into the identity that the second generation youth form. A micro culture pervades the world of Adjoah and her circle of close-knit girlfriends. This micro culture, or what one youth described as a "social club," is comprised of a group of six black immigrant girls in Adjoah's community who come together to express their femininity, and talk about friendship, boys, and problems with their first generation immigrant parents. There is a remarkable mix of ethnicities, social classes, and nationalities in this group. The group engages in talking, mostly about males, and also about hairstyles, music, jewellery, and clothing. The girls mix together and participate in social activities more regularly than their first generation parents who for the most part remain isolated and marginalized. It did not matter to the girls whether they were from Nigeria, Ghana, Haiti, or from other nationalities. The group's identity as second generation immigrant girls trying to carve a cultural and social niche for their lives in America's mass culture is based on the new epoch offered to the girls as a result of the migratory experience. New vistas of opportunities are being opened and presented to the girls in their new environment that they otherwise would not have experienced if they had stayed in Ghana or anywhere in Africa. In coming together as immigrant youth in America to find a collective expression for their identities, the girls are affirming the contents of their immigrant youth landscape. Central to this landscape and identity are group loyalty, cohesiveness, and a strong sense of loyalty, trust, and cooperation. The tie that binds them together is their status as second generation immigrant youth. More importantly, they are friends.

Compared to Adjoah's experience of identity, the youth identity that is constructed by Kwesi, another Ghanaian-American teenager (whose parents migrated to the United States in 1995) is reflective of the different cultural forms of expression that the second generation immigrant youth portray. Unlike Adjoah who was born in the United States, Kwesi was born in Ghana and was six years old when his parents came to America. I first met Kwesi and his parents during a Taste of Nations festival in Minneapolis-St. Paul. He spoke to me about the past, the present, and the future, particularly the pride and richness that he saw in African as well as in Ghanaian cultural traits. Now sixteen, Kwesi's youth identity is based on his strong black African centered perspective. "African culture has given me a place, a ground to stand on and look into the future with all its possibilities. I am an African and a product of her rich culture, which a lot of people look down upon or dismiss as unimportant. Without a place to stand, you cannot anchor your culture," he said. To Kwesi, the efficacy of his Ghanaian-ness and his penchant to observe and cherish everything Ghanaian and African is rooted in his core belief that African principles of social and cultural production are usually neglected in favor of European, Asian, and North American cultural systems. African culture, and by extension Ghanaian culture, are often times viewed as backward. The kind of identity that he is trying to create is one that is entirely African. "I am first of all a Ghanaian African. I am a pan-Africanist. I am following in the tradition of notable African scholars and world personalities, particularly Dr. Kwame Nkrumah. My dad made me read about him. The brother is a scholar of unmatched abilities. Above all, he is an African. His identity is reflected in his African-style clothing. He is a role model for several of my friends. The same as Hakeem Olajuwon, distinguished novelists like Nguyi wa Thiongo, and many more. These people live out their African-ness first. These are the people who are giving meaning and context to my African and Ghanaian culture. I have formed a strong solidarity with all of them, even including the ones that I have not met or read about. I believe in protecting black American and African institutions. As blacks, we are fast losing our cultural heritage by blending too much with white America and incorporating white values. I believe desegregation messed up black culture. That is why I embrace African culture and emulate African principles. Some say my people in Africa have no future. I have a future because I have always had a past."

Kwesi's identity is also based on the affiliative ties that he has formed with other immigrant youth who attend his local high school. He is particularly drawn to the Caribbean and South American immigrant kids who play football and basketball on weekends at the local gymnasium. Kwesi did not encounter any problems identifying with the members of this immigrant group due to the stated objective of the group to foster inter ethnic relations among the immigrant youth. A shared goal of using sports to bridge the ethnic identity differences of the youth and promote group solidarity was very appealing to Kwesi. In the course of his interactions with this group, Kwesi was able to find validation for his belief that during the early stages of migration, second generation immigrant youth face similar problems of identity formation because of the difficulties involved in finding new roles and statuses to differentiate the youth from their first generation parents. Over time, Kwesi's group was able to create the flexibility that allowed the youth in the group to link up with other minority youth groups in the community. The fluidity of the group's boundaries allowed its members to foster inter group relations with other peers to promote a common identity, and to define a common space and forum for the sharing of innovative ideas on a wide range of subjects related to their immigrant youth experiences. In forming social cliques that are permeable and that have fluid boundaries, the immigrant youth are able to tap into a broad range of social and cultural activities to enrich their immigrant experiences.

Muniru is a 15-year-old second generation immigrant whose parents arrived in the United States in the early 1980s. His father is a Lebanese-Ghanaian, and his mother is from Tamale in northern Ghana. Muniru was born in Chicago and is an American citizen. When his mother died, his father remarried a Nigerian woman who operated a hair salon near downtown Evanston, Illinois. Muniru's father and stepmother are both devout Moslems. As a child, Muniru always accompanied his father to the mosque to participate in religious rituals. Unlike Adjoah's parents, Muniru's parents prefer that he adopt a black American identity. A year ago, his parents enrolled him at an all black preparatory school which he attended for only three weeks. "I hated that school," he said. "I have nothing in common with the other kids. The students poke jokes at me because I profess a Moslem faith. They taunt me, often pulling my clothes and depicting me as a terrorist because I read Arabic fluently and they don't. I carry a copy of the Koran in my book bag and once someone chased me to grab it from me. The teachers don't do anything about it as I have complained several times."

For Muniru, the accentuation of his youth identity in the United States is largely influenced by his religious faith and not by adhering to a particular youth subculture. From his perspective, class, race, and gender are important in defining the cultural identity that people will adopt. But so is religion. "I read a lot of Arabic books. I have a lot of interests in the Arab and Moslem world. I like the religious lifestyles and the way Moslems help each other." Muniru's parents' desire is that he adopt a racial identity (black American identity) as oppose to a religious identity (Islamic). The clash between Muniru and his parents over identity has hampered his relationship with them parents. "I used to be very proud telling people about my parents and their devotion to Islam, but not anymore. They brought me up in a strong Islamic tradition and then after 9/11 they changed completely. They stopped going to the mosque. They are afraid of identifying as Moslems. My dad is afraid he will lose his job if he came out and professed his faith publicly. Our Moslem friends stopped coming to visit us. He stopped taking me to the mosque. I had become friends with several

Moslem children whose parents are also immigrants. Now my parents forbid me to have any contact with them. I do anyway. He gets angry with me but I don't care. I want to become an Islamic scholar and one day move to Europe to practice Islam. I will be free there."

For Stella, the expression of her immigrant youth identity is dominated by her perceived sense that the patriarchal system that defines Ghanaian family life hampers the advancement of immigrant girls. Stella finds the lives of the Ghanaian immigrant women she has come to know during the last seven years culturally constraining. Now 17 years old, Stella and her mother came to the United States when she was nine years old to reunite with her father who was already a naturalized citizen. The family's life was dominated by charges and counter charges alleging abuse, drinking problems, and lack of financial support. According to Stella, her mother tried to leave several times but could not do so because she had not yet secured her permanent resident status. Since Stella's father had sponsored them to come to the United States, the visas that Stella and her mother were given were based on the immigration status of Stella's father. Sensing that Stella's mother might leave, her father confiscated their passports. After interventions from family members and immigrant friends, Stella and her mother were able to get their passports back. Stella and her mom applied and obtained citizenship. Subsequently, the marriage ended and Stella stayed with her mother, refusing to see her father.

The purpose in referring to Stella's story is not so much to highlight the hegemonic control that some of the immigrant men have over their families but rather to suggest how the formation of identity is sometimes influenced by the lived experiences and the subjective realities and meanings associated with it. For Stella, what is emerging in her consciousness as she forms an identity is not an obsession with youth music, or an interest in milling around the malls and shopping centers on weekends with her teenage friends, or discussing the latest dressing trends and hairstyles, or even her racial consciousness of being a young black girl. Hers is an identity that is based primarily on gender and the imperative of empowering women to assume full control of their destinies. "I grew up witnessing my father coming home drunk, and to yell and scream at us at home. I always saw my mother wipe streaks of tears from her face all the time. I witnessed the gradual transformation of my mother from an upbeat person to a person of despair. I could only console her that one day everything will end and the abuse she suffered will be over."

Hinting that her social relationships suffered because she always had to stay home and protect her mother, Stella described the poignancy of her gender-based identity as a feminist activist who is committed to educate herself so that she can better understand and advocate for changing the worldwide customs that makes it possible for men to dominate and subjugate women. She attaches considerable significance to the sociocultural and economic mechanisms that permit the economic and social marginalization of women. In emphasizing the need for collective resistance on the part of young women to affirm their place in the global culture, Stella's intention is to forge an identity that crosses the gender divide between men and women and to work toward the dismantling of the forces that institutionalize the entrenched interests of men over women. "I cannot live with the thought that there are several women who are subjected to the same abuses that my mother endured. The identity that I want is one that builds a legacy of hope for a better world for all women, my future daughter included."

The manifestation of a feminist identity has drawn the attention of her friends who perceive that Stella's efforts are in vain because she cannot alter the circumstances that brought about the systematic abuse she and her mother suffered at the hand of her father. The expressions and representations of her gendered identity find a voice and a cultural place and space in the formation of the Young Women for Change group that she was instrumental in setting up at her local high school. "It is not just about wearing blue jeans and expressing femininity and going to the malls everyday after school to meet boys or to shop. It is about gaining control of our lives in order to support the collective burdens of women," she said. The support she receives from her mother solidifies her firm belief in maintaining her feminine identity. The experience of physical and psychological abuse perpetrated by her father lives in Stella's memory and is the guiding principle motivating her to strive to become economically independent. In her words, "you have to have something tangible like your education, to back up the identity and the beliefs that you are trying to live by. The identity of a feminist youth ought to be backed by a good education because people are going to reject you and think you are weird."

For some of the immigrant youth, the construction of identity hinges on how to create or seek membership in a reference group whose values and beliefs the youth identifies with. This theme is illustrated in Adu's quest to define his black identity. Adu is 14 years old. His father migrated from Ghana to the United States in 1981 to pursue postgraduate studies at a major university in the American Mid-West. Upon the completion of his education, he was approved for labor certification by his employer and subsequently received his green card. He married a white woman, and they had three children all born in the United States, the oldest of which is Adu. The family resides in a suburban community that is predominantly white. There are pockets of blacks from the Caribbean and Hispanics who have started moving into Adu's neighborhood to take advantage of the quality schools. The few minority parents in his community do not mingle with the white population. Neither do they mingle and interact with each other. At the neighborhood sports and recreational center, however the children often interact freely and uninhibited.

Being a mixed-race son of a black father and a white mother, Adu finds himself having to explain his identity. His black friends avoid him because they perceive, according to Adu, that he is "not black enough for them." He feels marginalized and alienated from the black youth at his predominantly white suburban school. His only friends are three classmates he plays basketball with who are immigrant children from the Caribbean and South America. The four teenagers often meet after school to do their homework together and go to the mall or the video arcade across from their school. His white friends have little or no interactions with him because he was told that he was different even though they thought he could easily pass as white.

For Adu, the notion of his identity was not an issue until he noticed that his parents were also dealing with the same problem of identity and exclusion in their community. The couple felt ostracized, and despite the fact that they had gone out of their way to widen their network of social friends, the response had been less than favorable. With the exception of the members of their Seventh-Day Adventist

Church who openly and receptively embraced them, the family did not have any close knit acquaintances. Extended family members live far away on the east coast of the United States. Adu feels that he is just like any other teenager; he likes to listen to a variety of music, dress according to the latest fashion fad, spend weekend afternoons in the mall or at the cinema, and eat at fast food restaurants. The sense of alienation that Adu felt from other youth caused him some consternation. "I just wanted to be liked no matter my skin color. Deep inside me, I identify as a black American. My role models are Dr. Martin Luther King Jr., Bill Cosby, Oprah Winfrey, Nelson Mandela, and Colin Powell. These are very powerful people who belong to my black ethnicity. All my values and beliefs come from this culture. But it hurts that the group that you identify as your ethnic heritage feels that you are not one of them." Even the visible symbolisms of his blackness did not endear him to his black or white friends. "I wear my hair Afro style. I follow the latest hip hop music and spends a lot of money on CDs which I share with a few friends. Above all, I am a good student. I get very good grades. And this kid who seems to be the self-appointed leader of this group of young lads at school told me that I cannot hang out with them because I make good grades and my parents drive very expensive cars while the rest of them walk to school everyday. If I am not black, then who is? Maybe it is because I am of mix race. Black is beautiful. White is beautiful. You need both black and white notes on the keyboard to make a beautiful concerto."

Role and identity differentiation occurs in varying degrees among the immigrant youth. For those who join multiple social and cultural organizations as a way to promote and facilitate adaptation and incorporation into the affairs of the host society, the pattern of identity formation tends to be extensive and holistic, usually encompassing multiple cultural sites and the blending of divergent belief systems. The degree to which the immigrant youth are willing to open themselves to other identity options proves significant in accounting for the scope and range of the identities that some of the youth construct. For those who have limited social circles or have joined youth networks in which the boundaries of membership remain somewhat fixed, the range of identity choices and options prove to be limited. On the other hand, for those who were willing and open to adapt to new identity patterns by forming a wider circle of peer group associations, the process of identity formation tends to be highly cosmopolitan and often trans-cultural.

For the youth chronicled here, identity is multifaceted, predicated on difference and diversity. A common theme in the accounts of the immigrant second generation youth is that the multiple identities that they forge are intended to highlight the complexities involved in defining a youth culture in the United States. Some of the immigrant youth hope to retain some form of Ghanaian or black African identity, but with time they come to realize that their status as immigrants and foreigners compels them to adopt new identities and roles which are different from the roles and statuses that their parents will have them adopt. For a few of the adolescent immigrant girls, migration has become the mechanism whereby they have been able to redefine gender identity and roles to secure a more egalitarian relationship in their affairs at home. In coming into contact with the body polity of American society, some of the young girls have been successful in constructing a gender identity based on values that lie outside the domestic and traditional boundaries of male–female relations in Ghana. This means that some of the adolescent girls have been successful in rejecting traditional Ghanaian gender identities that limit young girls to motherhood and domestic roles that deny them access to education, unlike their male counterparts. The adolescent immigrant girls often rely on each other for friendship. The network of friendship later develops into formal groups that advocate for better resources and equal opportunity for immigrant girls. Certainly, migration has made it possible for some of them to forge new identities outside of the domestic arrangements their first generation parents are accustomed to.

The social construction of identity among the second generation Ghanaian immigrant youth is complicated by the intersections of race, ethnicity, and class. The immigrant children will continue to face questions about how they express identity. Ultimately, the type of identity they choose to express is going to be determined by continued immigration to the United States and the ever-changing landscape of identity in relation to ethnicity, gender, class, religion, and race in the United States. For all the immigrant youth, parents' education, length of stay in the United States, and the racial and ethnic composition of their neighborhood or community-at-large serve as major determinants of identity. So does the vitality of the first generation immigrant community and the commitment it makes to maintain its heritage and culture. For those immigrant communities that succeed in developing institutions that makes it less dependent on the host society, the manifestation of identity among youth will reflect the values and beliefs of the first generation. Outside forces operating in the host society (minority–majority group relations, access to housing, educational resources, transportation, economic opportunity structure, and labor force participation) have the propensity to influence the form of identity that immigrants carve for themselves. Changes in residential planning and the rising cost of housing means that there is a strong possibility that immigrant groups are going to be steered into less desirable housing subdivisions where criminal proclivities and delinquent subcultures thrive. The immigrants may also choose to segregate themselves from other groups by creating their own institutions. This may alienate the immigrant and foreign-born groups and cause intra migrant conflicts. As a group, the immigrant youth who reside in communities that are more racially and ethnically diverse tend to adopt broader characterizations of identity than their first generation parents. The boundaries of the identities that the youth construct are not static. They change in consonance with cultural and social trends. In this regard, the identities that the youth negotiate have a frontier landscape where everything and anything is possible.

For the majority of the second generation youth, life in America is an expression of their desire to seek modernity in a fast changing world whose boundaries are becoming increasingly fluid. The pressure is to live in the present with some glimpses into what the future holds. Group identity is as important as individual identity. The peer affiliative culture informs their styles of dress, taste in music, and even the way they wear their hair. The intermesh between self directed as opposed to group-directed identity in defining youth values, norms, and mores is very strong. At the macro level, the social and cultural space in which they find and create identity is a well contested terrain. Immigration and the cultural transformations that it produces are only one aspect of this contestation.

For some of the second generation youth, identity formation incorporates the acquisition and learning of multiple cultures other than one's own and using that group's culture or values as a frame of reference to evaluate one's behavior. For other youth, identity is based on a homogeneous culture, possibly to the exclusion of all other cultures. For the range of identity options that the Ghanaian immigrant youth construct, we find that the preference is for the youth to form multiple identities drawn from multiple settings. The direction toward the social construction of second generation Ghanaian immigrant youth identity is not a homogeneous end point. Identity among the group connotes the parallel existence of multiple cultures that converge to define and shape the identities of the youth. In a cultural mosaic such as the United States, there is a constant blending of multiple ethnicities in delineating how different groups define or rationalize identity. For the Ghanaian immigrant youth, the outright separation and exclusion from the core of American society is not often the norm. It is the exception.

Irrespective of how they choose to manifest identity, the youth recognize the importance of education as a means of achieving social and economic mobility in the United States. The pressure to succeed in America through education is a dominant and constantly occurring theme in the identity of the youth. Education is seen as the means of achieving intergenerational mobility and as the vehicle for achieving the American dream. There is a pervasive belief among the immigrant youth that they cannot expect that achieving their cultural and economic goals as minorities in America will come to them with ease. Rather, the shared consensus is that the same motivation, drive, and eagerness to succeed that has propelled most of their parents to middle class status in America is needed if the second generation youth are to also become successful in America. Listening to the circumstances and the environment in which their parents grew up with in Ghana, a majority of the youth are determined to acquire an economic status higher than that of their parents. In their quest to attain success, the youth share the same values as those of their parents: that only a strong motivation, ambition, and drive can propel them toward the achievement of the American promise. As they mix and remix their identities to find their place in American society, the majority of the youth spoke in reverberating tones reiterating a commitment to the tremendous opportunities, responsibilities, and challenges that living in America presents. The multiple identities that they are forging reflect the interdependency of the world and the shared responsibility and challenge they face in promoting a global culture where tolerance and diversity of identities flourish. These youth are actively engaged in the process of creating meanings to capture the core essence of their American identities. They rationalize that the ideas and ideals of American youth culture ultimately have resonance because they appeal to the creativity and artistic expression of youth from all walks of life. The opportunity to live and flourish in American society is viewed as a tremendous opportunity to resolve pressing issues such as child abuse, homelessness, enslavement, access to healthcare, and housing and hunger, which confront youth worldwide. And as they live out their identities, they remain cognizant and sensitive to the problems that youth face the world over. Rather than adopt an identity that isolates and marginalizes them, I see the Ghanaian immigrant youth embracing and not wholly rejecting black American culture. At the same time, the construction of their identities will continue to reflect the specific social and cultural contexts of their migratory experiences in the United States. In essence, these youth will broaden and bring internal diversity to the black American ethnic and racial quilt. They will engage in a process of cultural hybridization, blending and mixing ethnicities, and ultimately a contestation of the outcome of the ethnicities in terms of what it means to be black, African, foreign, and American. At the end of the focus group sessions with the second generation youth, I was left with the image of identity formation described by Iain Chambers that identity is always in transit, on the move, evolving and sometimes without a goal or an end. In this sense, the ethnic identities that will be constructed by the immigrant youth will rest on a melange of cultures, some based on the Afro-Caribbean experience; the African experience; the Third World experience, and the Ghanaian experience. Collectively, the immigrant youth will all speak from a particular experience that is unique to their experiences in the USA.

Chapter 8

Remittance Flows: Sending Money Home and Sharing the Migration Dividend

Importance of Remittances

Sebastian Cofie, a 36-year-old Ghanaian from the Volta Region of Ghana shows me the picture of his father and mother he has carried in his wallet since he came to the United States 15 years ago. While I looked at the picture, he reached inside a drawer near the television set, took out a photo album, and opened to the page with pictures of his wife, children, and seven brothers and sisters who are living in Ghana. He then looked at me and said: "The faces shown in these pictures are the reasons why I came to America after living in the Middle East for five years working in Tripoli, Libya. I labor here so that I can save money to send home to them every month. They depend on the money I send. It is their life-blood. Without this money, they will not have enough food to eat, a place to stay, and money to pay for school fees or take care of elderly grandparents."

The story of Cofie was told by nearly every Ghanaian who participated in this study. Sending money home has become the most poignant aspect of Ghanaian migration to the United States. It is a manifestation of the chronic economic conditions and the poverty that beset the country. The strategy for dealing with the grinding poverty is to rely on family members who have undertaken the journey abroad to send regular remittances to relatives at home. Conceptually, Ghanaian immigrants view remittances as a moral imperative, a duty and a mutual obligation that the migrants establish with their extended family members at home. Depending on the family's economic circumstances at home, it is expected that anyone who travels abroad whether to study or to work will send regular remittances to support relatives.

Like other developing and poor nations gripped by poverty, Ghana is beset with a number of economic problems. Among these are unfavorable balance of trade receipts, huge foreign debt, inadequate savings by both the public and private sectors, low industrial output, limited foreign aid, and low gross national product per capita. The major source of foreign currency is revenue from export-driven products such as cocoa, timber, gold, diamonds, and bauxite. The prices of those commodities are often subject to fluctuations on the world commodities markets resulting in low foreign currency reserves. Additionally, the limited foreign reserves the country earns from international commodity prices are used in importing a wide range of consumer goods into the country since Ghana does not have a strong industrial and manufacturing base. Perennial fluctuations in world commodity prices, coupled with a weak industrial and manufacturing base makes it very difficult for Ghana to derive maximum economic benefits from international trade, thus leading to precariously low foreign exchange reserves.

The scarcity of foreign reserves is a major economic and political problem for most of the developing countries. A perennial constraint to economic and industrial development, the lack of foreign reserves is the principal cause of economic stagnation in Ghana. Due to the shortage of foreign reserves, the tools for economic and industrial investments decrease, causing difficulty in economic production and growth. Foreign aid from international donors comes with conditional and binding terms that sometimes do not favor the economic interest of foreign aid recipients. Its effect on the macroeconomic outcome and household economic well-being is sometimes questionable. Structural adjustments such as currency devaluation; removal of subsidies for utilities such as water, electricity, gas, and consumer goods; divestiture and privatization of state-owned corporations; and redeployment and mass reduction in civil service personnel often accompany foreign aid from institutions like the International Monetary Fund or the World Bank.

To minimize the impact of low foreign reserves and to generate capital for economic growth and expansion, Ghana, like other developing countries, must rely on its citizens abroad to fill the void of inadequate foreign exchange. International migration and the transnational movement of people from places of low economic concentration to destinations of high economic and industrial output is part of the panacea for the challenges and problems posed by underdevelopment in the emerging countries of the world. The millions of dollars that Ghanaian immigrants from around the world remit home have now become a major element in Ghana's national economic and industrial development. Remittance flows or the person-to-person income transfer has become one of the important aspects of the international migration of skilled and unskilled labor from peripheral (emerging nations) to core areas of economic and industrial activities (developed nations). Worldwide, the billions of dollars that transnational immigrants send home to their families has become a major source of foreign exchange for the migrant-sending countries. Immigrant families from India, Pakistan, Mexico, China, Egypt, Nigeria, and Jamaica, among others, have come to rely on the remittances their nationals send home as a source of investment capital. The impacts of these remittances on the economies of immigrant-sending countries have been phenomenal. A survey of the literature points to the fact that that remittances have become an important source of foreign exchange to several developing countries and that the impact of these remittances on the balance of payments is probably the most favorable aspect of the phenomenon of labor migration and on the gross domestic product of migrant-sending countries (Swami, 1981; Straubhaar, 1986; Nayyar, 1989). According to Lianos (1997) and Kandil and Metwally (1999), often, the remittances are seen as an investment that the family makes in the individual who is supported by the family to travel abroad. Other scholars have highlighted the investment potential of remittances and its role as a poverty reduction strategy, particularly in the less developed countries (Appleyard, 1989; Keely and Tran, 1989).

Immigrants who live in the United States are not the only beneficiaries of the opportunities to which they are availed in America. Immediate and extended family members at home also benefit from having a family member who lives and works in America. The remittances that Ghanaian immigrants send home have become a substantial part of the foreign investments that come into the country. In a country whose savings rate is very low (less than half of one per cent of net income) due to the low wages workers receive, there is often local and international investment and credit crunch. Entrepreneurs and government-owned industrial entities often lack the foreign exchange letters of credit to purchase production equipment and consumer items. The result is the frequent shortages of the consumer items that Ghanaians have become overly dependent upon. In the recent history of the country (especially during the reign of General Acheampong), these shortages have caused public demonstrations against the government, and have led to hoarding, smuggling, price inflation, and queuing even for basic items like toilet paper and sugar. Often, the government had to use the military and the police to enforce price control laws that arose out of the scarcity of foreign exchange reserves. Foreign remittance is a direct infusion of capital that is not encumbered by the hidden costs often associated with foreign aid or technical assistance that donor countries in the West provide to Ghana. Properly managed, the flow of remittances into the country can be a source of entrepreneurial capital to fund small scale and private-owned business initiatives (Rodrigo and Jayatissa, 1989; Abella, 1989).

The military government of General Acheampong tried unsuccessfully to regulate the sale and exchange of foreign currencies during the 1970s when foreign currency exchange became synonymous with economic and political corruption in Ghana. This was the era of *kalabule* when corruption permeated the entire fabric of Ghanaian society including the political hierarchy. Acheampong's attempt to use the military to stamp out the corruption associated with the illegal trafficking of international currencies woefully failed to ameliorate the fiscal crisis the country was experiencing at the time. Undaunted, many Ghanaians continued to engage in foreign currency transactions often defying the social control apparatus of the Acheampong military, because as Ghanaians then and now have come to realize, access to international currency is the only way to ensure the economic survival of the majority of people in Ghana.

Remittance flows into Ghana have become a major source of finance for imported goods into the country. They are also the major source of capital acquisition for small and large scale projects in the country. Institutional remittance flow is certainly one of the main sources of venture capital for the burgeoning private real estate developments in suburbs in Accra such as East Legon, Pokoase, and Tema. Ghanaian immigrants living abroad open accounts with private real estate developers and home finance companies and send monthly contributions to be deposited in these accounts. Home ownership is a primary goal for a majority of the immigrants. Once they have accumulated 25 to 50 per cent of the cost of buying a home, they enter into a formal contract with the real estate developers, and with the mortgage and home finance companies, to purchase their dream home in some of the exclusive neighborhoods and communities in Ghana.

Several Ghanaian immigrants indicated they have made arrangements with Home Finance Company (HFC), a mortgage financier, to transfer funds from their United States bank accounts to accounts they have set up with HFC. Others use the Ghana Commercial Bank or Barclays Bank. Funds transferred from the United

States to these banks are safe, secure, and easy to monitor. Such transfers also avoid the possibility that the remitted funds will be misappropriated by extended family members. One immigrant made reference to how the funds he remitted home for three years (about $4,500) were misappropriated by his brother. Whenever he inquired about the funds, he was informed that there was no need to be concerned and that the funds were being disbursed according to his instructions. According to this immigrant, "Some Ghanaians at home who receive remittance money for safe keeping do not understand what it means to live and work in the United States. They think America is a land of milk and honey, and Ghanaians in America are awash in money." This sentiment was echoed by another immigrant who stated that several of his relatives in Ghana have come to depend on his remittances to finance lifestyles that are very expensive and unproductive. Some of the immigrants who remit home regularly through Western Union mentioned that their relatives have become targets of robbers who loiter around the premises of Western Union in Accra and Kumasi, usually watching customers who enter the premises to withdraw funds.

Factors Influencing the Decision to Remit Home

Socioeconomic and demographic characteristics of immigrants influence the propensity to remit. Migrants' wages, marital status, the ratio of male to female migrants, household/family income, immigrant visa status, and the length of stay abroad all influence the propensity to remit. Beyond these variables are other factors that are noteworthy in explaining remittance behavior. Russell (1992) has proposed a theoretical model to explain remittance behavior among immigrants. His model highlights the effects of family income, disposable foreign earned income, political and economic conditions in both migrant-sending and migrant-receiving countries, foreign currency exchange rates, the fluctuations in currency rates, the safety of remittance transfer mechanism, and government policies regarding the exchange of foreign currencies.

Total family income and family size of Ghanaians in the United States are strong predictors of the frequency of remittance and the amount of money remitted. The average amount of money remitted by Ghanaian immigrants is $225 a month. This amount rises to an average of $326 among families with a combined income of $35,000. The amount of money remitted is highest among families earning more than $50,000 per year. Among immigrants who are single, the average remitted varies with income. The average monthly amount remitted is $175 for those immigrants who earn less than $20,000. For those earning above $20,000, the remittance averages about $200 a month.

Changes in the exchange rate of the US dollar to the Ghanaian cedi seem to influence the frequency and amount remitted home. Ghanaian immigrants monitor the exchange rate of the dollar to the cedi with keen interest. The demand for remittance from home coincides often with the erosion in the value of the cedi. The continuous slide in the value of the cedi against the dollar provides the immigrants the impetus to remit since more and more Ghanaians have now become dependent on remittance assistance from relatives living abroad, especially in the United States and Great Britain. Several of the immigrants cited the numerous telephone calls that they receive from relatives back home advising them to send more dollars to take advantage of the fall of the local currency. As the mechanism for effecting the transfer of remittance to Ghana has become more safe (mainly through Western Union and banks), so has the frequency of remittance.

Variations in family and household size influence the amount of money remitted. In immigrant households with two or more family members gainfully employed and fewer than three children, the amount of money remitted is approximately $400 every month. In some of the immigrant households where multiple patriarchs and matriarchs reside, the amount of money remitted home monthly is over $500. These households tend to have five or more children living in them. Generally, larger immigrant households with two or more married family members living in the same residence and sharing household expenses tend to remit amounts in excess of $455 and send their remittance home every three weeks.

Length of stay in the United States is frequently associated with remittance flows. This relationship is inversed, suggesting that the longer Ghanaian immigrants stay in the United States, the more they remit home, irrespective of their visa or residence status. For those who have stayed in the United States for five or more years, the transfer of money home also occurred frequently (once every two weeks) and the average amount sent is $300. For those who have stayed less than five years, remittance is lower, generally about $120 per month. Ghanaian students, non-immigrants, permanent residents, and those who have naturalized status remit home regularly regardless of their employment status. Non-immigrant Ghanaian graduate students who are receiving stipends for graduate teaching or research assistantship and often working no more than twenty hours a week remit home regularly but send smaller amounts, about $85 per month.

Educational background is a significant factor influencing remittance behavior among Ghanaian immigrants in the United States. The data collected from the Ghanaian immigrant community suggests that when variables such as length of stay, marital status, age, and gender are held constant, immigrants' educational attainment and occupational classification proved to be very significant in predicting immigrant remittance behavior. Ghanaians with less than high school education remit between $75 and $110 per month to their relatives in Ghana. Those who completed postsecondary education prior to their arrival in the United States remit on average $200 a month. For those who have pursued advanced graduate degrees upon arrival, the remittance home is higher, roughly $300 per month. Every category of occupational classification remits home whether they are professional or non-professional immigrants.

Age-specific cohort effects can be discerned in the data on remittance behavior among Ghanaian immigrants in the United States. Remittance flows drop in frequency and in the amount of money that is remitted with age. Immigrants in the 20–40 age group remitted more often than any other age group. Remittance flows continue at all age groups but begin to show significant dips in the amount and frequency of remittance between ages 50–59. Beyond age 60, the amount of money and the frequency of remittance drops precipitously, from $150 to $65 and the interval between remittances becomes more prolonged, sometimes lasting between three and six months. However, the majority of the immigrants aged 60 and above mentioned other pressing needs that led to them remitting less money. Concern about future retirement objectives, declining health, and rising financial obligations puts a limit on the amount and frequency of remittance. For those in the older age group and above who have had the opportunity to sponsor younger relatives to come to the United States to join them, the responsibility of meeting the remittance obligation is passed along to the younger relatives.

The frequency and amount of remittance sent home is influenced by the immigrants' work and occupational status. As expected, Ghanaians who work full-time remit more frequently than those who work part-time or are seasonally employed. However, the data suggest that the difference in the amount remitted by Ghanaian immigrants who work full time versus those who work on a part-time basis is negligible, about $30 more per month in favor of those who hold full time jobs. Even when they are not certain about whether or not they want to repatriate, Ghanaian immigrants of all age groups and occupational status do send money home at regular intervals. But as they near retirement, the frequency of remittance diminishes considerably.

Even when they establish their own families in the host country with all the attendant financial obligations that maintaining a family entails, the immigrants do not lose sight of the moral obligation to remit to other family members at home. This moral obligation to remit is culturally buttressed by social norms that prosperity would attend to the affairs of those immigrants who are very generous and remit regularly to their relatives at home. In the Ghanaian cultural ethos, giving and sharing one's resources with less fortunate members of the family unit is considered desirable. Immigrants who remit are said to receive blessings not only from the living but also from the departed ancestors. Remittance support thus touches and benefits the immigrants and their families.

The examination of the remittance behavior of Ghanaians in the United States reveals a number of interesting conclusions. First is that remittance has become a major form of monetary transfer and exchange between migrants and migrant-sending communities. Second, irrespective of their employment or visa status in the United States, Ghanaian immigrants recognize that without the monies that they remit home to their relatives, the economic well-being of their family members at home would be more precarious than it is currently. Third, although the amount of money and the frequency of remittance vary significantly, one thing remains clear: no amount of money is considered too paltry to be remitted. In most cases, even smaller sums of money have made a major difference in terms of providing for the basic sustenance of relatives back home in Ghana. Fourth, the remittance has allowed the Ghanaian immigrants to stay connected with their families at home and has enabled them to maintain bonds of affinity. Though living far away in America, their remittances have given them a place and a voice at the table of family decision-making back home. Fifth, the flow of money between the Ghanaian immigrants and their relatives back home is a way for the immigrants to define the future outcome of their migratory experience. After all, the benefits of the remittance do not always accrue to the family members alone. The immigrant also benefit because the monies sent are sometimes set aside for the acquisition of land, to purchase a home, start a business, or to provide financial security in time of old age, assuming the immigrant repatriates to Ghana.

Uses of Remittance Money

The disbursement and utilization of remittance money reveals some very interesting findings about the role of the Ghanaian family in economic and cultural production. Since the family is an economic production unit in Ghana, families that receive money from immigrants living abroad become the direct beneficiaries of remittance flows. Through migrants' remittances, some families are able to maintain a standard of living that is relatively higher than families that currently do not receive any remittances from abroad. The mainstay of family income remittances are mainly used to meet family personal consumption needs as well as provide the "seed" money or capital for economic production ventures. Whether it is used to meet consumer demands or provide capital for investment projects, the remittances that Ghanaians send home are hard cash that provide temporary economic relief for the recipients.

The bulk of foreign remittances (33.3 per cent) that Ghanaians send home are earmarked for meeting the day-to-day needs of the family. This includes housing, food, clothing, tuition, and healthcare. The faltering of the country's economy has put a big burden on many Ghanaian families. With a gross per capita income of less than $500 a year, many Ghanaians find themselves earning on average less than $1.50 a day. Depending upon where they live in the city of Accra or surrounding suburbs, the cost of transportation and food alone will wipe out their daily minimum wage. This means that they cannot afford to rent a room in a house or that they have to share one. In most instances, however, they end up finding accommodation in the city's sprawling squatter settlements. For the average Ghanaian who is receiving minimum wage, the economic outlook is dire, especially for those who do not have relatives living abroad to make remittances to them. The economic uncertainties and the precarious living conditions that prevail in the country provide the primary motivation to emigrate to seek a better life elsewhere. Remittance flows provide a temporary economic relief for the immigrants' families. However, it does not provide permanent alleviation of the prevailing economic stagnation, sharpened class inequalities, and the increasing poverty that plague many Ghanaians.

Remittance flows may trigger more outmigration to the West as more Ghanaians come to perceive the comparative economic advantage that living in the West provides. Many Ghanaians continue to chase after jobs in the West on the assumption that, if they are successful, they too can contribute to the well-being of their families. The high demand for expatriate labor (skilled or unskilled) in the Middle East, Scandinavia, Asia, and the United States, coupled with continuing economic dislocations, ecological frailties, ethnic strife, and political uncertainties means that for decades to come, Ghana and the rest of the countries in sub-Saharan Africa will become major labor-exporting nations. Additionally, as already pointed out, continued remittances from Ghanaians to relatives at home may strengthen the bonds of affinity and social networks between the immigrants and their family members. In fostering this network of contact with a relative abroad, the remittance flow can enhance the selectivity of migration by making it highly probable that sooner or later, the beneficiaries of the remittance will become potential candidates to emigrate. If the migration decision is acted upon, the potential migrant already has a network of support established in the United States to assist in the post-arrival and settlement process. Beneficiaries of remitted money may save their money instead of using it to pay for consumer goods. Eventually, the accumulated savings could be used to fund the expenditures associated with regional or international migration. Funds may be used to obtain a passport or open a savings account to show evidence of financial support which is a necessary requirement for procuring a visa to the United States. In addition, some of the beneficiaries of remitted money use the funds to pay for college admission application fees or for payment of the required admissions examinations, such as the Test of English as a Foreign Language or the Graduate Record Exam.

Remittance is changing the consumption landscape of Ghanaians by creating more public demand and preference for imported commodities to the detriment of local and indigenous consumer goods. Generally, as indicated, the bulk of remittance money is spent on productive enterprises such as establishing a business, building a home, paying for educational expenses, or it is used to meet consumption needs. A growing number of shopping centers and mini-marts in the Accra-Tema and Kumasi metropolitan areas cater to Ghanaians with access to foreign currency, stocking their stores with only imported goods in the expectation that their customers will make their purchases using foreign denominations instead of the local currency. The goods displayed in these stores are luxurious by Ghanaian standards and out of the economic reach of the majority of Ghanaians. With time, many people come to associate these goods and the acquired taste for them with international migration. After all, these imported goods symbolize, in part, what life is like in the United States and provide a basis for gauging the relative deprivation that the average Ghanaian faces in relation to those living in America and other Western countries. When aspirations for consumption of foreign goods are formed without the necessary economic resources, strategies for fulfilling these aspirations are developed. More than likely, leaving Ghana to go abroad features very prominently in any plans designed to fulfill unmet desires.

Money that Ghanaians in the United States send home is frequently used to establish family-owned business and economic ventures. Thirty per cent of the respondents in the study mentioned that the remittances they send home are the main source of capitalization for the operation of a business. Examples of businesses funded from remittance flows include transportation; iron works; brick manufacturing; home construction; and the retailing or wholesaling of consumer products, hardware, used garments, and auto parts. The day-to-day management of the businesses is entrusted to both male and female senior family members. Depending on whether the enterprise is labor or capital intensive, extended family members, including children, are often recruited to work. This reduces the overhead expenses associated with running the business and keeps the income generated by the business in the extended family unit. Profits are usually ploughed back into the business. Eventually, as borne out by the results of the interviews, some of these business ventures become self-sustaining and profitable enough to ensure the cessation of the remittances from the United States.

By far, the most profitable business venture utilizing remittance money is transportation. In the absence of omnibus transport services, Ghanaians have to rely on *tro tro* (mini buses) and taxis as the principal forms of city and inter-city transportation. Remittance money is often used in the purchase of a used *tro tro* or taxi and given to a family member to operate. Depending on the number of passengers they can carry (usually 15, 18, or 23), most of the *tro tro* drivers earn on average 120,000 cedis, approximately $15 per day.

In a growing number of instances, a lump sum is remitted from the United States to be used in establishing an import–export business. Recent encouragement by the Kufuor government to promote export production has caught the interests of Ghanaians living abroad. Liberal investment policies that grant tax incentives for Ghanaians and foreign investors who set up business ventures in the country continue to provide impetus for Ghanaians living abroad to bring substantial capital into the country to set up import–export businesses. The goal of the Kufuor government is to liberalize the laws dealing with capital investment in the country as a way to boost production for export and home consumption.

The impact of remittance flows is being felt on the manufacturing of finished and semi-finished goods for export to the Economic Community of West African States (ECOWAS). The relaxation of cross-border tariffs has facilitated the ease with which goods and services are traded in the economic zone. Light manufactured goods for export are thriving in the industrial parks of Accra, Tema, Kumasi, and Takoradi. The main source of funding for these privately-owned cottage industries are the remittance flows coming into the country from immigrants domiciled overseas, particularly from the United States, Canada, Germany, and Great Britain.

Whether paying for the tuition, room and board, or associated fees for the education of family members to attend primary, secondary or tertiary institutions of learning in the country, remittance money from the immigrants is a direct investment in the educational and cultural infrastructure of the country. By far, though, the bulk of remittance money earmarked for education is for children and relatives who attend private preparatory schools, and junior and senior secondary schools. Considered to be of better instructional quality than the public-sponsored schools, these schools prepare students for the long-term goal of gaining admission into any of the country's universities.

Remittance Flows, Land Acquisition, and Farming

Land acquisition has become a major form of investment among Ghanaian immigrants. Almost 75 per cent of the immigrants surveyed indicated that they own land at home. Another 15 per cent were contemplating purchasing land for agricultural production. This land is purchased with money that was remitted home. Prior to their migration to the United States, only 10 per cent of those surveyed indicated that they owned land in Ghana. Remitted money is often used in purchasing large tracts of land for farming. Among the immigrants who were surveyed, remittance flows earmarked solely for agricultural production is very common. Food production is a profitable venture in Ghana. Added to this is the financial and technical incentives and assistance provided by the government, non-governmental organizations (NGOs), and international donor countries to assist the country in boosting its agricultural production for domestic consumption and foreign exports.

Land purchased for agricultural production does not always end up being used for the intended purpose. Some of the immigrants cited frequent litigations and having to spend more money to ascertain rightful ownership. This is not surprising considering that land litigation in Ghana is fraught with corruption as it is not uncommon for the same land to be sold to multiple buyers. In that instance, the buyer who is able to develop the land first is able to establish claim of ownership even when that claim is fictitious or has no legal standing. The immigrants reported that efforts on the part of their families at home to protect the land they have purchased have been met with violence by machete-wielding land thugs.

While the use of remittance money earmarked for agricultural production is a laudable economic enterprise that has the potential to make Ghana self sufficient in food production, anecdotal evidence seems to suggest the economic viability of such ventures is questionable. Some of the families receiving remittance money intended for agriculture may divert the money to other uses because of the lack of interest in agriculture among rural youth and adults. Even where the land is cultivated, the acreage bought under food production is usually at a subsistence farming level. As older farmers retire, they are not replaced by rural young adults, who would prefer to migrate to the urban centers because they perceive agricultural labor demeaning or because of the low wages farm laborers receive. Dependency on the land for sustenance is diminishing due to the labor intensive nature of farming in Ghana. The responsibility of food production in Ghana has fallen mainly to women and children because of male outmigration and gender inequality. This has affected the amount of food produced. Also, there is a preference among the families who receive remittances to diversify the rural economy by channeling the remitted funds to other economic activities such as housing and water treatment or sewerage facilities. Moreover, the lack of water, irrigation facilities, agricultural extension services to assist farmers, marketing and storage services, and the low prices paid for agricultural produce by private and public procurement agencies render investments in food production unprofitable.

Remittance and Empowerment of Women

In Ghana, women's subordinated status relative to their male counterparts has been a major barrier to their inclusion in key economic and political matters. Their social positions are attached to the status held by the patriarchs and/or husbands in their lives. This dependency means that women are not free and independent to make their own individual and collective decisions. In Ghana, the women generally defer to males in matters of economic and political decision making, and even when they earn the largest share of total household income, women in Ghana continue to defer to their fathers and husbands in family matters.

Whether they were sponsored by extended family members to the United States or came on their own, for the majority of the Ghanaian immigrant women living in the United States, the journey to this country has been liberating. Their gender relationships have undergone significant transformation while living in the United States. Increasingly, their relationships with their male counterparts have become more egalitarian. Work outside the home, the chance to earn an income on their own and the opportunity to engage in secondary and tertiary education have given some of the Ghanaian immigrant women the opportunity to have a voice in all aspects of family life, a voice they are using to define new roles for themselves and at the same time dismantle the age-old patriarchal structures that dominated their lives in Ghana.

Exposure to new gender roles in the West, coupled with the opportunity to be away from home has provided the immigrant women with a new perspective of looking at women's issues back home in Ghana. In sending remittances home, some of the immigrant women channel the funds to the adult women in their respective families instead of sending it to the male head of the households. According to the immigrants in this study, decisions about how to invest remittance money have been made by male authority figures to the exclusion of the women in the family, although the responsibility for implementation of the decisions, once made, will fall on the women. This is especially true in matters of trading and operating small retail businesses. According to Abena, a Ghanaian immigrant, when the women in her family have received remittance money, they allot the money to income-generating ventures and to improve upon the educational and human capital of the children in the family. Again, the goal is to alleviate the poverty in the extended family unit and generate income-producing activities like trading. Other immigrants spoke about the mishandling of their remitted money that is entrusted to the care of patriarchs. Excessive drinking, speculative land ventures, and frivolous spending are only some of the ways that remitted funds, intended for economic and cultural projects, have been misappropriated by patriarchs and male heads of household. Family needs, including children's education and expenses for taking care of elderly parents are often neglected. When the "American money" (as locals refer to the remitted funds) arrives in Ghana, the young men who often receive the funds visit the local bars and restaurants first before they proceed home. Adoley went on to say that when the men in her extended family receive the remitted money, they usually allocate the money to projects that perpetuate the structured gender inequality, thereby widening the gender gap. From the perspective of this immigrant, sending money home to female family members instead gives the opportunity to change the balance of power between men and women in Ghanaian society by making the relationship between men and women more egalitarian.

In directing their remittance to matrifocal-based households and diverting the funds away from the men, the immigrant women are changing the status of women and children in Ghana, contributing to the breaking down of traditional gender stereotypes and thereby promoting the economic security of women and children. According to the immigrant women, remittance funds have contributed to the redefinition of familial relations and gender roles in her family. Previously, when the men were in charge of disbursing the remittance money, nothing happened as the men did not invest the money in economically productive ventures. When one immigrant woman decided to stop sending the remittance money to the males in the household, a noticeable difference in household economic production was felt once an aunt took charge and started receiving the remittance money. With the money she receives, the aunt has managed to set up a trading kiosk, opened a savings account at a local bank so other women in the family can qualify for a small loan to open shops, and pay the school fees of the young girls in the family, so they can enroll in school instead of working on the farms as sources of cheap labor.

Akosua, another immigrant woman from Ghana shared her experiences about the remittances she sends home to Ghana. Like other immigrants, she directed the remittances to her brothers, father, or uncles, even when the remitted money was intended for the use of her sisters, mother, and aunts. The men usually held on to the money and did not disclose the full amount that was sent. This buttressed her case that remitted money is often misappropriated by the men to better themselves economically while at the same time strengthening their control over women and children. The consensus among the immigrants is that funds remitted home directly to the women in their families are often put to the uses intended and usually benefit the women and children in the family.

For Ghanaian women who have access to remittances, regular foreign cash flows from the United States has aided in raising the economic standard of living. These remittances have afforded a growing number of women the opportunity to create more options for themselves and their children outside of the patriarchal domination structures that continue to hinder the bulk of Ghanaian women who find themselves eking an existence via labor intensive activities such as farming, street hawking, and working in restaurants. Rural and urban women who regularly receive remittances from abroad have used their money to open kiosks selling sundry items like soft drinks, food items, and used clothing.

The changes that have occurred in the lives of some of these women are phenomenal. Remittance money has enabled them to raise their earning capacity, providing them with a sense of independence in and out of their household structure, and permitting them to set up savings accounts for the education of their children. It has also enabled the provision of electricity and pipe-borne water for their homes. The female beneficiaries of remittance money raise their competitiveness in the local economic production system by transforming the economic viability of their households.

Types of Remittances

Remittance is not a fixed construct. The types of remittances that immigrants provide to relatives at home are influenced by economic, cultural, and political considerations in the home country. During the reign of Acheampong in Ghana, restrictions were placed on person-to-person foreign currency transactions, and sanctions were imposed on individuals who were apprehended for buying and selling in unapproved foreign currency exchanges. Foreign currency flows were monitored by the government to ensure that political enemies of the government did not have unrestricted access to funds to mount a threat to the government in power. The perception of the Acheampong military regime was that access to foreign money provided the financial wherewithal for those who opposed the ruling government to mount a challenge against the government, possibly plunging the country into chaos and political instability. Post-Acheampong governments liberalized the fiscal policies of the country to allow the sale and purchase of foreign currencies on the open market because of the futility of government controls in the past. Today, international currencies can be bought and sold everywhere in the country.

Cash remittance transfer is the common form of remittance flow. The dominance of cash transfer transactions is attributed to the fact that cash transfers are faster, reasonably inexpensive to send home, and can be used to meet an immediate need such as paying for food, medical or funeral expenses. With the advent of Western Union and the Forex bureaus, Ghanaians abroad can also transfer money home via electronic wiring. The electronic transfers through Western Union are received instantly and paid out to the beneficiary in Ghana. The fees charged by the money wiring companies are very steep, averaging between 15 to 20 per cent of the full amount that is wired to Ghana.

Some Ghanaians abroad use their banks as the main source for channeling remittance funds to Ghana. Banks like the Ghana Commercial Bank, Barclays, allow Ghanaians abroad to open savings and checking accounts for depositing foreign currency. Several of the immigrants have taken advantage of this to send money home on a regular basis. This money earns interest and is available for withdrawal when the immigrant visits home. This way, many of the immigrants do not have to carry large sums of money with them when they travel home to visit their relatives.

The term remittance suggests a monetized transfer. Remittance behavior among Ghanaian immigrants is very complex and varied. The transfer is not confined only to money. Non-monetized, humanitarian transfers to relatives and to public and private institutions have become a very popular form of resource transfer from Ghanaian immigrants to their home country. These transfers include diverse items like pharmaceuticals and medical supplies (mainly aspirin, bandages, and antibiotics) to local polyclinics and rural hospitals, educational supplies (used textbooks, computers, pens, pencils, crayons, notebooks, and science lab equipments), and water-filtration devices.

Ghanaian immigrant associations provide institution-to-institution remittances by adopting organizations at home and providing cash and non-cash assistance, sometimes through NGO's. Families, orphanages, schools, and hospitals are the beneficiaries of institutional remittances. Items remitted usually include healthcare related items such as bandages, antibiotics, and wheelchairs, as well as computers, textbooks, and resource materials for institutions of learning, and books for libraries. To the Ghanaian immigrants, this is a form of what one immigrant described as "national remittance or pay back remittance." This form of "national" remittance is often contrasted with investment remittance. Investment remittance is used for a wide range of business, manufacturing, and industrial production activities such as building a gas station, creating a cottage industry to process agricultural raw materials into finished or semi-finished food items, transportation services, shopping marts, and other infrastructure developmental projects.

Deciphering the Pros and Cons of Remittances

Ghanaian immigrants are great savers, and their remittance behavior is very well understood in the cultural landscape of the country. On the average, Ghanaian immigrants in the United States remit more than ten times the yearly incomes they would have made had they not immigrated to the United States. Whether they were university graduates, civil servants, business entrepreneurs, hawkers, unemployed, or underemployed prior to their departure from Ghana, the majority of the Ghanaians who remit were once low income workers eking out an existence on paltry wages and salaries that provided little or no fringe benefits. The practice of remittance flows has become a poverty alleviating strategy for the large number of Ghanaians who depend on the informal economic sector, where the bulk of economic goods and services are produced in the country. Generally, when remittance money is saved at home in local banks, this increases the liquidity of the banks and makes it possible for them to provide loans for both small and large scale economic development. As the country's economic fortunes have declined, remittances from Ghanaians domiciled abroad have become the dominant form of capital acquisition for the financing of projects. This trend, as was noted by the immigrants, cannot continue without long term repercussions for the country. The perspective of some of the immigrants is that, ultimately, it is imperative for the government of Ghana to institute economic development and growth policies that would structure the Ghanaian economy to make it more competitive and to promote export and international trade as a way of generating foreign currency reserves for the country. An increase in the production capacity of Ghana is critical for ensuring that the country enjoys a healthy balance of payment receipt. A positive balance of trade would make it possible for the government and the private sector to embark upon economic initiatives that would raise the gross national product and income earnings of Ghanaians. The continued reliance on immigrant remittances for private capital to fund social, economic, and industrial projects implies that for the millions of Ghanaians who do not have relatives living abroad to remit, participation in the economic recovery of Ghana is at best marginal.

Continued dependency on foreign remittances for economic survival in Ghana exacerbates the already widening gap of inequality between the educated and uneducated, urban and rural population thus making the task of forging national unity after decades of political instability very tenuous. As a major source for the financing of imports into the country, remittance flows have the unintended consequence of creating "artificial prosperity" in the country. The flow of Western goods into the country has been facilitated by greater access to remittance money. However, in the absence of a sustained national policy to reinvigorate the domestic economy using local resources, and as foreign savings continue to outpace domestic savings, the possibility of remittance flows drying up has the potential to spell more economic uncertainties and political woes for the country.

The structural problems confronting Ghana are very complex. As indicated, the inability of the country to gain a competitive edge in export production has meant that the country does not generate sufficient foreign reserves to accelerate its economic growth. Diversification of exportable commodities aside from cocoa, gold, and bauxite is imperative if the country is to arrest the foreign exchange receipt problems. In the short term, the moderate gains that the country is currently making due primarily to the remittances from Ghanaians living abroad are being sustained, providing economic impetus by boosting consumption and, to a lesser extent, invigorating the manufacturing sector. But in the long-term, sustained economic growth will have to come from the government's ability to promote and implement large-scale economic and industrial development projects in concert with bilateral and multilateral economic development partners. Remittance is merely a temporary solution to the gigantic task of nation-building. It takes care of the immediate consumption needs of individual families, but an over-reliance by the central government on foreign remittance flows to get the country out of its current economic doldrums will cause further stagnation and derail the long-term economic and political stability of the country.

The Future of Remittance Flows

The impact of remittance flows the economic development of Ghana is phenomenal. According to government estimates, the amount of remittance money that flowed from the Ghanaians abroad to the country in 2002 was $1.4 billion (Dr. Paul Acquah, Governor of the Bank of Ghana). In looking ahead to the future of remittance flows to Ghana, a sub-text is whether or not continued remittances will spur further outmigration of skilled and unskilled Ghanaians to the West. Evidence collected from the Ghanaian immigrants suggests that in the short term, remittances may potentially reduce the desire for more and more Ghanaians to go abroad. The majority of the immigrants perceive that their relatives back home are willing to stay in Ghana and not emigrate as long as they receive remittances that can be used for personal consumption or for an investment in an economic venture. This stems from the fact that it is very prohibitive for the relatives living abroad to come up with the funds to sponsor relatives to join them. The funds that otherwise would be spent to pay for a return ticket and sundry fees involved in applying for a passport and visa for relatives could be channeled into viable economic activities that would benefit members of the migrant's extended family.

Approximately 40 per cent of the Ghanaian immigrants in the United States responded that they frequently engage in discussions with their relatives in Ghana about the comparative advantages and disadvantages of staying in Ghana and receiving regularly remittance versus coming to the United States. Ultimately, the changes in homeland security and the tightening of visa applications for prospective immigrants and non-immigrants alike means that to stay home and receive remittance flows from their relatives living in America may be more beneficial than migrating.

The decision whether to remit or to sponsor family members to come to the United States is made more complicated by the tightening of American immigration laws in the wake of the terrorist bombings. For some would-be immigrants, plans to leave Ghana for the United States may have to be re-evaluated, postponed, or alternate destinations considered in light of the tightening of immigration laws in the United States. The tightening of visa standards is not only confined to the United

States. Several of the European capitals and Pacific Rim countries such as Australia, Japan, and New Zealand that attract Ghanaian immigrants have also tightened visa applications. For those who desire to come to the United States and secure employment, the prospects of securing a visa to enter is very dim. As before, the chances of securing a visa to come to the United States will prove more favorable for those Ghanaians who have relatives in this country and who are seeking to reunite with their families or enter the United States to pursue educational goals. In the near future, and as they wait for the world-wide ripple effect of the terrorist attack to subside, the direction of Ghanaian immigration will shift to countries in the Middle East, to Asian countries such as Malaysia, Taiwan, and Indonesia, and to new Republics in Eastern Europe.

While the tightening of immigration laws in the United States and elsewhere may dampen the migratory aspirations of prospective migrants initially, it will not eliminate the desire to travel abroad. For both skilled and unskilled Ghanaians, going abroad has become the principal way of achieving economic mobility, and notwithstanding the security screening and the streamlining of immigration laws, Ghanaians will continue to look to the United States because of the perception that life is always better in America than life in Ghana.

For families not receiving any assistance in the form of remittance flows from relatives living in the United States, life can be hard in Ghana. Frequently, these families feel a sense of economic deprivation as they see a growing gap between themselves and those who regularly receive remittance. These disparities are becoming apparent in some of the rural areas of Ghana. In the dam community of Akosombo, the beautiful homes and level of material comfort enjoyed by rural dwellers who receive remittances from relatives abroad is in sharp contrast to the homes and living standards of families that do not receive remittances. Some of the remittance-receiving families in the rural areas use the remitted funds to purchase large acres of land, displacing subsistence farmers, and holding on to the land for years without developing it. They own the hardware stores in town, control the bulk of the private transportation system, the smoked and dried fish markets, and the privately-run preparatory schools. In some of the small towns surrounding the Accra-Tema metropolitan area, shopping centers financed by remittance flows have created the "new rich" who are using their economic status to influence political decision making at the local district level. Some have used the remittances to build multi-story gated residences with 24-hour security.

The transfer of money from the United States and the West to Ghana is creating new aspirations for Ghanaian youth who have come to associate the new wealth with going abroad. For some, the remittance flows create material desires that cannot be met if one does not migrate. Anecdotal evidence from Ho and Keta in the Volta Region of Ghana suggests that the rise in prostitution and the trafficking of underage girls may be linked with the transfer of money, particularly from the United States and England. Recruiters use the remitted dollars and pound sterling to lure unsuspecting girls, looking for work and a better life abroad, into brothels in North Africa, Asia, the Middle East, and Europe. Most of these women never see their families again as they are moved around from country to country using falsified travel documents.

While it is acknowledged that remittance money sent home has the potential to improve upon the economic standing of recipients and thereby minimize their desire to emigrate, remittance flows can also serve as a pull factor by creating aspirations that, in the minds of recipients, can only be attained if one were to travel to the United States or abroad in general. In the estimation of many Ghanaians, remittance income is associated with the opportunities offered to live and work in the West. Remittance money is a cultural manifestation or symbol of the material affluence of the West relative to the deprivation and poverty that confront most people in Ghana and the rest of Africa. In the psyche of prospective "*ablotsi*" goers, the opportunity to travel abroad and possibly obtain employment is one way of ensuring access to foreign currency and by extension the chance to remit to relatives at home. The opportunity to have access to foreign currency is what is driving, in part, the mass dash among Ghanaians to go abroad. As the country's economic fortunes continue to deteriorate, the pressure to go abroad will mount as Ghanaians strive to improve upon their economic circumstances; and the physical mobility of people across national and international boundaries will continue to be one of the principal motives for international migration. Given that capital for funding economic and industrial development projects in Ghana is scarce, one might expect that remittance from Ghanaians abroad will continue to play a major role in the resuscitation of the country's frequently ailing economy. The motivation among Ghanaian immigrants abroad to send regularly remittances to their kin folks at home is very strong. Their desire to remit is culturally and psychologically entrenched in the social and moral ethos of Ghanaian society. This ethos specifies that the ultimate goal of international migration is the collective economic welfare of the entire family. According to Cofie, the Ghanaian abroad who regularly remits is "like the rising tide that lifts everyone out of economic misery and brings hope that the future will be better than the past." To remit is to show loyalty and commitment to the family that they are not alone in their fight against poverty. Ghanaians abroad always have to imagine home with all its burdens, promises, and hopes, and be a channel for making dreams come true." This commitment to the welfare of the family unit is considered to have a rational and utilitarian value: the strong belief among the families of immigrants abroad that a migrant who is successful abroad is expected to help shoulder the bulk of the economic needs of kin group members. In sending remittances therefore, the migrant enhances and maximizes their own utility as well as that of other family members.

Chapter 9

Homeward Bound: Return Migration and Repatriation to Ghana

Modeling Return Migration: Situating the Determinants

The bulk of migratory research has focused on the initial motivations that spur the movement of people from one geographic place to another. Little attention has been paid to the motivations that spur and form the decision to return home. The scope of return migration is very complex as there are several factors associated with this process. Structural and individual components operate to determine the circumstances of why certain individuals repatriate and others do not.

The volume of voluntary return migration from the United States to Ghana is not known. The government of Ghana does not collect data on the temporary or permanent return of its citizens who return home from abroad for a protracted period of time. The paucity of data on this subject at the national level makes it very difficult to determine the volume and extent of return migratory flows into the country. One has to rely on micro-level survey data to identify the proximate determinants of return migrants and their demographic features. Using the data collected from the Ghanaian immigrants who are domiciled in the United States, it is possible to delineate the proximate determinants of return migration and provide a general theoretical framework to fill the void in our current state of knowledge on this subject. Our primary purpose in this section is to provide a contextual exposé of the determinants of return migration to Ghana. The sociological understanding of return migration is very important in the formulation of governmental strategies to confront the short and long term problems associated with the management of Ghana's human resources and for the implications of return migration for national development and reconstruction.

The theoretical modeling of the determinants of return migration of Ghanaian immigrants has to address a number of key issues. First, to what extent do socioeconomic considerations in Ghana and in the immigrant country of residence motivate the decision to repatriate? Second, what role, if any, do immigrants' sociocultural and familial networks play in facilitating or hindering the decision to repatriate? Third, what is the current knowledge about the readjustment and settlement patterns of Ghanaian immigrant returnees? Fourth, once they arrive in Ghana, do the returnees consider their repatriation as temporary or permanent? What considerations determine whether the repatriation would be temporary or permanent? Finally, are there any policy implications of return migration for an immigrant-sending country like Ghana?

The phenomenon of return migration of Ghanaians started even before the country achieved self-rule. A cadre of notable returnees left Europe and the United States to come home and agitate for political self-determination and challenge British hegemony over Ghana. Among the returnees was Dr. Kwame Nkrumah, Ghana's first Prime Minister. He arrived in the United States in 1935 as a student at Lincoln University in Pennsylvania. There, he met Ako Adjei, and the two started mobilizing other students for political reforms in Ghana. In 1945, Nkrumah returned to England to study and hone his political skills. When he finally returned home, he organized with other previous returnees, including Dr. J.B. Danquah, to clamor for political reforms in Ghana, which ultimately forced the hand of the British to end colonial rule in the Gold Coast. Most of Ghana's political leaders were returnees who came home upon the completion of their studies in the United States or United Kingdom to assist in national reconstruction. Aside from Nkrumah, other notable Ghanaian returnees were Dr. Kofi Abrefa Busia, and Dr. Hilla Liman, both past Prime Ministers of the country.

Since attaining independence from Great Britain in 1957, international migration has come to assume immense significance in the Ghanaian body polity. Whether the migratory experience is international or regional, for short or long term, the bulk of Ghanaian émigrés intend to repatriate to Ghana after they have achieved their economic and cultural goals. Irrespective of their legal status in the United States, the majority of Ghanaian immigrants (79 per cent) consider themselves as sojourners and will repatriate sooner or later. Fifteen per cent indicated that they would probably repatriate but are not definite about the time line to return. The remaining six per cent were definite that they would stay permanently in the United States.

Two theoretical models offer insight into why Ghanaian immigrants, domiciled in the United States, return home after a short or lengthy stay. The first is the structural approach. This approach concentrates on the factors that spur return migration. From a structural perspective, return migration is explained as a function of the general contextual conditions prevailing at the transnational level and of the extent to which these relationships are incorporated into a unified system of international labor movements and exchange between core and peripheral countries. The structural component of return migration seeks to address issues such as why people return; streams, volume, or composition of the return; problems and issues associated with the reintegration and incorporation of returnees into the returning society affairs; and the overall impact of the return on the home society. In this respect, the explanation of return migration can be juxtaposed within the hierarchical paradigm of globally-structured inequality that forms the content of core-peripheral economies.

The second model is the micro or individualistic approach. This approach stresses and highlights the role of returnee personal attributes such as family network, motivation, psychological state, the perceived benefits of staying versus returning, and the formation of attitudes about the meanings of being a returned migrant. Similar to the human capital perspective in migratory research, this approach rationalizes the cost versus benefits of returning home or staying abroad with the sole objective of maximizing the best interest of the returnee. The decision to return is made only when the prospective returnee is able to configure the impact of a return migration on children and spouse, the costs associated with returning home, and the returnee's overall personal assessment and satisfaction with their migratory experience. For Ghanaian immigrant returnees, the decision or motivation regarding repatriation is multidimensional and is often nuanced by a complex set of social and economic variables that are specific (factors internal to Ghana) as well as those that are non-specific to Ghana (factors operating at the transnational level, particularly in the United States).

Motivations to Repatriate: General Reasons

In situating the multiple contexts of the propensity of Ghanaian immigrant return, we find that both structural and individualistic explanations provide valuable insights into this important aspect of migratory studies and policy formulations. As far as Ghanaian immigrants are concerned, the decision to repatriate is largely determined by economic conditions prevailing in the United States and in Ghana. The economic motivation to return home by far outweighs other considerations. Nearly 90 per cent of the returnees who were studied stated they returned home to Ghana to establish a business or economic venture, to manage a pre-existing economic or business enterprise, or to explore the feasibility of starting an enterprise. The type of business activities of the returnees are as varied as the economic reasons that motivated the returnees to repatriate to Ghana. Computer related businesses, tourism, import–export business activities, wholesale and retail of foreign consumer items, marketing and distribution, insurance, auto sales, food processing, restaurants, finance companies, and building and construction activities dominated the list of economic and industrial activities that the returnees are currently pursuing.

Globalization, spread of investment capital, and the concentration of economic activities away from the core to the peripheral economies have led to an increase in the establishment of subsidiaries of major industrial and manufacturing conglomerates in Africa. This has spurred return migration of Ghanaians because of the opportunities offered by international subsidiaries of major international firms who prefer to recruit personnel who have had experience living in the West. In this regard, return migration is seen as the modus operandi of economic and industrial incorporation of Ghana into the global economy. No matter the capital investments or the size of the business activities that the returnees engage in, one thing remains certain: that international migration of Ghanaians to the West and their subsequent repatriation is changing the economic landscape of the country by opening up new vistas of opportunities hitherto reserved for those with significant capital outlays.

Government incentive schemes, aimed at encouraging Ghanaians abroad with skills and assets to return home and assist in the national economic development effort, play a major role in the decision to repatriate. In concert with their local and international economic partners, the Ghana government has launched schemes to attract prospective investors who are willing to risk capital investments in such key areas as energy, transportation, housing, agriculture, and mining. Returnees who invest in these sectors of the country's economy are provided with technical support and, in some cases, the money to pay for the freight of heavy equipments from abroad earmarked for production. Small and large capital investors from the private sector are working with government and international donors to improve the economic infrastructure of the country. To facilitate this, the Ghana government has launched schemes to grant tax incentives to Ghanaians with private capital to invest in key sectors of the economy, especially healthcare, housing, transportation, and food production. As part of this initiative, the central government has indicated its willingness to provide the necessary infrastructure (especially roads and water) and other economies of scale for the affected projects. The government is also going to make it easier for the entrepreneurs to transfer their foreign money to Ghana without becoming encumbered in Ghana's bureaucratic thicket.

One-third of the returnees indicated that the primary motivation behind their decision to return was the liberalization of government tax incentives, usually in the form of bank credits, to assist entrepreneurs to locate their business ventures in the country. Still in its infancy, the goal is to harness the skills and assets of returnees by assisting them to create small proprietary enterprise catchments specializing in both service and manufacturing production. The majority of the Ghanaians who repatriated under this scheme have yet to receive all the financial assistance that was promised to them by the central government. A common complaint among some of the returnees was that the business assistance program for returnees is fraught with corruption, political patronage, bureaucratic entanglements, inadequate start-up funding, and lack of adequate feasibility studies and evaluation of outcomes. In addition, the inability of the government to provide adequate business extension services was cited as a common problem encountered by the returnees, including delays from the central bank in setting up lines of credit to import foreign materials required for local production.

In making the decision to repatriate, prospective returnees assess the economic, social, and cultural standard of living in the host society vis-à-vis the standard of living at home. In this connection, the human capital traits of the returnee (educational level attained, length of stay in the United States, age, and amount of money saved) become critical. For example, among returnees who participated in the study, the average amount of money saved prior to repatriation was $67,500 over a 20-year stay in the United States. This amount is over 150 times what the average Ghanaian earns in a year. The bulk of the money the returnees had saved was transferred or remitted home for safekeeping prior to repatriation.

Returnees with higher educational credentials perceive their services to be valued more at home in Ghana than in the United States. Possession of foreign credentials in Ghana is highly valued. Returnees come home to live in a culture that is rigidly stratified along class lines, and those with higher education dominate the political landscape and, by extension, become key figures in economic and political decision-making. Going back home is a way for returnees who have acquired substantial human capital in the form of higher education and savings to gain rapid social mobility, prestige, and status. Returnees with advanced degrees who are able to secure employment with the civil service or with corporations gain rapid social mobility and status, becoming part of the elite class. In most cases, they are provided with subsidized accommodations at some of the choicest locations in town with modern amenities (telephone service and streets lights) and, at times, with free company or government transportation, a chauffeur, maidservant, and security personnel (night watchman). As senior personnel, most of them also get the chance to travel abroad to attend conferences where they represent their respective government or private agencies. While returning home from their visits abroad, they bring with them commodities that are in short supply or too prohibitive to purchase in Ghana.

In addition, having lived abroad for a while provides returnees with access to a network of friends and associates who provide them with gifts, mainly material goods. They also have the opportunity to send their children to the best preparatory schools as well as to the prestigious junior and secondary schools in the country. For those returnees who still have access to their foreign accounts, cost is usually not a hindrance to sending their children to the elite prep schools in the country. At home, the returnees live a life that is far removed from the lives of the average Ghanaian. They have access to modern telecommunication devices (satellite dishes and internet services), and some of their children travel on charter flights to Europe and America during the summer. Most of the returnees have been successful in duplicating the material comforts and amenities that they are used to having in the United States. Hence, they have the best of both worlds: living in their own country and enjoying a standard of living that is out of reach for more than 90 per cent of the population of the country. This is part of the migration dividend that was alluded to earlier; having migrated to the United States is an economic pay off. Returning home to Ghana with assets is even more economically rewarding.

The income of returned immigrants is relatively higher than that of their Ghanaian counterparts who have not emigrated. To a large degree, the returned immigrants have become part of the Ghanaian bourgeoisie, living in relative affluence and enjoying a level of financial security due to their access to foreign capital and currencies. Meanwhile, the majority of their Ghanaian counterparts who are semi-skilled or unskilled are living on below $1.25 per day. With their relatively high income and standard of living, the returnees continue to shape the cultural geography of Ghana and create their Ghanaian dream in several respects. New and exclusive subdivisions near the Kotoka International Airport, East Legon, Pokoase, McCarthy Hill (all located in Accra), and Community 22 near Tema, cater to and replicate the living standards returnees are accustomed to having domiciled in the United States and other Western capitals. Prices for these housing developments are often quoted in foreign currencies. For the majority of Ghanaians, these real estate projects are far out of financial reach. The units near East Legon, the airport area, and those off Spintex Road average between $77,000 and $150,000. Houses developed by Emefs (a private developer), located near the Sakumono Lagoon and Community 22 are selling between $70,000 and $180,000 range. Housing units developed by the Tema Development Corporation near Community 22 are similarly priced. A common feature of these subdivisions is the service amenities they provide, such as landscaping, schools, libraries, shopping centers, and recreational clubs.

For some of the returnees who are able to afford a home in one of the exclusive subdivisions in the regional capital centers, coming back to Ghana is like a dream come true. While the return home has definitely led to a reduction in income, this loss has been compensated for by new opportunities for social and economic advancement. For those returnees who have managed to save their money, the cost of living in Ghana is very favorable, and this is one of the key incentives for returning home. Living conditions in Ghana are favorable if one has the means to afford the services they desire. For those with children, the return has made it possible for them to take advantage of the high quality educational systems available in most of the regional urban centers across the country. While Ghana does not boast of the same infrastructure as the United States, at a minimum, the returnees have access to their basic needs, and relative to the standard of living enjoyed by other Ghanaians, they are doing very well economically and have adjusted adequately to the new environment. Having an access to foreign resources enables the returnees to live a life that Ghanaians who never had the opportunity to travel abroad can only dream about. But with this status also comes a defined cultural expectation; that returnees will continue to share their assets with extended family members in need. Sharing the migration dividend with extended kin does not come to an end because of voluntary repatriation. Providing assistance to meet the economic needs of family members is expected to continue following repatriation. It is a duty and an obligation.

The decision to return is also influenced by the frequency of remittances and homeward transfer of money accumulated in Ghana during the stay in the United States. Usually, the remittances were sent to family members who then opened bank accounts once the money was exchanged. The remittances and cash flow that immigrants had forwarded to Ghana became the "seed" money that the returnees used as capital to start their entrepreneurial activities. One returnee sent $150 every month during the 13 years he lived in the United States. When he finally returned to Ghana in 1999, he had accumulated about $24,000. With this money in hand, he started a home construction business in Tema and now employs about 25 workers. Another returnee had money withdrawn bi-weekly from his bank account in the United States to a bank in Ghana. When he finally repatriated, he had accumulated nearly $40,000. He used this money to start three businesses: a preparatory school located near Kaneshie, a suburb of Accra; a mini-mart with a pharmacy attached located at near Kotobabi (also a suburb of Accra); and finally an import–export business specializing in African cultural artifacts, electronic equipments, and spare auto parts.

Decisions regarding future repatriation are problematic for Ghanaians abroad who have experienced persistent unemployment and underemployment. For those immigrants who are laid off and eligible to collect unemployment compensation or receive social welfare assistance, the economic pinch of unemployment is somewhat minimized as long as they remain in the United States, though they cannot save enough or send money home to expedite their return. The decision to repatriate at a future date may hinge on the chronicity of unemployment. In instances where persistent unemployment has led to downward mobility because one cannot find a comparable job to the one they were laid off from, the decision to return home is delayed considerably. Most of the immigrants would rather stay in the United States where they can tap into institutionalized safety nets for those who are laid off and cannot find employment. In addition, some of the immigrants prefer to take advantage of job re-training to hone their work skills and better the odds of obtaining stable employment.

Among the Ghanaian immigrants who are not eligible to receive unemployment assistance, mainly due to their undocumented status, being laid off can alter the decision to return home. Usually, it has taken a longer time for these Ghanaians to obtain employment because, in most instances, they have to find an employer who is not going to check their visa and work authorization status. This is becoming more and more difficult since the 9/11 attack as most employers are now required by law to check the employability of all their workers by completing immigration forms to show proof of work eligibility. The decision to go home will never materialize for these undocumented immigrants because of their perception that they have not achieved enough social mobility and occupational security to be able to afford the trip home. Plans regarding the decision to return may have to be revised and probably will be placed on hold permanently. For this group of immigrants, repatriation is a dream that may not be fulfilled because of the economic uncertainties associated with not having saved enough money to support themselves and their families upon repatriation.

For the growing number of Ghanaians in the United States who have to rely on the work permits of relatives or friends to secure employment, returning home is fraught with problems. These Ghanaians become indebted to those people whose papers they are using to get work. Sometimes, they have to pay exorbitant monthly or quarterly fees to the legitimate owners of the work authorization documents, which leaves them little money to spend on themselves, let alone the money to set aside to defray the cost of going back home. For these immigrants, involuntary or forced repatriation in the form of deportation proceedings is what will eventually facilitate their return home. Meanwhile, they intend to stay in the United States and keep working until their luck runs out and they are apprehended by the authorities.

For legal immigrants, the most suitable way to prepare for the return home is by starting a remittance plan. Whether they send the remittances directly to family members or arrange for a bank in Ghana to hold their saving deposits in a trust, the transfer of money by Ghanaians living abroad has become a major source of capital funding and a principal source of foreign currency in the country. External transfers that the returnees in the focus group interviews had sent to Ghana over their total period of stay in the United States when combined, add up to over five million dollars. Some of the returnees in the focus group remitted between one-third and two-thirds of their income while living in the United States. In some instances, returnees had worked multiple jobs while domiciled in the United States, lived frugally, and saved their money to facilitate their future repatriation.

A recurring theme in the motivation to return to Ghana is the cultural and social fragmentation of American society along racial lines. The majority of the returnees expressed concern about the black and white racial polarization and the continued struggles by Black Americans and people of color in general to overcome discrimination. Their black skin color serves as a marker which brings them face-to-face with white antipathy toward dark-skinned people no matter their country of origin.

Attitudes toward blacks of African descent in general and their exclusion from mainstream society and segregated status inevitably cast a negative shadow over any possibility of the immigrants remaining in the United States permanently. The expectations of returning home to Ghana are formed within the broader context of the struggles that blacks and people of minority status in the United States have had to endure over the years. The returnees did not see the need to stay in America permanently only to be marginalized and exposed to the deep-seated legacy of racial tension that characterizes black–white relations in the United States. Despite the tremendous economic opportunities America provided them, the returnees were unanimous in their assertion that the opportunities offered by the United States pale in comparison to the struggles against negative perceptions and antiblack sentiments that pervade the general body polity of the United States.

Race relations have become an enduring legacy of the American landscape. As stated previously, the immigrants are not immune to this social canker. As members of a visible minority group, the immigrants encounter racism, discrimination, and prejudice in a variety of forms: denial of employment opportunities, unprovoked harassment by agents of law enforcement, discriminatory practices by real estate agents and landlords, and a general perception of being second class citizens. Structural discrimination is of big concern to several minority populations in the United States because they experience its interlocking nature and consequences. While they have adapted to the racial tension in this country by developing various strategies and institutions, such as the immigrant associations, to cope with it and minimize its impact on their daily lives, a majority of the immigrants still feel insecure about their presence in the United States. While most Americans believe that these discriminatory practices are a thing of the past, to many minorities (including immigrants), these *de facto* discriminatory practices are entrenched and very real in the lives of those who become its victims.

The climate of racial antagonism and uncertainty was brought to the fore by the returnees as a major contributing factor to their repatriation. To a majority of the returnees, the opportunities that America affords its citizens and immigrants are unrivaled anywhere in the world. But this same system also treats people of color, especially those of black ancestry in a dehumanizing way. According to one returnee, in spite of all his accomplishments as a nuclear engineer, he was still made to feel that he was not welcome in the United States though he never got into any trouble with the law or disrespected anyone. This lack of validation was very problematic for this returnee and for many of his immigrant associates while they lived in the United States. Eventually, they decided to pack their bags and return home to Ghana. In the words of one of the returnees, "the advantages of living in the United States are tremendous. But the persistent encounters with racism, humiliation, disparagement by the wider society or being made to feel psychologically inferior to whites is very difficult to withstand. I returned home because in Ghana I am treated with dignity, and I am not constantly reminded in subtle ways about my blackness. Here, my blackness does not count against me, and I am free of this poverty of dignity that America tags its black population with irrespective of their accomplishments. Being black in America is a lot of baggage and a heavy load to bear."

For some of the immigrants who were studied, the racial and ethnic status of peoples of black African descent in the United States was a motivating factor behind the reason to repatriate. For others, the decision to repatriate was influenced by family considerations. A number of returnees with non-Ghanaian spouses stated the primary reason for coming back home was the opportunity for the spouse to live outside the United States and experience Ghanaian and African cultures. This was especially the case among returnees married to American spouses. For many of these returnees, what started as a temporary visit to Ghana soon became a protracted stay and eventually a permanent relocation and departure from the United States. A majority of the returnees in this category are retired and spend the bulk of their time traveling across Ghana and the rest of Africa to share in the Continent's rich cultural panoply and heritage traditions. To one immigrant who repatriated home with his American-born wife, the repatriation was viewed as a "cultural renaissance of tremendous historical and spiritual significance, a reconnection with one's past heritage." This returnee couple did not show any intentions of returning to the United States, and as for other returnees, the relatively slow pace of life in Ghana, the warmer weather, the hospitality of Ghanaians, and the low cost of living compared to the United States are the primary reasons for the decision to repatriate.

The data collected from the immigrants revealed that retirement planning and economic security in old age are closely linked to the motivation to return to Ghana. Again, pecuniary factors (amount of money saved, investment securities, number of quarters earned for social security, existence or non-existence of company or agency funded pensions, currency exchange rates, and transferability of assets) are critical factors influencing the decision to repatriate. Prior to returning home, Ghanaian immigrants ensure that they have taken care of their retirement and other fiscal matters. For those who are eligible to receive social security, this includes filing the necessary papers at the Social Security Administration (SSA), completing the interview with the SSA, and instructing where the funds should be deposited. Nearly 80 per cent of the returnees in the focus group interview indicated that they receive some money regularly from the United States in the form of a pension, social security, personal savings, or investment dividends. The average amount of money received from the United States is about $3,600 quarterly or a total of $14,400 per year. Meeting the economic expenses associated with the return process is a daunting task. In general, the eventual outcome of the return experience must be determined economically viable before the decision to repatriate is made because the chances of receiving adequate monthly Social Security payments from the Government of Ghana are unlikely. Returnees must therefore prepare themselves to face any economic obstacles that come their way because they cannot rely on relatives, and neither can they rely on the government of Ghana for economic assistance if times become dire.

The results of the survey and focus group interviews revealed that some Ghanaians repatriate from the United States, live and work in Ghana for a while (the average stay in Ghana is about five years), and then migrate again, this time to Europe, particularly Great Britain, Germany, and the Netherlands. This time, the stay abroad is not too prolonged (average stay about two years). The trip to Europe is made relatively easier because the majority of the returnees possess United States permanent resident documents or certificates of naturalization. While in Europe, they stay with friends and relatives, work multiple jobs, and then repatriate back to Ghana. In a number of instances, there are returnees who initially went to the United States, stayed there for about 15 years, returned and domiciled for about four years in Ghana, left for Germany and the Netherlands for a brief period, and then finally repatriated to Ghana. This transnational identity that a growing number of Ghanaians are assuming stems, in part, from the precarious economic and political conditions at home and the relative ease of crossing international borders using immigration documents secured in the United States.

To deal with the frequent shortages of economic and consumer goods in Ghana, some of the returnees make frequent trips abroad for a quick "tour of duty" and then return with capital goods which they sell, ploughing back the profit into an existing business enterprise. Cars, farming equipment, clothing, electrical appliances, auto parts, and educational supplies are some of the common items that the returnees bring home.

Every return migration of Ghanaians is tentative. Many of the returnees want to connect with home and become part of the national reconstruction effort. At the same time, they perceive that the possession of valid immigration papers from the United States is a tremendous asset that they intend to utilize to the maximum. The cyclical nature of some return migration leads to opportunistic migration. This is the form of migration that occurs when migrants return home for a brief period and then migrate again to another destination where they stay for a short period before returning home. If and when embarked upon, the primary purpose of opportunistic migration is to work for a brief period (usually one to six months), acquire a lump sum of money to finance a project, or to buy capital equipments. Increasingly, a growing number of returnees may travel abroad for medical reasons or to attend graduation ceremonies of their dependents, if any. This form of migration is facilitated by the fact that when Ghanaians repatriate, they never sever ties with their adopted countries.

The propensity to return home and live for a while spurs additional migration. When Ghanaian émigrés come home for a brief sojourn and then repatriate only to come back after two or three years, it creates a cultural expectation among the youth that migration is the optimal means to achieve mobility. For some returnees, there is ambivalence about whether to become fully immersed in the social and political discourse of Ghana or whether to remain aloof, detached, and marginalized outsiders looking in from the outside. Though some of the returnees have acquired citizenship from the United States, the majority of the returnees feel that their native ties with Ghana confer on them specific rights and privileges to become full members and participants in the affairs of the country. These returnees perceive that they could make a meaningful contribution toward the development of Ghana. The general perception is that leaving Ghana to go abroad for a temporary sojourn and returning home later after accomplishing their goals should not be construed by the rank and file of Ghanaians as a betrayal to Ghana.

The high unemployment rate at home does not seem to influence the decision to return since the bulk of the returnees (75 per cent) become self-employed or establish business and economic ventures requiring them to hire workers. Business, educational, and cultural skills acquired abroad prove beneficial once a returnee settles in Ghana. The majority of returnees do not seek service employment. Those who do so seek senior or executive positions in the civil service so that they can qualify for the benefits and gratuities that come with senior civil service jobs in Ghana, especially a state car and subsidized housing. For those returnees who have already built a home, the common practice upon landing a senior civil job is to rent out their own place and live in the government subsidized housing. Even when they are able to obtain lucrative positions in the civil service or a private corporation, several of the returnees prefer to operate their own business alongside their regular full-time employment. The *raison d'etre* behind this is that the economic situation in the country is very precarious and volatile, as fortunes can shift without any notice, such as a military coup d'état or civil unrest. To cope with this, some returnees regularly transfer part of their incomes to the West for safe keeping. This way, if they have to leave the country all of a sudden, they will have something to fall back on.

In probing why some of the returnees had come home instead of remaining in the United States, a number of the returnees stated that they had failed to find gainful employment in the United States upon the completion of their education. They were unfortunate in that they did not find an employer who was willing to sponsor them for their labor certification and permanent residency or green card. Some of the returnees had tried to cope with the chronic unemployment by doing odd jobs, which sometimes called for them to travel far away from their family to seek temporary employment, which may last only a couple of days. A minority of the immigrant returnees (12 per cent) had spent thousands of dollars to pay attorney fees to file for permanent residency only to be turned down by the immigration office. Prior to their return home, some the immigrants were able to work jobs that paid at or below minimum wage and often had to struggle to make ends meet. For this group of returnees, the perception is that the money spent on attorney fees could have been brought to Ghana to be invested in a business venture. However, most of them had no regrets for their decision to repatriate to Ghana.

The constant fear associated with the risk of deportation for working without the necessary authorization papers also occupies the minds of the returnees, especially those who are not citizens of the United States. Before the 9/11 attack, swoops by immigration enforcement agents in factories were infrequent, and employers were rarely suspected of using illegal and undocumented workers. However, as part of the legislation that authorized the establishment of the Homeland Security Administration, provisions were made to fund more immigration personnel in a bid to find, prosecute, and deport illegal aliens living in the country. Moreover, the social and political climate following 9/11 has made the work of the underground green card and social security card brokers very difficult, if not impossible. Scores of these brokers are now being rounded up and their activities shut down permanently in the major cities across the nation. Thus, for those who may want to stay on in the United States and work for a brief or extensive period of time, this possibility has dwindled due to the new political reality associated with the war on terror.

A number of the returnees also stated that paying thousands of dollars to find a spouse to marry for the purpose of claiming immigration benefits is even riskier given the events surrounding the war on terror. According to one returnee, "most of the people who otherwise were willing to help are now very afraid and even where they are willing to risk for you, they charge so much, more than $20,000 to enter into a false marriage relationship." This returnee went on to say that given the amount of money involved, "it is prudent to bring the money home to Ghana to set up a business because even if you find someone who is willing to take this money, there is no guarantee that your application for permanent residence would be approved."

The investigation of the motivations behind return migration is very difficult to conceptualize because the process involves the specification of the underlying psychological and ideological meanings that the migrants associate with the journey that they have undertaken to the United States. If the objective of the migration is a temporary sojourn expressly designed to accomplish an instrumental goal, then the return process is not hard to conjecture. A problematic aspect of international migration is that while many of those who undertake the journey do intend to return home in the future, the decision about when to return and the circumstances under which the return home will be initiated are amorphous due to the several intended or unintended considerations that may mar any proposed return plans. Feelings of nostalgia about home and the constant sense of loss of contacts with family members often occupy and shape the thoughts of immigrants about the prospects of returning. In this regard, immigrant statements about returning home may be masked by feelings of homeland abandonment and the nostalgic feelings that emanate from persistent feelings of having been absent from home for too long.

For some of the Ghanaian immigrants, prolonged absence from home has made the heart grow fonder, and the prospects of returning to Ghana have become a myth because the thoughts about going home have become merely a coping strategy, an adaptive tool to find solace in the belief and knowledge that, perhaps, a return home is not going to occur. Talk about going home is seen by some as a diversionary tactic to ease apprehensions associated with being in a voluntary diaspora that is characterized by entrenched racial and ethnic subordination and powerlessness. The rationalizations associated about being homeward bound one day are a temporary fix for unmet aspirations, lack of full citizenship, and delayed integration into the host society.

Another central issue is the timing of the return. At what point in the migratory sojourn does the immigrant decide to go back home and resettle? While a majority of the Ghanaians expect to fulfill their economic and cultural aspirations prior to returning home, most were not able to clearly articulate when that goal would be reached. Additional considerations include whether or not there are any specific motivating factors that define the timing of the return. While the need to see aging parents or grandparents before they pass on is important to all the immigrants, most feel that the desire to see their children grow up and become successful in the United States is also a major consideration. The general pattern is to repatriate after children are grown and have completed post-secondary education. In instances where they have grand children of school-going age, it is not uncommon for returnees to come home with their grandchildren for a temporary sojourn. While in Ghana, the children attend school and usually visit their parents in the United States during the summer. The goal is to have the immigrant families stay connected to both Ghana and the United States. For the children, the opportunity to live in Ghana as well as in the United States for brief periods at a time is considered culturally reinvigorating. The children get to learn Ghanaian and African culture. For the parents, the temporary sojourn of the children in Ghana has educational benefits since the children attend elite college preparatory schools in the country. This improves the chances of securing admission to nationally ranked institutions of higher learning upon the children's final return to the United States.

Gaining Re-Entry after Repatriation: Impediments to Integration

Due to their relatively higher educational credentials compared to most Ghanaians and the experiences they have garnered from living and working in the United States, several of the returnees can be described as very successful by Ghanaian standards. Nevertheless, re-entry and integration into Ghanaian society after a long period of absence can be problematic. The voluntary returnees I encountered in Ghana came from different social and cultural backgrounds. In sharing their return experiences, a recurring theme was that a majority of returnees reported being alienated or looked upon with suspicion, or having their motives questioned and maligned.

Feelings of antipathy from the general public toward people who have lived and worked abroad often persist. Returnees are sometimes viewed as traitors who left the country to seek greener pastures abroad when things were very difficult and unmanageable in Ghana only to return home to live lavishly on their imported wealth. Living in gated communities, many of the returnees feel they cannot contribute to the social and economic development of the country because of the erroneous perception that they have returned home only to exploit the precarious economic misfortunes of the country to their financial advantage. One of the returnees, feeling shunned by his associates, summarized his frustration and the level of resentment encountered in his community: "Often in my conversations with people, I make contrasts (positive contrasts) between Ghana and the United States. However, my friends think I am too critical of the situation in Ghana and that I always elevate the United States as a model that we should emulate." Another returnee who obviously was having some problems gaining access to political brokers in his community stated, "Sometimes it is very difficult to tell others who are less fortunate than you are that you really want to help them and make their standards of living better. Everyday when the lights go out of the community and I happen to be the only one with power because I own a generator, people think that you cannot be one of them, that you don't feel their pain and are oblivious of their plight. So they ostracize you, and even the ideas and ideals that you want to introduce are second-guessed not based on merit but on suspicion." In the words of one returnee, "You become a minority in your own community and among your friends and family. You have a strong feeling that people are envious of you and that your success abroad, while laudable to some, has become a sore point with some in the community because you have become a person of privilege."

A main obstacle to the full integration of returnees into the social, political, and economic affairs of the country stems from the public perception that returnees are elitists who go to great lengths to separate themselves from the rest of Ghanaians, especially from those who have not had the opportunity to travel abroad. To provide a forum and voice for discussing and finding solutions to their unique problems, returnees have formed associations based on the country where they previously domiciled. By far the largest of these organizations is the Ghanaian-American, British, and German Associations. Through these associations, the returnees are able to develop a sense of shared identity and common experience as defined by their individual and collective experiences of living in the West. Like the immigrant associations referred to earlier, these organizations provide the necessary information and resources to enable its members to readjust to the new roles, challenges, and opportunities they face as a result of returning home. The associations also provide charity and support for community projects. To some Ghanaians, however, there is a sense that the returnees belong to an exclusive club whose members are too class conscious and out of touch with the daily social and economic realities that Ghanaians experience.

A frequent concern is that the social circles of returnees are limited to other returnees who share similar cultural and economic experiences. Concerns that returnees often live separated lives and only interact with their immediate family members are commonplace. In this respect, the common perception is that while the returnees are making significant contributions to the development of the country, this development is limited in scope and pertains only to issues at the household rather than at the national level. This concern is not shared by the returnees who see their contributions to the national development effort to be critical. Additionally, the concern that they live separate lives and tend to associate with other returnees is dismissed as baseless because of the belief that they have the right to choose their friends and associates.

When returnees first arrive in Ghana, they are filled with vigor and enthusiasm about the ideas and ideals they learned from the West. They believe they have the panacea for resolving the myriad of social problems ailing the country. But the results have sometimes been dismal. Efforts on the part of returnees to integrate their ideas into the body polity of Ghana often fail because of a number of reasons. First, returnees who want to change the social, cultural, political, and economic arrangements of Ghanaian society do not have a full grasp of the depth of the problems facing the country. Often, they have tended to adopt a piecemeal approach to finding solutions to perennial problems confronting the nation. Second, they have tended (especially political returnees) to apply British or American models to Ghana's situation, and for the most part, the results have not been successful. Third, the institutionalized role of endemic corruption has made it very difficult to implement programs and policies that benefit the majority of the society; coupled with this is the lack of social or political accountability. The end result is that returnees with good intentions end up being co-opted by the entrenched social and political interests in Ghana, often to the detriment of their ideas and principles.

Antipathy and feelings of resentment toward returnees are often expressed at the community level of social and cultural organization. Returnees who actively pursue inclusion in community social organization are sometimes rebuffed by political power brokers in the community. Statements like "what you learned in the United States cannot hold here" and "your dollars do not give you total control over others who have not had the opportunity to go and live in the white man's world" refer to the inexperience of returnees in finding solutions to local issues due to their long absence away from home. This problem is exacerbated by the fact that for some of the returnees, the skills they have acquired while domiciled in the United States are not easily transferable to Ghana. Even where the skills are directly transferable, the pay structure is very low in relation to what the returnee can earn if they stayed abroad.

As much as they are willing to engage in the national reconstruction effort in Ghana, the returnees encounter frustration when things seem to move very slowly, oftentimes becoming entangled in patrimonialism, corruption, and static configurations that are strongly embedded in a traditional ethos that defies progressiveness and change. Here, the returnee finds they have to confront an undifferentiated system of division of labor and a social structure that as a result of its past (chiefly due to militarization of social and political discourse) has managed to, consciously or unconsciously, institutionalize corruption, nepotism, and avarice. In this system, upward mobility or advancement sometimes only come to those who have relatives who are well positioned in the economic and political hierarchies of society.

Gaining re-entry to one's place of birth after a protracted stay abroad is often filled with apprehension when the returnee has become a naturalized citizen of the host society. Even when they do hold dual citizenships, returnees find themselves in a "foreigner status." The first sign of this status is evident at the arrival terminal when passengers have to go through customs and immigration. There is a sense of consternation when those returnees recognize they have to queue in the category marked foreign nationals to have their entry papers processed though they were born in the country. In addition, they have to become reacquainted with the old ways of doing things prior to their departure. Naturalized citizen status in a foreign land may serve to both constrain, and facilitate entry and access to the society. When Ghanaian-Americans who have become citizens of the United States return home for short or long visits, they often have to deal with re-acculturation issues in terms of language, mannerisms, and social expectations. Cultural and normative beliefs practiced in the host society cannot be imported or easily adapted to the local scene in Ghana. It is imperative to strike a balance between the expectations of the two contrasting cultures. Sometimes, returnees act according to the values, norms, and beliefs they have internalized in the United States. One returnee who showed too much public display of affection for his American-born spouse in the presence of his elders found himself being sanctioned for his behavior. A few days earlier, his wife had been approached by family matriarchs who felt that she was dressed inappropriately, although according to her husband, she was properly dressed considering it was in the middle of the tropical summer.

Although some returnees may experience cultural clashes with some extended family members concerning how they blend American and Ghanaian cultures, overall returnees are generally accorded respect by the majority of family members and friends. Returnee migrants who have acquired citizenship status in the United States have a different status in Ghana. United States citizenship confers on them a unique opportunity, which facilitates entry into the affairs of Ghanaian society. Citizenship insulates the Ghanaian-Americans from political victimization and assures that when potential conflicts arise with authorities, at a minimum the American government may intervene and seek a resolution. Ghanaian-American returnees with a naturalized status often feel unrestricted in their challenge of Ghanaian political authorities. Some of these returnees recounted their experiences during the reign of Jerry Rawlings and the PNDC. One returnee criticized the government for unlawfully detaining him at the Kotoka International Airport in Accra for rebuffing a security agent who had openly asked him for a bribe. Upon refusing and threatening to report the matter to the security agent's supervisor, he was arrested for allegedly violating custom regulations and smuggling a controlled substance into the country, which later turned out to be prescribed medication. He was detained for three days, and upon his release went to the American embassy and the Ministry of Foreign Affairs to launch a formal protest. Not satisfied with the outcome, he sought an audience with the Chief of Staff at the Castle (the official seat of government) who formally issued a written apology on behalf of the President. While having a naturalized status may offer some degree of political protection, it does not offer economic security to the returnee. Returnees who have given up their Ghanaian citizenship may encounter difficulties purchasing land or applying for business permits. In addition, employment opportunities may be limited and very cumbersome to obtain for those who have to seek a work permit.

As the immigrant returnees in this study have affirmed, the process of repatriation is daunting and challenging, often filled with unanticipated outcomes. On its part, the central government of Ghana does not have the institutional resources to incorporate return migration into national economic planning schemes. For a developing nation like Ghana, the systematic collection of data is central to an understanding of the objective and subjective factors that continue to shape return migration. To specify the correlates of return migration of Ghana's citizens who have been living abroad, micro and macro-level studies are needed to explain the implications of return migration on the economic, social, and political development of the country. National samples of return migrants must be drawn to provide a gauge of the volume of return migration to the country. Such a database would form the basis of surveys to primarily collect information on return migrants, and secondarily to provide some insight on how to mobilize return migrants for collective national economic development.

Issues concerning the direct and indirect impact of return migration on the country would have to be ascertained. Such an analysis would have to develop appropriate theoretical models and paradigms for disentangling the complex issues involved in return migration. More specifically, there is a critical need to determine what kinds of policies and practices must be implemented by the central government in an effort to monitor the return of its citizens or immigrants from abroad. It is imperative to document the contributions that return migrants are making to the economic, social, and political development of the country. There is a need on the part of the central government to understand the problems associated with the return process and the integration of returnees into the body polity of the society. Public discourse on the role of return migrants in sustainable development must be initiated, and the input of the public solicited in the design and implementation of programs to better tap the skills and resources that returnees bring with them. Return migration, a form of reverse brain drain, has to be approached with the same degree of urgency that attends to the processes of outmigration. Both approaches must not be separated as the sociological, political, cultural, and economic reasons that spur these processes are interwoven and are not isolated or discrete events.

The impact of return migration on national development and reconstruction is very difficult to quantify. At a minimum, any assessment and analysis of the benefits that have accrued to Ghana from the return of its citizens from abroad would have to consist of an examination of the impact of return migration first, at the household or community level and second, at the national level. To date, return migrants are making significant contributions to their various households by improving the standard of living of individual family or household members. The financial support in the form of remittances that they have provided to their households has certainly changed the economic conditions of many families in the urban and rural areas of the country. By providing funds for the education of household or family members and setting up small capital or labor intensive business and manufacturing enterprises, they are also contributing to the social welfare and development of their communities. Some returnees have made it possible for family members to have a steady source of income by making available the capital to engage in petty trading and the sale of consumer items to the public.

At the national level, the contributions of the returnees are yet to be felt. Though they are utilizing their human capital skills (acquired abroad working in diverse capacities as engineers, pharmacists, doctors, and business entrepreneurs), the collective impact of these contributions at the national level has yet to have any significant measurable impact on the society at-large. The foreign money they spend enters the local and national economies, bringing added value to consumption and ultimately assisting in the economic development of the country. As more returnees come home in response to favorable social, political, and economic climate conditions in Ghana, it is expected that the collective contributions returnees make to national development will increase. A stable environment in Ghana also means that some of the returnees who have yet to repatriate their investment holdings from abroad back to Ghana will eventually do so, thus adding more value to the economy.

The governance of returned migration should consist of policies designed to ensure the reintegration of migrant returnees into the affairs of their country. Consistent with the need to ensure that returned migrants play a meaningful role in national development is the necessity for the central government and private stakeholders in Ghana to coordinate policies that will ensure greater consultation and cooperation toward a better understanding of the relationship between return migration and national development. An assessment of the human and fiscal capital that returnees bring with them to Ghana is warranted. A national consultative process whereby central government would work with regional centers in the country to identify critical areas of manpower and capital shortages and assist in directing migrant-returnee resources is equally important. Hitherto, the lack of centralized administrative planning to incorporate migrants into the task of national economic development had been a major stumbling block in regional and national development in Ghana. Strategic initiatives to harness the human and capital resources of returning migrants with the goal of closing the unequal gap in economic development projects between rural and urban Ghana is sorely needed. A major component of such a strategic initiative is for the national government to have a centralized role in facilitating return migrant resettlement schemes by directing return migrant resources and capital to identifiable sectors of the economy that need an infusion of innovative small scale investment schemes.

On the whole, Ghanaians who travel and live abroad ultimately have the desire of returning home. The repatriation process is often embarked upon in multiple stages. During the first or initial stages, the prospective returnees visit home, obtain an assessment of what it would take to implement the return journey, and weigh the expected outcomes if the decision to repatriate is to be implemented. Some of the immigrants are ambivalent about permanent repatriation. They continuously weigh the pros and cons of returning while shuttling back and forth between the United

States and Ghana. Some return home and stay briefly, and then move again not only to the United States but to other Western nations. Most of the immigrants in the study affirmed that, all things considered, they would eventually like to return and settle permanently in Ghana. In spite of moderate improvements in living standards and the sustained progress toward the stabilization of democratic institutions, the majority of the immigrants remain ambivalent about whether conditions are conducive for permanent repatriation. To encourage more Ghanaians currently residing abroad to return home, the socioeconomic conditions of the country would have to change to reflect the imperative of sustainable national development utilizing all the available resources of the country. The government recently has come to recognize the imperative of harnessing local resources (human and physical) rather than relying on the West to generate the internal capital needed to maximize economic and industrial productivity and to arrest the problem of low standards of living and poverty that have characterized the landscape of Ghana since its independence. As they wait for this transformation to occur and eagerly look forward to the day when the cloud of economic uncertainty lifts, the Ghanaian immigrants remain in a migratory "limbo," suspended between two countries. While the vast majority of Ghanaians living in the United States have cast their vote in favor of repatriation, often, as indicated, structural and individual impediments at home and in the host society may enhance or thwart the intention to return.

Chapter 10

The Ghanaian Diaspora: Transatlantic Continuities in the European Union

Ghanaians are forever on the move. Even before the mid-1960s when the country had a buoyant economy, Ghanaians engaged in regional, inter-regional, and international migration to other parts of Africa for trade. In the early 1970s, the country itself also became an economic magnet, attracting citizens from mainly Nigeria, Burkina Faso, Liberia, the Ivory Coast, Lebanon, and Syria. Cocoa production and related services brought migrant workers from the West African sub-region to the country. Relative to other countries in the region, Ghana was an economic gold mine. During this time the country's infrastructure compared favorably with Singapore, Malaysia, and South Korea; and in areas such as education, its institutions of higher learning were noted for their quality instruction. Its hospitals, notably Korle-Bu, were among the best in Africa. However, the relative economic prosperity the country enjoyed during this time did not hinder Ghanaians from casting their eyes beyond the country's borders. Those Ghanaians who could afford to travel abroad looked beyond Africa for possible destinations, often choosing the United Kingdom (UK) as the place to fulfill their economic and cultural dreams.

The phenomenon of Ghanaian and by extension African migration to the West, in general, is very important because it has broad implications for the economic and social development of the countries of the region. In this chapter, I present a description of the Ghanaian community in the British West Midlands and in southern Italy. The goal is to assess whether there are aspects of the migratory experiences of Ghanaians in the USA that parallel the experiences of immigrants from Ghana who have settled in the UK and Italy. Confining the immigrant and diaspora experiences of Ghanaians to the USA, while insightful, ignores differences in diasporic patterns in other parts of the world. This section juxtaposes the experiences of the Ghanaian immigrants by drawing comparisons with the Ghanaian immigrants who have settled in the UK and Italy.

Transatlantic Parallels of the Ghanaian Diaspora

As Ghana forged ahead to achieve economic independence, it continued its historical ties to the UK. Today, the UK is a major business partner of Ghana, supplying Ghana with consumer goods. British-made capital goods continue to be imported into the country by Ghanaian businesses and organizations. The UK has made significant contributions to Ghana's healthcare system, rural infrastructure developments, the training of doctors, and civil servants. When it comes to debt relief schemes, the UK has been pivotal in supporting Ghana's efforts to service its massive foreign debt or having the debt forgiven by the donor countries.

The UK has attracted Ghana's brightest and best, and Ghanaians are not newcomers to the UK. Before the country attained its independence from Great Britain, thousands of Ghanaians came to the UK mainly as students to pursue undergraduate and graduate education. Emigration for higher education goes back to the last century. The first Ghanaian university was founded in 1948, and there were British-trained Ghanaian lecturers teaching at the University of Ghana at Legon before the country gained independence in 1957. After the country gained its independence, Ghanaians continued to favor British higher degrees and flocked to the UK to receive postgraduate credentials (Peil, 1986; 1995; Jenkins, 1985). Also Ghanaian civil servants who worked with the British colonial administration were sponsored to the UK for further training, and several religious organizations, such as the Methodist and Anglican churches also sponsored Ghanaians to travel to Britain to receive further training to work in the missions in Ghana. Individual Ghanaians who could afford their passage and living expenses also came on their own, often to look for work, seek medical treatment, or simply to visit. Whether they were skilled or unskilled, sponsored by public or by private organizations, to most Ghanaians who lived during the colonial era and the period immediately following independence, going abroad meant going to the UK. Principal cities of the UK, such as London, Birmingham, Manchester, Liverpool, Edinburgh, and Cardiff attracted Ghanaians from all walks of life. Eventually, as more and more Ghanaians encountered difficulties securing visas to the UK, several started looking for greener pastures in other Western European countries like Holland, Germany, Italy, Sweden, Denmark, as well as the countries in North America.

The Ghanaians who come to the UK are part of a stream of people whose countries had been under the British sphere of colonial administration. From Africa, the Ghanaians have joined others coming to Britain from Nigeria, Kenya, Malawi, Uganda, Sierra Leone, the Gambia, Egypt, South Africa, the Zambia, and Tanzania. A common membership in the British Commonwealth means that visa and passport provisions are not as stringent as those of other countries in the West. As a result of Ghana's close relationship to the UK, many facets of Ghanaian society have been influenced by Great Britain culture. At all levels of education beginning from the primary to the tertiary level, Ghana's educational system was modeled after the British pattern, as was the civil service. English became the official language of the country, and it afforded Ghanaians the opportunity to travel to England to pursue cultural and economic goals. A strong sense of shared cultural history, similar institutional structures and frameworks (law, education, and language) coupled with trade relations singles out the UK as the preferred destination for many Ghanaians. The UK is the preferred destination because Ghanaians recognize that they will encounter and meet several Ghanaians living in the UK. Additionally, the journey by air is a mere six hours and for most Ghanaians, this keeps them closer to home. Globalization and the concomitant economic incorporation of the country into the world's economy also facilitated the linkage of Ghana and the rest of Africa into the complex network of international division of labor, trade, finance, and technology as the capitalist countries came to dominate the world commodity and exchange markets, and to rely on the developing countries for the production of primary raw materials (Gordon, 1998).

When Ghana became independent, the total number of Ghanaians living in the UK was very small. According to Census data, in the early 1960s, the number of Ghanaians numbered approximately 11,000. At the beginning of 2002, the total number of Ghanaians living in the UK was estimated by the Census to be 56,000, a five fold increase since the early 1960s. However, estimates suggest that the number of Ghanaians who are officially registered with the Ghana High Commission in London is about 1.5 million. Of this number, 850,000 live in London boroughs (Ghana High Commissioner, Ghana Embassy: London). The peak period of Ghanaian migration to the UK was from the late 1970s to the end of 2000. This period was marked by political and economic instability and the erosion of civil liberties in Ghana. It was during this period that Ghanaians started flocking to Britain and other Western countries to seek better standards of living. Asylum migration from Ghana to the UK became an important feature of Ghanaian migration to the UK. Structural adjustment policies of the government and the International Monetary Fund added to the country's woes, forcing thousands to flee to the UK (Peil, 1995). Cyclical fluctuations in the economy, the deterioration of the country's foreign reserves caused by corruption and dwindling commodity prices, and increasing population pressure on the land all converged to force thousands of Ghanaians out of the country.

The expulsion of all Ghanaians by the Nigerian government during the early part of the 1980s created a hiatus in the international migratory behavior of Ghanaians. Estimated by the United Nations to number over one million, the forced returnees repatriated to a country with a crumbling economy and infrastructure. Those returnees with marketable skills did not settle in Ghana permanently. Several found their way to the UK, aided by the sums of money that they had saved while working in Nigeria. The strong value of the Nigerian currency (the Naira) made it relatively easier for some of the returnees to secure travel papers, purchase their tickets, and head mostly to the UK or to the USA. Though some of the repatriated Ghanaians went back to Nigeria after the expulsion order, for a majority of them, the UK and the USA offered better economic and cultural opportunities than Nigeria. Many of those with significant savings and who had completed post-secondary education obtained visas to come to the UK to pursue various academic programs and ultimately stayed.

The majority of Ghanaians living in the UK reside in the London metropolitan area, concentrating in the boroughs of Hackney, Lewisham, Croydon and Brent, Lambeth, Southwark, and Haringey. In the British West Midlands, the preferred settlements for the immigrants are the Birmingham–Liverpool–Manchester corridor, including towns and municipalities located in Worcestershire, Warwickshire and Gloucestershire. Like their counterparts who have migrated to the USA, the residential patterns of the immigrants reflect a tendency to locate in major metropolitan centers. This enables several of them to tap into the urban employment market opportunities where they stand the chance of receiving high wages. An added advantage of locating in the larger metropolitan centers is to afford immigrants the opportunity to meet with and associate with kin groups and associates from the same secondary schools, universities, or towns. The immigrants also derive gain a collective sense of economic and psychological security when they establish residence near other

Ghanaians living in the larger cities. Structural distances among the immigrants and the home country are bridged. In the large urban metropolitan centers, news and information about current happenings in Ghana can be shared. The cultural advantage is equally immense. The immigrants have access to ethnic stores and markets (such as the Kejetia Market in London) catering to the palates and cuisines of the home country. Fiercely political, Ghanaian immigrants in both the USA and the UK often invite political leaders from home to discuss a wide range of domestic and international issues of concern to the immigrants. Government officials who attend these presentations often share information with the immigrants about current political and economic policies of the central government to rebuild Ghana. In this process, sociopolitical linkages are forged with the homeland. Often, there is an appeal to the immigrants to contribute their skills and financial resources toward the betterment of the country.

Celebrations and festivals spanning a wide range of political and religious rituals are staged by the urban residents while living in the UK. As already indicated, this may include the celebration of ethnic festivals such as *Homowo, Odwira,* and *Fetu Afahye,* to mention a few. Parties are frequently scheduled to celebrate Ghana's Independence Day. Alumni from the various educational institutions often organize parties often to catch up on news from the alma mater. It is also at these gatherings that funds are collected to be remitted to the immigrants' institutions of learning. Secondary migration is common, and if it occurs, the destination is to another urban or suburban community where the immigrants expect to take advantage of affordable housing or quality schools for their children. A common reason for engaging in secondary migration is also to avoid high urban crime rates. When they move, they still maintain close ties with the large urban centers where they have established a cadre of associates and networks of patronage that serve to connect them to the homeland and at the same time anchor them in the affairs of British society. In this regard, their experiences are similar to their counterparts in the USA. Their transnational identity places them in two cultures, British and Ghanaian, strongly connected to both but flexible enough to allow them to adapt to Western institutions and ideals. Ultimately, the formation and continuity of the Ghanaian diaspora is going to reflect the incorporation and synthesis of new ways of thinking, feeling, and acting that the immigrants acquire abroad, mixed with their Ghanaian cultural ethos to carve an identity niche unique to the immigrants' individual and collective experiences. The convergence of the ideas and ideals acquired in the migratory transnational identities and journeys are brought back to Ghana and applied by the immigrants. The immigrants become agents of innovation and are the vanguard in the sociopolitical, cultural, and economic transformation of Ghanaian society.

Ghanaians in the British West Midlands: Broadening Transnational Identities

Like their Ghanaian counterparts across the Atlantic in the USA, the Ghanaian immigrant community in the UK is not monolithic. There are significant internal differentials in education, economic and class status, family formation, gender and age, and attitudes toward immigration. Economic motives dominate the reasons for leaving Ghana. Irrespective of the number of years they have lived in the UK, a majority of the Ghanaians in the West Midlands (74 per cent) came to Britain to pursue economic goals. The attainment of economic goals is mediated through cultural goals, that is, the pursuit of education. Over two-thirds of the immigrants arrived in the UK to undertake graduate and postgraduate education. The expectation is that upon the completion of their studies, opportunities will open up to enable them to find employment and stay in the UK until the decision is made to repatriate to Ghana. Among those residing in the West Midlands, one-third had completed undergraduate education prior to their arrival in the UK. Another 38 per cent had completed a postgraduate education since arriving in the UK. The remaining respondents entered the UK to find employment, seek refugee status, or reunite with extended family members. For those who have not been able to pursue higher education, employment prospects are dim and where they have secured employment, job losses tend to be common, pushing several of them to depend on welfare and social service agencies to make ends meet.

For the Ghanaian immigrant population in the UK and the USA, education is considered a valuable asset and the main conduit for achieving social mobility in the West. For those Ghanaians who are able to acquire specialized skills, the chance of obtaining a lucrative job, especially in the sciences, is very high. Education affords the opportunity to become part of the global migration of skilled workers from the developing countries who are flocking to the West, particularly to the UK, Canada, and the USA. For these Ghanaians, their fluency in English, due to an educational system modeled after the British system and immigration policies in the West that favor the retention of highly skilled immigrants has worked to their advantage. Ghanaians in the West Midlands who entered the UK with only secondary school credentials frequently go on to pursue vocational–technical skills in high demand jobs working as plumbers, electricians, carpenters, and masons. Some of the immigrants find jobs as taxi and bus drivers, parking ramp attendants, school teachers, and auto technicians. Service sector employment is common among those immigrants who possess secondary school credentials, particularly the Ordinary and/or the Advanced Level Certificate of Education. A smaller proportion of the immigrants can be found in professional areas such as marketing, accountancy, insurance, real estate management, and banking. Ethnic entrepreneurial activities and self employment are not as common among the Ghanaians in the West Midlands as they are among Ghanaians in the USA. In the UK, when they have established their own businesses or have become self-employed, the tendency among the immigrants is to specialize in the marketing of Ghanaian-based consumer goods or services that cater to the immigrant population. Ethnic grocery stores and the sale of clothing, textiles, and apparel imported from Ghana tend to be common among the self-employed.

Doctors, nurses, and allied health workers form a significant percentage of the total Ghanaian immigrant population in the West Midlands who were studied. The majority of the nurses and allied health care workers were recruited in Ghana by employment agencies in the UK. The rest initially came to the UK as visitors but later managed to find employment in the health sector. Lured by the prospects of earning higher salaries and improved benefits and an immigration environment favoring the migration of skilled professionals, several of the nurses consider themselves economically successful. In one hospital in the West Midlands, Ghanaian nurses work alongside other Nigerian, Filipino, Caribbean, and Asian émigrés who are all connected to Britain as skilled transnational workers who have left their countries to seek better economic opportunities in the West. This group of healthcare professionals compare favorably with their counterparts from Ghana who have settled in the USA. A common link among this group of Ghanaian immigrants is that they are part of the larger transnational movement of specialized labor from the poor to the rich countries. For those healthcare workers who have not been recruited directly by employment agencies to work in the UK, there is a strong reliance on family and social networks of Ghanaians who have successfully transplanted in the UK. They share information about job prospects in the healthcare sector and provide moral and financial support to prospective healthcare workers who are desirous of finding work in the UK. The numerous Ghanaian associations operating in the UK provide assistance in the integration of the Ghanaians into British society.

The pattern of chain migration among some of the Ghanaians in the West Midlands mirrors that of their USA counterparts where the initial migration targets another country for a brief sojourn before final resettlement in the UK. This certainly was the case among some of the lesser skilled Ghanaians living in the West Midlands. Initial destinations for settlement include Nigeria, the former East Germany, Italy, and the Middle East before migrating to the UK. As previously stated, Ghanaians engage in chain or stepwise migration in order to improve upon the chance of securing a visa to the West. Nearly one-third of the Ghanaians in the West Midlands study arrived in the UK from countries other than Ghana. Furthermore, as the diaspora gathers momentum, so has the tightening of visa requirements at the British and American consular offices. For those who engaged in the chain migration to get to the UK, a common practice is to enroll at an institution of higher learning immediately upon arrival. This practice enables the migrants to attend school and work at the same time while preparing toward the acquisition of permanent resident status and work permits.

Among the Ghanaian healthcare and allied workers living in the UK, the reasons cited for leaving the Ghana Health Service for the UK include the opportunity to receive higher remuneration (37 per cent); the poor conditions of service in Ghana, including having to work with obsolete medical equipments and appliances (26 per cent); the opportunity to train in other healthcare related specialties (21 per cent); and the chance to reunite with families who have acquired British citizenship or hold a permanent resident status (16 per cent). Favorable visa and work permit visas from the Home Office made it relatively easier for several of the healthcare workers to immigrate to the UK. A Ghanaian nurse practitioner employed at a West Midlands hospital near Warwickshire stated that nearly all the students in her graduating class at the Nurses Training College (NTC) at Korle-Bu are employed by the NHS Trust hospitals. According to one respondent, "the healthcare system of Ghana is a feeding trough that feeds hospitals and clinics all over the world, not just the UK though most of us prefer to come to the UK because we speak good English and have been trained at institutions similar to that here in England." At a nearby residential home for elderly retired UK citizens in Warwickshire, scores of Ghanaian health operatives (12 in all), including social workers, gerontologists, and healthcare technicians work alongside nurses and other allied health staff from Africa. For the Ghanaian healthcare workers, the migration of skilled healthcare workers to the UK is caused by the inability of the government of Ghana to offer conditions of service parallel to what is offered them by the British government. This sentiment is shared by four Ghanaian pharmacists who work for a major chemist chain in the Black Country in the West Midlands region. According to these immigrants, nearly 90 per cent of their mates from the Kwame Nkrumah University of Science and Technology (KNUST) in Kumasi have either relocated to the UK, Canada, or the USA. In the words of one chemist from Ghana living in Perry Bar near Birmingham, "I cannot dispense drugs in Ghana because when I left the country in 1989 to come here, all the shelves in the drug stores were empty of drugs. Instead, we were selling chewing gum, candles, and soaps. The country told me in essence they didn't need my services after paying for me to attend KNUST. The situation has not changed by much today."

Coupled with these issues are political problems caused by military intervention and the suspension of civil liberties. Six per cent of the Ghanaians left the country because of political reasons. The political destabilization of the country coincided with the departure of thousands of skilled and unskilled Ghanaians who were escaping the military rule of Acheampong and later Rawlings. The general atmosphere prevailing in the country cast a dark cloud over Ghana's future. Like those Ghanaians who headed to the USA, the UK based Ghanaians fled from a country that could no longer take care of the basic necessities of its citizens. Though conditions have significantly stabilized and moderate progress has been made in stopping the economic hemorrhage of the country, a majority of Ghanaians have not lost the motivation to come to the UK to live and work. For some, the situation is dire and every possible method for leaving, such as stowing away to the UK in the cargo hold of a Ghana Airways aircraft is considered. Hundreds also risk crossing the Sahara Desert to enter Morocco illegally in the hope that they can enter the European Union through Spain and ultimately head to the UK.

Like their counterparts in the USA, Ghanaian immigrants in the West Midlands have a strong presence in the British labor force. Even though several of them start at the bottom of the economic system of UK society, the majority of them do not stay at that level for very long. Continuous education to upgrade their skills coupled with taking English classes to improve upon their language skills has enhanced their occupational status in the UK. Moreover, their flexibility in adapting to labor and employment trends in the UK has served them well. When some of them have found themselves in minimum wage jobs with little or no benefits and with no prospects for further advancements, the response has been to retrain in high demand areas such as electrical work, carpentry, masonry, and plumbing where employment and pay structures are very high and usually accompanied by benefits. Some who have retrained in plumbing and electrical repairs have been successful in starting their own businesses catering to the ethnic minority population in the West Midlands. For a majority of the immigrants, a commitment to lifelong education means that even when they are laid off temporarily or permanently, the immigrants are able to find substitute employment. Recognizing the value of higher education, the immigrants stress to their children the importance of achieving high scholastic credentials. As indicated, the shift in immigration laws in the West, particularly in the UK,

USA, and Canada to a skill-based system that gives preference to immigrants with marketable skills and good education, has served the Ghanaians very well in the West Midlands. However, there are consternations on the part of the immigrants that the system whereby visas are made available to immigrants with marketable skills to migrate to the UK will change due to the expansion of the European Union and recent proposals in the UK to hire EU nationals. Unless trained in the UK, several Ghanaian professionals in the healthcare sector will find it very difficult to legally migrate to the UK.

To enhance their job prospects and take advantage of regional differences in economic opportunities in the UK, several of the immigrants engage in secondary migration, usually moving from Scotland and Wales to look for better paying jobs in the boroughs of London, the Southeast region in general, and the West Midlands. Family networks facilitate this secondary migration as job information in employment districts are shared with friends and relatives living in cities and towns where jobs are hard to come by and wages are low. When they migrate from Scotland and Wales to the Southeast and the West Midlands, the Ghanaians settle in communities with a large number of Ghanaian and other African-Caribbean immigrant populations. First, Ghanaians are attracted to these areas because of the strong manufacturing-based employment. A second attraction of the West Midlands is the close proximity to London and its surrounding cities by bus or rail. The immigrants can get to London in two hours to visit friends and family members. Third, the cost of living is relatively less expensive than it is in the Southeast, including the London boroughs. Housing and the cost of long commutes to and from work make the West Midlands an attractive place to live, work, and raise children.

Demographically, the West Midlands Ghanaian population shares similar characteristics with their USA counterparts. The bulk of the immigrants tend to be young, with the average age being under 40 years old, predominantly male, living in households with children who are teenagers and with both spouses present, and well educated. Household units of single-parent families with children form 15 per cent. Of these, 75 per cent are female-headed, 15 per cent headed by a male, and the remaining households are occupied by single, widowed, or separated persons. As a group, the majority of the Ghanaians, like their USA counterparts have completed secondary or postsecondary education prior to leaving Ghana. Nearly 20 per cent of their households have elderly family members who are grandparents and who assist in child socialization, baby sitting, and household management. Children are entrusted to their care, and it is expected that they will be home when the children come home from school. Couples are expected to work and contribute to the household budget. The social organization of the immigrant households are based on the shared belief that every member, with the exception of young children and the elderly, must contribute to the economic well-being of the family unit. In this sense, like their counterparts in the USA, the West Midlands based immigrants view the family as a unit of economic and social production whose resources are to be harnessed to meet the needs of all its members, including those who have been left behind in Ghana.

This cooperative spirit forms the bulwark of the remittance system. Sending remittances home is a feature of the Ghanaian diaspora and the UK domiciled immigrants are no exception. Like their counterparts in the USA, the remittance is targeted primarily for consumption purposes though in a growing number of instances, the money is being used to set up businesses, fund education for extended family members, purchase land, build a home, or support aging parents and grandparents. Remittance is a way for the immigrants to share the gains from their migration with relatives at home. The primary motivation is to assist in reducing the economic hardships confronting many Ghanaians. For Ghanaians in the West Midlands and across the Atlantic in the USA, international migration and by extension the remittances that the migrants send home, has become the dominant mechanism of global incorporation of Ghana into the world's economy. More recently, Ghanaians in the diaspora have extended their remittances to include schools, colleges, charitable organizations, non-governmental organizations, and even government institutions.

Core to the diasporic experiences of the community in the West Midlands is the notion that the lived experiences of the immigrants is a reflection of and an extension of the relationships that they have formed but have left behind in Ghana. And as to be expected, the dominant theme that defines the contents of this cultural community is the pervasive sense of economic altruism which provides the psychological rationale for the institutionalization of immigrant remittance. It is this sense of altruism that captures the deep spiritual connotations that Ghanaian immigrants have always attached to the sharing of their means with relatives and non-relatives alike. Like their counterparts in the USA and elsewhere, the subject of remittances evokes strong sentiments among the immigrants. A recurring theme that emerged from the social encounters with the subjective world of the immigrants is that to remit home regularly is not only obligatory but necessary for the preservation of the spiritual continuity of the entire family, even including the ancestors. Immigrants' sentiments about the material and non-material items that are regularly remitted are often based on the notion and recognition that in the Ghanaian cultural ethos, sharing one's resources with those who are less fortunate is considered a moral duty, underpinned by the norm that those who remit become benefactors of spiritual blessings, overall well-being, and life satisfaction.

In the end, the portrait that emerges from a cross-section of the Ghanaian community living in the British West Midlands is that irrespective of their class or economic status, the cultural fabric of the immigrant community is constructed in such a way as to include aspects of both British and Ghanaian society. This inclusiveness and the crossing of traditional boundaries is intended to promote community integration of the immigrants and at the same time to reduce the social distance between the immigrants and other minority and majority ethnic and non-ethnic groups in the West Midlands as well as in Ghana. For some of the immigrants though, an enduring dilemma is how to broaden the scope of their identities without relinquishing cherished Ghanaian values, especially those that are intended to buffer their children from the deleterious effect of racism and discrimination. The perception is that as foreigners in a strange land, it behooves the immigrants to create a cultural community whose realities are grounded in Ghanaian values of altruism and collective empowerment, designed to ensure the viability and sustainability of the entire social system. To the majority of the immigrants in the diaspora, the boundaries of the community are perceived as broad and elastic in order to allow for the formation and strengthening of ties that transcend specific cultural entities.

Encountering and Confronting Racism and Discrimination

Though the Ghanaian immigrants in the West Midlands constitute a visible minority, they perceive that having a foreign and black identity in the UK has not hampered their integration into British society. The majority of the participants in the focus group study described the racial climate in the UK as favorable. In Leicester, some of the immigrants spoke about having a harmonious relationship living alongside Caucasians, Indians, Pakistanis, and Caribbean blacks. The majority of the Ghanaians in Leicester and Coventry expressed the view that though they have experienced racial harassment in their communities, the problem is not as institutionalized and widespread as it is in the USA where race continues to be a culturally divisive issue separating blacks from white America.

Living in a welfare state such as the UK further insulates the Ghanaians from institutionalized racism and discrimination as the immigrants seek access to opportunities and resources. Safety nets provided by the UK government and local authorities in services such as healthcare, housing, and education has meant that for those Ghanaians who are legal residents, gaining access to opportunities has been relatively easier than the experiences of their counterparts in the USA. The added advantage of living in a European Union country is that it provides the immigrants with additional safeguards from human rights abuses and the exploitation of workers and residents. The image that is portrayed by the Ghanaians regarding racial and ethnic divisions in the UK is that like every society, overt and covert discrimination and racist behaviors and attitudes can be found if one looks for it. However, the Ghanaians do not allow racial and ethnic discrimination to thwart their goal of achieving economic and cultural success in the UK. From their perspective, the expectations regarding the delivery of social services have been clearly delineated by a set of governmental-issued guidelines that local authorities follow when making decisions regarding education, housing, and welfare benefits for the public. Agency discretion is important, but strict guidelines for the delivery of social services are monitored by government and non-government agencies that are accountable to the British government. In this regard, the Ghanaian immigrants in the West Midlands perceive that their integration into society has been enhanced by the protections that they have received from watchdog groups, human relations organizations and immigrant associations that monitor the delivery of services and the distribution of opportunities for the British public-at-large.

Though the majority of the Ghanaians have resided in the UK for a decade or more, cultural identification and affinity with Britain is very weak. Most of the immigrants perceive a disconnection and marginalization with British culture even though unlike their American counterparts, there is a strong sense that the disconnection with British society and culture has yet to manifest itself in racial polarization and tension between ethnic minorities and the core of British society. The feeling of marginality and disconnect with British society and culture was especially common among second and third generation British youth of Ghanaian descent. This group of youth, mainly young males, tend to reject their British identity while at the same time embracing an African-centered and black identity.

Despite their favorable perception of race and interethnic relations in the UK in general, there was unanimity among the study participants that a major problem confronting them is how to curtail the negative stigmas often associated with their black teenage youth. The general perception among the white majority culture is that black teenagers are uneducatable, belligerent, overly aggressive, threatening, and trouble-prone. This negative and stereotypical image filters down to social service agencies, including teachers, social workers, and law enforcement personnel. Whether in the streets of the USA or UK, minority black teenagers are often portrayed as fatherless, lacking male role models, and growing up in single-parent homes that are dysfunctional and economically deprived. Mainly urban and confined to the inner cities, several of the youth experience high rates of unemployment, attend underachieving schools with poor infrastructures, and often lack access to community leisure, entertainment, and after school educational programs. The majority of urban black teenagers who are law abiding, attend school regularly, and achieve high scholastic standards are often unfairly associated with the gangster image typically associated with black urban teenage boys. Ghanaian immigrant parents in the UK and the USA struggle to change this cultural image. A common strategy among the immigrant parents with young male teenagers in the UK and the USA is to create conditions at home and in the community conducive for high scholastic achievement on the part of their children. This includes taking a keen interest in the education of their children, hiring tutors to provide additional instruction in mathematics and science subjects, monitoring with vigilance the associates of their sons, and fostering in the youth a sense of positive self esteem and identity. The immigrant families usually bond together to share resources, and they support one another by adopting a cooperative spirit in nurturing their children and alerting their children to some of the negative antiblack sentiments and stereotypes pervasive in the West. The parents are aware that the negative stereotypes commonly associated with black teenagers in general will persist and that more often than not, their children are going to be stigmatized, and could become caught up in these stereotypes by virtue of their skin color. Try as they might to insulate the children from these antiblack sentiments, the parents believe that a strong moral and educational foundation anchored in traditional African values of altruism, respect for others, and service to community will serve their children well no matter the disharmonies caused by racial and ethnic intolerances.

For most of the Ghanaian immigrants living in the West Midlands, the social construction of a black or pan-African identity is facilitated and made somewhat easier by the immigrants' perceived sense that as a country, a majority of British citizens know more about the cultures and peoples of Africa because of the colonial legacies Britain shares with her former colonies. These former colonial territories have been incorporated into the British Commonwealth. In a sense, the Africans in the former British sphere of influence were part of the British identity and heritage. Learning and being able to speak English fluently is a mark of identification with Britain. Schools in Ghana were structured to learn about British culture and society. In their encounters with the British public-at-large, the Ghanaians feel that they do not have to explain a lot about Ghana or about Africa to their British associates. Ghanaian national affinity with the USA is not as strong as it is with their British counterparts.

By all accounts, the immigrants believe this special historical relationship with the UK tends to minimize conflicts and sharp racial divisions, which dominate black and white relations in the USA. Despite this special relationship, Africans and Ghanaians living in the UK do experience racism and discrimination on account of their black identity and skin color.

Struggles with how to define an identity permeates the fabric of the immigrant community. Like the Ghanaians in the American diaspora, the strategy for dealing with issues of marginality and segregation is to concentrate on the achievement of economic goals while being aware that discrimination and racism abounds but their effect can be minimized when the migrants orient themselves toward their primary objective for being in the UK: to work, save money, build a house, set up a business in Ghana, and ultimately repatriate. Even when they encounter racism and discrimination, the immigrants allay their concerns by taking satisfaction in the notion that they are not the sole targets of racial prejudice and bigotry. Other immigrant groups from the former British colonial territories, mainly Indians, Caribbean, and Pakistanis, are also forging their distinct identities in the UK, and by all accounts, several of them have become economically and culturally successful in spite of all the discrimination and racism they have encountered upon moving into the suburbs and competing for highly skilled and well paying jobs. Although some of the immigrants acknowledge the existence of racism and racist attitudes in the UK, most of them feel that their current racial and ethnic experiences are incomparable to what blacks endured under the vestiges of the Jim Crow era in the USA. Above all, there is a sense among the Ghanaian immigrants that even if they encounter discrimination and racism, the effect on their lives pales in comparison to the dire social and economic problems they left behind in Ghana where some of them did not have access to healthcare, lived in substandard housing surrounded by open sewers filled with trash, faced violent victimizations at the hands of the police or military, and failed to adequately feed themselves and their families. Comparatively, the standards of living of the immigrants have gone up considerably. Like their USA counterparts, a majority of them are living their dreams in the West and have lifestyles most Ghanaians at home aspire to have one day. The opportunity most of them have to share their income with relatives at home and help alleviate the abject deprivation and poverty confronting their families in Ghana makes it imperative for the immigrants to develop strategies to confront the insidiousness of discrimination and racism in the UK or in the USA.

In constructing their ethnic and racial identities, the immigrants tend to stress achievement and meritocracy, believing that ultimately, the contents of their relationship with the rest of Britain will be measured by their accomplishments and contributions to British society in general with less emphasis on their blackness or African identity. The perception is that obstacles to equality engendered by institutionalized racism can be offset by acquiring high educational credentials and qualifying for jobs that provide ample opportunities for economic advancement and mobility. As experienced by their counterparts in the USA, the quest for high credentials is often accompanied by a frequent assessment of employment and labor conditions in the UK, always seeking to maximize and derive the utmost economic benefits from their education, including exercising options to relocate or move to labor centers where jobs are plentiful. This flexibility to move around to more favorable locales for economic gain has been pivotal to the success and upward mobility of several of the immigrants in the West Midlands. The expression of black racial and ethnic identities among the immigrants has been facilitated by the increasing multicultural-ness of the UK. The mosaic of identities that are being forged by the millions of immigrants from all over the world who currently call the UK home have eased the fears and concerns that the immigrants have about racism and discrimination. The Ghanaian immigrants living in Leicester, a community in the West Midlands that is predominantly Asian, find themselves forming interethnic alliances with their Asian neighbors to promote cultural understanding and to bridge the cultural chasm between Asians and Africans. Similar inter-racial linkages have been established by the Ghanaian and Caribbean residents in Leicester to mobilize community resources and work in concert with law enforcement agencies to ward off social problems like youth crimes, underage drinking, and vandalism. Such inter-ethnic coalitions have the manifest consequence of achieving community integration, fostering a sense of belongingness, and assisting the immigrants to feel safe at home as they go about pursuing their economic activities and raising their children.

In forging interethnic alliances with other immigrant groups in the UK, the Ghanaian immigrants embrace the view that community integration and social participation constitute important aspects of their immigrant experiences in the UK. Achieving community integration and social participation serves as an indicator of the extent to which the immigrants embrace the values, norms, and beliefs of the host society. For Ghanaians in the UK and USA diaspora, a significant aspect of community participation can be found in the wide range of social activities that the immigrants engage in as members of their respective communities. Unique in their experiences is a high degree of social volunteerism and civic incorporation. In the West Midlands, Ghanaian immigrant parents of school age children take a keen role in Parent Teacher Association (PTA) activities, often working in tandem with educational proprietors and local education authorities to strengthen the quality of education their children receive. Ghanaian nurses and other professional occupational groups volunteer their time to teach English to new African immigrants and refugees in the community to enhance their educational and job prospects and thereby facilitate their social integration. Volunteerism and civic participation such as working with disabled people, visiting elderly citizens at home or in the hospitals, and taking initiatives to build strong police–minority community cooperation has become a poignant aspect of the lives of the Ghanaians in the West Midlands. Crime in the predominantly minority communities and the high exposure of minorities to criminal victimization underscores the need for the immigrants to explore ways to improve police and minority relations in their respective communities. For those Ghanaians who arrived in the UK during the 1960s and 1970s, images of racial tension and community fragmentation in both the UK and the USA caused by growing public discontent with the influx of immigrants, high unemployment rates, xenophobia, economic depression among whites, and a general feeling of antipathy towards the government are still etched on their minds. The opportunity to actively participate in community affairs through civic engagement and volunteerism is an affirmation of the immigrants' growing orientation and involvement in community affairs. For the émigrés in the UK and the USA, building community through citizen participation is personally enriching even though the immigrants may also have the perception of being outsiders whose daily lives are characterized by marginality, self-segregation, and alienation. The Ghanaians in the West Midlands remain aware that their skin color marks them for scrutiny and sometimes discrimination by agencies of government and social fringe groups who perceive that immigrants are taking away jobs from British citizens and changing the cultural mix and ethnic landscape of the country. Some of the immigrants spend a great deal of time finding ways to confront the negative antiblack sentiments they encounter. While experiences with antiblack sentiments have led to a greater awareness and consciousness of the importance of race and ethnic relations in the UK as a whole, these sentiments have not led to a significant threat to Ghanaian immigrants gaining an economic and cultural foothold in the UK.

Immigrants' Attitudes Concerning Social Conditions in Ghana

Generally, there is a confluence of attitudes held by Ghanaians in the diaspora about the social conditions of their country. When it comes to identifying the problems confronting Ghana and the steps or measures that ought to be taken to ameliorate these problems, Ghanaians in both the UK and USA show an excellent understanding of the continuum of pressing socioeconomic and political issues that have resonance for the future of Ghana. Whether they live in the UK or in the USA, Ghanaians seem to be unanimous in their sentiments about the internal factors at home that spur the migration of trained and untrained workers and students to the West. To a vast majority of the immigrants, entrenched political cronyism, arrested development, economic mismanagement, and overdependence on foreign aid are a major hindrance in the country's quest to create and sustain a vibrant economy and establish a political culture that is rooted in civility, rule of law, and the nurturing of democratic institutions.

The underlying similarities in the collective experiences of the immigrants in the UK and the USA have been influenced by the fact that for a vast majority of the Ghanaians in the diaspora, the internal conditions at home which necessitated their departure from Ghana also serve as the rallying call for the marshalling of their resources to alter the course and future direction of their country toward economic empowerment and political transparency. The economic and sociocultural strains at home make it imperative for the Ghanaians abroad to become successful in the West. The Ghanaian immigrants on both sides of the Atlantic are united in their shared belief that the opportunities that come to them while in the diaspora are intended to offset the myriad of problems that continue to hinder economic advancement at home. Irrespective of their ethnic affiliation, educational occupational background, age, gender, and outlook on life, for a vast majority of the Ghanaians in the West, the opportunity to live and work in the UK or USA is interpreted as a chance to seek economic advancement and social mobility. For those who are pursuing higher education, the collective sentiment among the Ghanaians on both sides of the Atlantic is that upward mobility in the West via education is seen as paramount and necessary for attaining a higher living standard and status. Among those of them who are self-employed, the prevailing attitude is to carve an ethnic entrepreneurial niche that would unable them to compete favorably with other immigrant and ethnic entrepreneurs in their respective communities.

As a group, Ghanaians are very nationalistic and proud of their country. This nationalistic fervor manifests itself in the eagerness and interest that the immigrants take in following events back home as well as in discussing openly and publicly the issues that affect Ghana. For the vast plurality of Ghanaian émigrés in the UK as well as the USA, concerns about the future economic and political direction of Ghana weigh heavily on their minds. The need for Ghana to maintain a sustained economic growth to consolidate and stabilize the country's economy is a major preoccupation with the immigrants. Finding permanent solutions to the economic and political conditions that force thousands to leave the country every year is seen as the first step toward economic revitalization and the creation of wealth in the country. From the perspective of the Ghanaians in the diaspora, key sectors such as education, healthcare, housing, rural electrification, road construction, and the expansion of the private sector must be given priority in the national development process. Economic diversification coupled with the promotion of light industries in depressed rural communities across the country is viewed as a step in the right direction to revitalize the rural economy of the country. The creation of light industries to process agricultural raw materials into semi-finished goods for local consumption will bring added value to the rural economy and at the same time help retain the rural population by giving the youth options to find gainful employment upon the completion of their education. In particular, the expansion of the private sector to create jobs for secondary and postsecondary graduates is warranted to stem the tide of the brain drain.

Rising public discontent concerning the inability of the public and private sectors to provide adequate drinking water, quality roads, affordable housing, and a livable public wage structure threatens the country's economic future. The sluggish domestic economy, which is currently agricultural-based and employs over 60 per cent of the total labor force is in need of a massive overhaul to create opportunities for raising the living standards of Ghanaians. From the immigrants' perspective, sustainable economic development and a revitalization of the rural economy, coupled with improved road transportation networks and employment opportunities, would assist in stemming the flow of population to the urban regional centers of commerce and culture.

Improvements in the physical infrastructure of the nation were identified by the immigrants as pivotal in ensuring and sustaining economic and social development in the country. In particular, the immigrants feel that steps need to be taken and programs implemented to improve upon the road and transportation systems of the country. This, as the immigrants pointed out, is a prerequisite to economic development in that it will facilitate the unimpeded movement of people, goods, and services throughout the country. Of particular interest to the immigrants is the construction of feeder roads to link areas of food and agricultural production to distribution and market sites to ensure that agricultural produce are not left to rot in the hinterland due to lack of transportation or poor and inadequate road network systems. The construction of feeder roads and the development of a national transportation interlink system will ensure that small towns in the country are integrated into the national economic system. This will have the added advantage of helping to retain the population of small towns by opening up economic and business opportunities for the youth who otherwise may be compelled to move to Accra or engage in transnational migration. In essence, population retention is perceived by the immigrants as key in Ghana's march toward economic efficiency and toward the maximization of resource distribution to bring about an improvement in living standards.

The country's educational system was also cited by the immigrants as a major source of the brain drain and migration of the unskilled. In the view of the immigrants, if the brain drain is to be curbed and national economic development implemented, concerted efforts must be undertaken to resuscitate the educational curriculum of the country's educational system. The goal of revamping the country's educational system is to develop a system of education that has relevance for the modern age of technology and innovation. Of particular concern to the immigrants is the belief that the current system of education, from the primary through to the tertiary level has been designed and modeled after the colonial system of education without any consideration given to the training of skilled personnel in vital areas such as engineering, healthcare, technology, and agricultural production. The result is that the majority of graduates at all levels of education find it difficult, if not impossible to obtain employment in their fields of study. Graduate unemployment is a major problem facing the country today. This has caused labor redundancy and underemployment among secondary and university school graduates. In the absence of having jobs that matches their skill level, several of the graduates look beyond the shores of Ghana in search of job opportunities. As it stands now, the country's educational system is seen as preparing graduates who end up taking jobs overseas. This jeopardizes the manpower resources of the country, further impeding the economic and social development of the country.

A majority of the immigrants expect the economic stagnation of the country to persist, resulting in the continual migration of both skilled and unskilled Ghanaians. The immigrants agree that as visa requirements are tightened in the UK, USA, and in other Western destinations, more Ghanaians who desire to leave the country will look elsewhere. Already there is a growing stream of Ghanaians heading to Southern Europe, particularly to Greece, Malta, Gibraltar, Spain, and Portugal. Unlike their counterparts who are successful in making it to Great Britain and the USA, a majority of the new immigrants to Southern Europe consist of uneducated and unskilled Ghanaians. Many of them are able to find jobs as agricultural farm migrants, seasonal laborers, cleaners, and meat packers.

When Ghanaians migrate to the West, they never sever ties with their communities and extended family relations living in Ghana. Highly transnational in their migratory patterns, yet nationalistic in their outlook, Ghanaians take a keen interest in the socioeconomic and political affairs of Ghana. As a group, the immigrants manifest a dual attachment and loyalty to Ghana as well as their host society, often interpreting social events in the home country by finding meaning and rationality in a new social context based on their diasporic or transnational identities. Nearly 80 per cent of the Ghanaian immigrants in the UK follow events in Ghana, often relying on the print and electronic media to obtain current information about the social and political situation in the country.

Irrespective of where they live, for a majority of the immigrants, the propensity to engage in international migration is seen as an opportunity to close the wide gap and structural inequality between the rich and poor countries of the world. From their perspective, Ghana as an immigrant-sending country stands to gain as more of its citizens migrate abroad to seek better economic and cultural opportunities for themselves. Etched in the consciousness of the immigrants is the notion that international migration has the potential to alleviate the country's economic problems by making it possible for Ghanaians abroad to share their incomes and assets with their relatives at home. While acknowledging that the country is loosing its skilled and unskilled labor to the West, the immigrants perceive that, ultimately, the country will derive maximum economic payoff as more and more people in the Ghanaian diaspora repatriate and transfer their assets as well as their skills back to Ghana. There was consensus among the immigrants in the study that social and economic conditions in the country will need to improve before mass repatriation of Ghanaians in the diaspora can occur. Specific improvements called for by the immigrants include quality healthcare, liberalization of fiscal and monetary policies to allow for the transfer of immigrants' assets, affordable housing, a political atmosphere conducive for political stability and participatory governance, and the promotion of civic order and the rule of law. If properly managed, the immigrants believe that the brain drain has the potential to become a brain gain for the country. But that is assuming that return migration and repatriation will become an integral component of the Ghanaian diaspora and that the central government will implement policies to harness the human and capital resources of returning Ghanaians. This aspect of the Ghanaian diaspora and the role of central government in formulating migration policies have yet to attract the full attention of the Ghanaian government.

Attitudes of the immigrants have shifted considerably regarding the role of international migration in the development of Ghana. Specifically, a majority of the immigrants are supportive of the efforts of the government of Ghana to give Ghanaian immigrants a voice and representation in the political and economic systems of the country. The introduction and passage of the dual citizenship legislation and the right of persons abroad to vote in all elections in Ghana is seen as a positive sign of inclusiveness and of the empowerment of Ghanaians in the diaspora to make significant contributions to the national development effort. However, the immigrants perceive that the right to participate in the political process does not go far enough because it failed to incorporate an institutionalized mechanism whereby Ghanaians in the diaspora will have access to current information about the issues that define each election cycle in the country. In essence, giving Ghanaians the right of representation and participation in the electoral process without a corresponding process and forum for educating and disseminating the key issues defining elections in the country is viewed as a cosmetic offering designed to give the immigrants abroad a false sense of political participation and representation.

Prospects for Return Migration

For Ghanaians in the USA and the UK, a common theme that resonates with several of the immigrants is whether or not they intend to repatriate home to assist in national reconstruction. A second theme concerns the manifest impact of the brain drain on national development. Citing information from the World Bank (2000), Savine Ammassari and Richard Black state that nearly about a third of all the skilled professionals trained by African governments are domiciled abroad. The loss in terms of human capital and subsequent impact on economic development and national reconstruction is immense. Ghana is no exception to this brain drain. The migration of Ghana's skilled and unskilled workers is a major problem confronting the government. Unable to secure well-paying jobs in Ghana, several of the skilled workers and graduates cast their eyes to the West where their skills are in demand and where they can attract higher wages and have a standard of living significantly better than what they are accustomed to in Ghana. On their part, the unskilled also look outside the borders of Ghana to accomplish their economic dreams even if it means that they are going to find employment in the West as cab drivers, parking ramp attendants, migrant farm workers, and the like. The expectation and hope of the Government of Ghana and those in the diaspora is that sooner rather than later, the push-pull economic and political factors that forced them to leave Ghana will be ameliorated and conditions at home will improve enough for them to return to Ghana. However, it is nearly four decades since the Ghanaian diaspora commenced, and the economic and social factors that have motivated Ghanaians to leave and seek greener pastures elsewhere have yet to be tackled to reverse the brain drain.

Leaving Ghana to go abroad for a temporary sojourn while waiting for economic and social conditions to improve in the country has become a permanent feature of the Ghanaian diaspora. Like their USA counterparts, the Ghanaians in the West Midlands consider their stay in the UK as temporary. Coming to the UK mainly as economic and cultural migrants, a majority of the immigrants have plans to return to Ghana for permanent settlement after they have accomplished certain economic goals, chiefly to build a home and save enough money to support them in time of old age. The stay in the UK is regarded as a temporary sojourn because of immigrants' perception and certainty that in the long term, economic and political conditions in Ghana will improve. Through their networks of extended family members, friends, the mass media, and the internet, the immigrants stay abreast of economic and political developments in Ghana, often weighing the pros and cons of return migration. Nearly 85 per cent of the Ghanaians living in the West Midlands intend to repatriate at some time or another.

Although the decision to repatriate is affected by several factors already noted (age of children, spousal relationships, and owning a home in Ghana), there is evidence also to suggest that economic and political conditions at home are key considerations as well. Nearly 80 per cent of the immigrants in the West Midlands cited economic conditions in Ghana as the main factor they will consider as they deliberate on the pros and cons of returning home. Another 73 per cent mentioned improvements in the country's political culture as a major determinant in the decision to return. Home ownership was cited by 62 per cent of the immigrants as a factor they will consider when they make plans to repatriate. While the amount of money remitted or saved in Ghana and in the UK influences the decision to repatriate, only 49 per cent cited this as a reason to return. Psychological variables (feeling home sick, need to be near kin folk, nostalgia, and eminent death) were cited by only a third of the immigrants as having an impact on their decision to return.

These findings mirror the findings among the Ghanaians in the USA, that economic and political factors in Ghana are major considerations in the decision to return. For a plurality of Ghanaians in the diaspora, plans of returning home are influenced by the perceived need to go back home and assist in the task of national reconstruction. Nearly 77 per cent of all Ghanaians in the UK and the USA perceive that the skills, education, or savings that they acquired abroad will make significant contributions to the economy and political development of the country. In this regard, returning home is rationalized on the part of the immigrants as beneficial for Ghana. This benefit is far more significant than any bilateral or multilateral assistance programs that Ghana receives from her partners or donor countries. A reversal of the brain drain from the West to Ghana is seen by the immigrants as a major contributory factor aimed at improving the standard of living of Ghanaians. The immigrants in the diaspora decry the fact that the Ghana government has yet to put in place sustained and systematic policy initiatives to tap into this reservoir of wealth and resources that Ghanaians have amassed abroad.

For the immigrants who do not intend to repatriate, a major reason cited is the apprehension that they will not be able to achieve a full reintegration and incorporation into the affairs of Ghana. Additionally, consternation about political instability still dominates the thoughts of some of the migrants. Many are concerned that the recent economic strides the country has made are going to wane due to poor planning, unrestricted population growth, corruption, and fiscal irresponsibility. The obstacles faced by returnees who had repatriated only to come back to the UK are still fresh in the minds of those who are reluctant to repatriate. Nearly 65 per cent of the immigrants who indicated that they will not repatriate mentioned that they know Ghanaians who went back home to resettle permanently only to return to the UK after a couple of years. Reasons cited for returning include persistent financial demands made by extended family members, problems adjusting to social expectations and meeting obligations, poor planning resulting from inadequate savings prior to repatriation, bureaucratic encumbrances encountered in the process of setting up a business, and the erosion of the value of their funds. Social ties and networks of relationships formed in the UK also make it difficult for some Ghanaians to repatriate because of commitments to children, spouses, and weak social ties at home.

The opportunities presented for prospective returnees to re-engage in the affairs of the sending country are enormous but so are the challenges and obstacles. The opportunities and challenges of repatriation often dominate discussions among the immigrants. The majority of the immigrants are willing to utilize their newly acquired skills and capital to assist in the economic and social development of Ghana. However, most of the immigrants perceive that currently the key to a successful return depends on the type of skill acquired or learned during the period of stay in the UK coupled with the amount of investments or monies saved. There was agreement among the immigrants in the West Midlands that the absence of a coordinated national scheme to assist in the resettlement of returnees is a major setback to prospective returnees. Though the central government recognizes the skills and the investments that the returnees bring to the country, the immigrants perceive that national economic development planning policies have not integrated return migration into economic models.

The social psychological meanings that Ghanaian immigrants attach to their migratory experiences are least understood by the central government. From the perspective of the central government, Ghanaians engage in international migration often for two main reasons: to seek education and to raise their living standards. Least understood by the central government and national economic planners in the country is the notion that once they have met and fulfilled these expectations, a majority of the Ghanaian immigrants focus their energies and their aspirations higher to fulfill other dreams and goals, primarily the hope to achieve economic security and define a transnational identity and space that offers Ghanaian returnees protection against the vagaries of poverty and economic malaise. Living, working, and interacting within the framework of the kin group networks that the immigrants form, the Ghanaians in the diaspora project an identity and image that focuses on regional and continental African integration in addition to their strong nationalistic attachment to their country of origination.

In sum, an important aspect of the Ghanaian diaspora in the West is the fluidity and dynamic nature of the diaspora. When they migrate to the USA and the UK, the most salient aspects of their migration include the formation of cultural communities that reflect a strong belief in, and a commitment to their Ghanaian-based immigrant social institutions as vehicles for fostering solidarity, shared essence, and cultural affinity. This diaspora resonates in how the immigrants pursue economic and social objectives. Economically, a common theme in both the Ghanaian diaspora in the USA and in the UK is the pursuit of employment and high rates of labor force participation as a means of achieving status and mobility in the West. The economic benefits that have come to the immigrants as a result of their strong work ethic are immense. Several of the immigrants have seen their economic fortunes change since arriving in the West. For the first time in their individual and collective lives, some of the immigrants are able to earn enough money to share with their extended family members at home through regularly remittances. From their perspectives, the opportunity to live and work in the West is the main embodiment of their success. The fulfillment of economic goals facilitates the structural integration of the immigrants into the body polity of UK and American societies respectively. By far, the main similarity and parallel between the Ghanaian diaspora in the UK and the USA is the continued recognition among the immigrants that opportunities abound in the West, and that with sheer determination and assiduousness, the immigrants can alter the economic misfortunes that dominated their lives and those of their families in Ghana prior to their emigration to the West. Their strivings to become successful has become an institutional component of the diasporic experiences of the Ghanaians. The confidence that the immigrants portray in the economic opportunities offered to them by the West is unparalleled. Despite dwindling economic opportunities for immigrants in the West as a whole, a majority of Ghanaians on both sides of the Atlantic are of the firm conviction that any type of work in the West is far better than the horrific economic conditions that most of them had experienced in Ghana. And though they may encounter racism and generalized antipathy towards people of color and blacks in particular, the immigrants are never daunted by the continued challenges of racial hatred, alienation, and marginalization that some of them continuously experience in the West. Etched firmly in their consciousness is the belief that racism can be overcome through self empowerment and a value orientation that is modeled on economic advancement and individual improvement. For some of them, the entrenched legacies of racial discrimination, coupled with years of antiblack denigration in both the UK and the USA directed toward people of the black African experiences in the West strengthens their resolve to prove to skeptics that blacks are capable of achieving upward mobility no matter the institutionalized structural barriers that are imposed on them by virtue of their race.

The focus of the Ghanaians on achieving economic upward mobility is buttressed in their common acknowledgement of the importance of maintaining or constructing a social identity that is reflective of their Ghanaian and by extension, their African cultures. And whether they are domiciled in the UK or in the USA, to the immigrant, identity connotes negotiated space, place, and sense of being. The identities that are formed by the immigrants in the UK and the USA are intended to preserve the cultural heritage of blackness and promote strong bonds and affinity among the immigrants. In the course of shaping and mapping their identities, the immigrants recognize their minority status in the West and therefore, proceed to negotiate an identity that is transnational but fluid enough to recognize differences while at the same time celebrating and promoting a common cultural ethos. Generally, Ghanaian immigrants recognize notions of racial and ethnic discrimination in the West as problematic. For blacks in particular, the vestiges of institutionalized forms of racial discrimination have consequences and outcomes as they forge membership in predominantly all white cultures and societies. For most of the Ghanaian immigrants, encounters with racial polarity and inequality are treated with great concern. This concern stems from the collective awareness among the immigrants that while discriminatory practices continue to persist in the UK and the USA, often, its deleterious effect can be minimized through self and group cultural affirmation and empowerment through hard work and the cultivation of identities that promote socioeconomic advancement. To these immigrants, a proven and time tested outlet for weathering racial and ethnic polarization and marginality in the West is the formation of strong networks of kinship and the establishment of bonds that cuts across social, cultural, and economic lines. Ultimately, the immigrants in the diaspora come to recognize that despite their differences and the variances in the motivations that form their transatlantic immigrant journeys, they are all connected to one principle: the harnessing of collective resources to achieve economic security for themselves and their relatives at home. To many Ghanaians in the diaspora, migration to the West offers this opportunity.

Chapter 11

Conclusion: The Continuities of the Ghanaian Diaspora in the New Global Migration

Economic and political factors play a large role in the migration of Ghanaians to the West. In the economic realm, two forces have shaped the outmigration of Ghanaians to the United States and other Western destinations. The first is the process of economic and technological globalization brought about by the incorporation of the economy of Ghana into the world's economy. As this study shows, the continued integration of Ghana's economy into the world's economy has enabled those Ghanaians with marketable skills in the West to carve and fill a labor market niche in the United States and Europe. When migrating abroad, the majority of Ghanaians arrive as non-immigrants, often on student or visitor visas. Ultimately, they change their nonimmigrant status to immigrant status using various provisions in American immigration law such as family reunification and amnesty, and also through the possession of educational credentials and skills in demand by American employers; occasionally Ghanaians achieve immigrant status on humanitarian grounds as asylum-seekers. Only a small number of Ghanaians arrive in the United States with pre-approved permanent resident status. The initial pressure to migrate to the United States is brought about by deteriorating economic "push" factors such as unemployment and underemployment among secondary and tertiary institution graduates in Ghana. The "pull" factors include favorable economic conditions in the United States and the prospect of achieving higher social mobility through the pursuit of education and labor force participation. The results from the study show that an increasing number of Ghanaians have come to realize that they can make more money working in the United States and in the West than they will make if they stay in Ghana. In this regard, migration to the West has become the dominant means whereby Ghanaians are able to improve upon their economic circumstances and raise their living standards.

The second factor shaping Ghanaian migration to the United States and Europe is attributed to decades of political morass and the deterioration of political civility coupled with the erosion of democratic institutions. The persistence of these problems created a favorable climate for people to leave the country. The failure of democratic institutions to preserve the political order of the country and create an atmosphere conducive for the nurturing and exercising of political rights has compelled some Ghanaians to look beyond the borders of the country in search of a relatively better political atmosphere. Today, economic and political forces converge to influence the continued saga of the Ghanaian brain drain to the West. This unfolding brain drain has come to represent every sector of Ghanaian society, and it involves skilled workers such as doctors, nurses, pharmacists, engineers, teachers, and civil servants. Moreover, large numbers of unskilled workers are also leaving the country in search of better living standards in the West.

Upon their arrival in the United States, several of the immigrants join or create ethnic and transnational cultural communities to provide networks of mutual support to assist them cope with the realities of their new environment. In this regard, this study demonstrates that for Ghanaian immigrants in the United States and in the West as a whole, the creation of a cultural community has been the dominant form of social integration with the host society. In general, the evidence presented in this study show that for the bulk of Ghanaian immigrants, the enduring legacy and theme in their individual and collective transnational diasporic experiences has been the creation of an identity that is distinctively black, African, and yet global. And as their numbers increase in the United States, the Ghanaian immigrants are able to establish differentiating forms of expression of identity that match their ethnic fervor. And no matter what form(s) the expression of their identities take, one thing remains certain: the continuity of the Ghanaian diaspora in the West is going to be shaped by how successfully the immigrants are able to create and preserve their panoply of cultures they import from Ghana to sustain them in their adopted countries.

The interactions between both external and internal factors (in Ghana and in the West) converge to define the tapestry of identities the immigrants carve and construct for themselves. The evidence presented in this book shows that though the immigrants will continue to construct an identity that is mainly African and or Ghanaian, some of them will continue to associate and identify with American–born blacks and Caribbean blacks in the collective diaspora. Increasingly, several of the immigrants are coming to recognize the interconnectivity between them and other blacks in an America that is highly heterogeneous in its ethnic and racial composition. For the second generation Ghanaian youth, the formation of identity is a continuum, often based on the blending of multiple ethnicities to create a unique identity that transcends black and Ghanaian-American identities. The emerging identities of this group reflect the divergent ethnic groups that are emigrating to the United States. The pressure to become an American is intense among the second generation immigrants as they explore ways to balance the cultural expectations of their parents (to embrace Ghanaian values) with the simultaneous pressure from the generalized society to adopt the values and mores of American youth culture. Among the first-generation, identity is structured solely upon the need to preserve Ghanaian cultural traditions. For this group, there is guarded assimilation coupled with increased separatedness, fragmented identities, and sometimes self-imposed segregation in an effort to preserve Ghanaian heritage and culture. In contrast, the second generation immigrant children are beginning to embrace American cultural identities, often mixing and borrowing from the new minority ethnicities being formed in the United States due to massive immigration from Asia, Latin America, and the Caribbean.

Fiercely nationalistic and cognizant of their African heritage, the Ghanaian immigrants will continue to resist being defined by the general negative stereotype that Americans often associate with black Americans. The immigrants' rejection of the generalized antipathy towards people of the black African diaspora in America will lead several of the immigrants to construct a detached identity that is based upon redefinition of what it means to be black in a race-conscious society such as the United States. As the findings from this study reveal, the immigrants will continue to stake a position that affirms the historical bonds and affinity that they share with their black American counterparts. This is not to imply that the two groups of blacks do not have their differences. Stark differences exist, but both sides agree that their collective destinies are linked to the preservation of their unique identities in the United States along with the marshalling of their collective wills to ward off the disparaging and negative connotations often associated with being black. In the end, the identities constructed by the immigrants will involve a negotiation of cultural values learned in the West, those that are imported from Ghana, and more importantly, those that have transnational foci. The subjective fluidity in the manner by which the Ghanaians negotiate these complex identities speaks to a larger theoretical issue: the ascendancy of transnational but fragmented identities that are designed to optimize the economic and cultural interests of people migrating from the developing to the developed nations of the world. Ultimately, the form of identity that the immigrants negotiate is one that seeks to find ways to transcend the black–white racial gap in America. The goal is not to bridge this gap because the immigrants perceive they lack the power and the institutional resources to redefine the contents of black and white relations in the United States. Their goal is to look beyond this racial divide in the hope of capturing the promise of a better economic future.

The analysis of the immigration experiences of Ghanaians living in the United States demonstrates immense diversity in terms of how the immigrants construct their cultural, economic, and political communities and create identities that span national and geographic barriers. The portrait of the Ghanaian immigrant living in the United States and other Western countries is one is based on a transnational identity. By living and re-creating their lives in several societies including their country of origin, Ghanaian immigrants abroad manage to engage and compete in the global economic system that is characterized by increased social and political differentiation. In keeping their options open as to where they choose to call home, for example, the immigrants are able to capitalize on the social, cultural, political, and economic benefits of their migratory experience by taking advantage of the full range of opportunities offered to them in both their countries of destination and origination. This way, they manage to become active participants and contribute their quota in the affairs of multiple societies irrespective of whether they identify themselves as Ghanaians or American citizens.

The central government in Ghana must seek an understanding of the processes involved in the social and cultural creation of transnational identities in order to harness the global human capital of the Ghanaian immigrants toward the monumental task of national economic, social, and political development efforts. An understanding by the central government of how the immigrants assist in the resuscitation of the fragile economy of Ghana is central in the formulation of policies to ameliorate the myriad of problems affecting the country. Such an understanding will assist the government in the future mobilization of local and international capital resources to expand the economic and industrial base of the country. In seeking to retain their Ghanaian-ness in addition to a transglobal immigrant identity, many of the Ghanaians broaden their social and cultural ethnicity. This co-mingling achieves two goals: it provides the immigrants with a shared sense of pan-black identity rooted in afrocentric principles whose goal is to re-center the cultures and rich heritages of the peoples of black African descent and it enables the immigrants to redefine the notion of blackness in America by stressing achievement, merit, and the commitment to alter the negative stereotypes and antipathy often associated with blacks in the United States.

Managing International Migration in Ghana

International migration has become a sociological phenomenon and a source for social, economic, cultural, and political change in Ghana. As an immigrant-sending country, Ghana has had to cope with the deleterious impact of the outmigration of skilled and unskilled labor. During the past five decades, economic and social development has become stagnant. The result is that the country is compelled to look to international donor countries for foreign assistance, which further exacerbates the debt burden of the country. In this section, I attempt to map out strategies for macro-contextualizing international migration in Ghana. Public discourse has to be initiated to find meaning for the mass exodus the country is facing. Providing a broad, social structural context for illuminating the issues affecting this exodus is a critical aspect of national reconstruction. Hitherto, national public debate about the exodus of Ghanaians has been approached from the perspective that given the opportunity, a majority of Ghanaians would like to emigrate. Therefore, strategies to ensure that potential émigrés stay at home and assist in national development have yet to be incorporated into national development planning initiatives.

To derive the utmost benefits from her citizens who engage in international migration to the United States and elsewhere, the central government of Ghana must embark upon a systematic initiative to ascertain the volume of outmigration with a goal of understanding the demographic and economic characteristics of leavers. This is best accomplished by a census and registration of prospective travelers at the national port of departure and entry. A social program to encourage increasingly more Ghanaians to register with Ghanaian foreign missions abroad must be attempted. On its part, the central government can tap into the already existing Ghanaian immigrant associations and affiliated networks by providing them with institutional support to encourage the registration of all Ghanaians abroad.

It is imperative for the government to begin monitoring Ghanaian emigration with the objective of gathering demographic data about who is leaving, why they are leaving, the impact of emigration on social and economic development, migrant plans for the future, and the role of the government in facilitating the resettlement of Ghanaians abroad who want to return home. Toward this end, a comprehensive national policy designed to achieve a balanced and integrated approach to economic development is sorely needed. The goals of such a policy are twofold. The first is to reinvigorate the public sector to encourage private capital in all aspects of economic and industrial development. Under this policy, sustained emphasis will be placed on rural population retention, rural economic self-sufficiency, and the provision of the necessary infrastructure such as feeder roads, clinics, education, electricity, and water facilities. Second, rural economy diversification programs relying on appropriate technology will have to be implemented. The expansion of the rural agricultural infrastructure to process finished and semi-finished goods utilizing rural raw materials will assist in providing sustainability to the rural economy and by extension, population retention. Previous approaches to rural development in Ghana that stressed a capital intensive approach failed, in part, due to a shortage of machinery parts, lack of technical know-how, and failure of the central government and international aid donor countries in developing marketing and distribution strategies to link producers with consumers.

To improve their competitive edge with the urban centers, intra-rural economic cooperation in Ghana must be fostered. This cooperation should be designed in such a way as to create economies of scale and comparative advantages for rural communities as they compete with the urban sector for resource allocation and industrial projects. Parity in the distribution of economic and industrial projects between the urban and rural sectors of Ghana is light years away. However, current policies, where relative to their urban counterparts, the rural areas of the country are viewed as "hewers of wood and drawers of water," have certainly not enhanced the economic production capacity and potential of Ghana's rural areas. To become viable and equal partners in national development, a seamless integration of the rural economy into the national economy is imperative. At the cusp of Ghana's independence, the rural sector held the promise for a vibrant agro-business and light industrial production for home consumption and export. But nearly half a century after independence, Ghana's rural areas are stymied, often lacking in necessities such as water, electricity, and income-generating jobs. The result is a higher per capita ratio of poverty relative to the urban centers.

Poverty reduction has to become an integral component of national policy on migration and economic development. Rural outmigration to the urban centers by Ghanaian youth has had deleterious consequences for the rural sector as food production has declined while thousands of youth have flocked to the metropolitan centers to hawk on city streets and thoroughfares instead of working on rural farms. The rank and file of the street hawkers forms a large pool of surplus labor in Ghana and ultimately will engage in international migration, often to the Middle-East, Asia, and subsequently to the United Kingdom or the United States. In the principal streets of Accra and Kumasi, these street peddlers often trade and exchange information about the mechanisms involved in embarking upon international travel. They come to acquire the contacts, motives, and the resources (in the form of falsified papers) that they may need to implement the journey to the West.

Once the youth leave the rural areas and are fortunate to migrate to the United States or Europe, their principal motive is to earn enough money to send remittances home. These remittances have become a major reason behind the motivation to emigrate. As this study demonstrates, these remittances have become a major component of foreign capital flows into the country. To ensure that it benefits from the remittances or foreign currencies that Ghanaians abroad transfer home, the central government must design policies to harness the economic benefits of remittances must be implemented. And whether these remittances are sent to migrant families or to support educational, health, and small-scale economic projects in the country, there is the need for a national coordination to direct how these remittances can be marshaled to sustain economic development in the country as a whole. The central government, working in concert with financial institutions in the country, may be able to provide leverage and added value to the remittances that are sent home by the immigrants. For projects deemed in the public interest, the central government can provide top up funds to assist private entrepreneurs and individuals who regularly receive remittances to set up small scale, low capital business ventures in economically depressed rural areas of Ghana. The goal of these small scale business ventures is to provide employment for middle and secondary school graduates in the rural areas. A second goal is to assist in the retention of the rural population through the creation of employment opportunities to stem the tide of rural to urban migration in the country. The management of this aspect of the international migration of Ghanaians to the West is important for two reasons: first it will institutionalize and incorporate remittances into central government planning; second, it allows the government to create an environment conducive for the harnessing and mobilization of the human resources of Ghana's citizens abroad. These remittances must be seen by the central government as an investment in the future of Ghana. Consequently, it behooves the government to implement policies that will support private sector initiatives at poverty reduction through income generating microeconomic projects funded with remittances received from abroad.

Tapping International Migration to Promote Economic Development in Ghana

International migration is a complex and dynamic process. In migrant-sending countries such as Ghana where issues associated with migration have yet to be incorporated into public and national development, the establishment of systemic linkages between international migration and social development has the potential to yield outcomes that can serve as modules for implementing sustainable development. Interconnections between international migration and national development policies geared toward the understanding of the full ramifications of migration have dual implications. Such interconnections provide a conceptual framework for understanding international migration as a process and not an isolated discrete event undertaken by individuals who are driven to seek better economic opportunities in distant destinations. There is a critical need for government to recognize the impact of international migration on national development instead of the current perception that migration is only a minor aspect of a larger system of social transformation. Policies emanating from the impact of migration on Ghana's social structure have historically been placed within a micro-level perspective where an actor, the prospective migrant, is seen as responding to a set of stimuli completely unrelated to national development. In point of fact, the interconnections between migration policy and the implementation of sound economic development measures, when managed properly, becomes a *sine qua non* in resource mobilization and economic growth. Past and current governments of Ghana have rarely been interested in the issue of migration per se, viewing migration instead as a means to address structural imbalances associated with cultural, political, and economic production.

Understanding the multidimensional issues surrounding international migration in Ghana requires an analytical conceptualization, on the part of central government planners, of the global forces that are shaping the mass migration of skilled and unskilled labor from the developing to developed countries. In the case of Ghana and the rest of Africa, international migration continues to be a perennial issue. There is a critical need for the formulation of regional and continental strategies by the governments of the sending countries to develop institutional mechanisms and responses to the economic and political implications of the changes associated with the global dispersion of migratory labor. A two-pronged approach emphasizing the interplay of why people leave (outward migration) and why they return (repatriation) is central in delineating the contours of the impact of migration on developing societies: how does outward and return migration impact important demographic, socioeconomic, and political variables for the original sending society as well as the actors (migrants) who undertake the journey?

Central government initiatives to better comprehend the "psychology of migration" are critical toward the formulation of policies to stem the tide of outmigration of Ghana's best and brightest. Migrants everywhere, including Ghanaian migrants in the United States, form an ideology or mind set about their sojourn abroad. In the case of Ghanaian émigrés, the ideology that undergirds this mindset is that the stay abroad is going to be temporary, maybe no more than five years, and that as soon as economic and political conditions improve at home, the return migration process will be undertaken. The mindset of Ghanaian immigrants abroad about the prospect of future repatriation is the least understood aspect of the relationship between the immigrants and the Ghana government. A systematic effort to restructure the educational system of the country to bridge the gap between education and access to jobs is sorely needed. The international migration of Ghanaians is fueled in part, by the desire of students and low skilled workers to improve upon their skill level. The push to leave Ghana is stimulated by the high rates of unemployment and underemployment among secondary school, college, and university graduates, and the inability of both the private and public sectors of Ghana's economy to absorb the graduates. This has made Ghana a major supplier of skilled and well-educated labor force for the rest of the world. Hard-earned foreign exchange is spent by the government to produce an educated labor force, a vital necessity for economic take-off. But the Ghana government is yet to derive any measurable and significant return on the cultural investment in education. Ghana's tide of outmigration cannot be stemmed by the central government because policies designed to reinvigorate the economy and expand its absorptive capacity have been woeful and uncoordinated. A comprehensive plan that would ensure the mobilization of all the available human resource of the country must be carried out within the context of gaining more understanding about the structural components of regional and international migration.

This mobilization would minimize the country's perennial brain drain problem. More importantly, such mobilization is critical for the development, implementation, and rationalization of policies designed to alleviate the economic problems that confront the country. A goal of this mobilization should be income enhancement initiatives designed to improve upon the wage and emolument structure of the country. The mass exodus of skilled and unskilled Ghanaians to the West is magnified by the search for relatively higher wages and benefits in the intended countries of destination. The current wage structure that Ghanaian workers receive are problematic because they do not rise to the level of providing basic necessities for millions of Ghanaians who depend on government initiated wage structures for their livelihood. On average, Ghanaian minimum wage workers earn about $1.10 a day or less than $400 per year. The salary structure of both public and private institutions leaves many professionals and non-professionals alike unable to make ends meet. Several skilled men and women in the country are forced to accept jobs that are not in their field of training, and therefore, receive much lower salaries than what they are qualified to earn. For those few who are fortunate to find employment in their fields of training, salaries and compensation still remain low due to low productivity and the absence of incentive-based programs to reward meritorious work.

There is a strong case to be made about the inability of the system of economic and industrial production in Ghana to utilize the professional talents of their skilled citizens. Most of them perform at a sub par productivity level because of the persistent underemployment that confronts them. This is a major cause of poverty in the country, which in turn is fueling international outmigration. Though moderate improvements have been made in agricultural production and light manufacturing, this growth lacks any sustaining capacity to ensure the long term alleviation of poverty. Coupled with this is the fact that efforts to accelerate the rate of agricultural output are stymied by the lack of technical input and ecologically sound policies that integrate land tenure reforms into food production targets. This has pushed people off the land, depressed rural agricultural food production, and has caused mass migration of rural youth to the urban centers in search of employment.

The ability of the central government to organize domestic and international capital resources for large-scale economic and industrial projects is usually fraught with problems. A climate of political uncertainties coupled with corruption have rendered most economic and job creation projects in both rural and urban Ghana ineffective; they fail to provide Ghanaians with livable incomes and are usually cost prohibitive, often resulting in frustration and the desire to migrate. The complex processes involved in re-focusing Ghana's economic and industrial development strategies present a daunting challenge. Our conviction is that political factors that have operated in the country in the last three decades or more have severely hampered the ability of the government to formulate long lasting policies to arrest the issue of spiraling underdevelopment, poverty, and economic stagnation.

The lack of comprehensive national data to form the basis for rationalizing the economic and political motivations behind the constant stream of Ghanaians going abroad hampers any systematic effort made by central planners to incorporate migration into national development schemes and models. The motivations of Ghanaian migration to the West can be conceptualized broadly at two levels. First, there are those macro-structural triggers of migration that operate at the aggregate level to push out masses of people who are constrained by poverty, low incomes, lack of opportunity to advance, or political oppression. Second are the micro-level traits of individuals that motivate people to migrate. This component consist of psychological variables such as family reunification considerations, the symbolic meanings of migration for the individual, sheer curiosity, and the wanderlust associated with traveling to and taking up residence in a foreign land. Ghanaians react differentially to the macro and micro-level factors that motivate them to emigrate. Knowledge about the intersections of the macro and micro-level determinants of international migration from Ghana is critical toward the understanding of the expected economic and cultural benefits that accrue from emigration.

Governmental efforts that target the development of policies to retain the educated, skilled, and unskilled class of workers in Ghana must show an appreciation for the direct and indirect factors associated with the decision to emigrate. More specifically, policies to manage population mobility has sometimes been undertaken in piecemeal fashion often without attention given to problems associated with underdevelopment such as poor infrastructure, population growth, and lack of jobs. For instance, in efforts to check the rural to urban exodus of population in Ghana (a major factor influencing international migration from Ghana), current and previous governments have attempted to reform land, provide pipe-borne water and other amenities for rural dwellers, embarked upon agricultural revitalization, and even implemented frontier settlement initiatives. All told, these approaches, while laudable, have frequently been implemented only in specific regions of the country with no effort made to spread development projects evenly across the nation. A shining oasis of development that is surrounded by large scale underdevelopment and impoverishment only encourages migration to the place(s) with better resources. Toward this end, a policy of intermediate development at the national level that would ensure community-based self-sufficiency and sustainability is critical in minimizing the structural economic imbalances in the distribution of government and private sector economic development projects in Ghana.

The internationalization of capital (both human and physical) coupled with the structured inequality between nations, which are at varying degrees of economic and technological development, will continue to spur the migration of skilled and unskilled labor from the developing and peripheral countries to the advanced and core countries. As more and more Ghanaians depart the country and establish new cultural and economic moorings, the meaning of Ghanaian citizenship and nationalism will become very amorphous. The new ideas, identities, and the material and nonmaterial artifacts that Ghanaians create as members of the transnational migration community and bring with them home to Ghana will be tested against the background of the entrenched interests of political regimes in Ghana and Africa in general. A critical issue will be how the nation-state can manage the incorporation of the immigrants in the task of development, as well as show some understanding of the processes and consequences involved in transnational labor migration, while at the same time preserve the sovereignty of the country.

Despite the fact that the country stands to gain from increased international migration as a result of the remittances migrants send home, the process of engaging in international migration is also fraught with perils and uncertainties. There is need for the central government to embark upon programs that will ensure safe passage and travel for those Ghanaians who continue to engage in perilous journeys abroad in search of economic opportunities. The promotion of safe travel protocols is warranted. In the short and long run, policies designed to ensure the safety of Ghanaians who emigrate must be addressed by the central government. Institutional resources and the development of protocols of understanding at the bilateral and multilateral levels involving the Ghana government and the governments of the intended destinations of Ghanaians must be incorporated into national development planning goals and objectives. The goal of such a protocol is to ensure that Ghanaians who travel abroad, particularly those who travel with valid documents are guaranteed safety and security. Dire economic circumstances continue to force many unskilled Ghanaians to travel abroad without possession of valid papers. In some instances as this study demonstrates, young Ghanaian men and women migrate on foot across the Sahel with the hope of making it to the Mediterranean and subsequently to the European Union. In this regard, the enforcement of border crossing regulations on the movement of people, goods, and services must be incorporated into the protocol used by the Economic Commission for West African States (ECOWAS) and the African Union (AU). Government-sponsored program of civic education should seek to educate Ghanaians about the perils and pitfalls of traveling abroad without valid papers. Existing protocols and arrangements with other governments regarding the repatriation of Ghanaians who are rescued by immigration authorities abroad will have to be implemented or strengthened to safeguard the security of migrants. And bilateral and multilateral agreements with Ghanaian immigrant receiving countries must be expedited to allow the safe return of those immigrants who encounter hardships in the migratory process, such as those who are arrested, detained, or imprisoned abroad due to violation of immigration laws.

Innovative programs to implement public and civic education of Ghanaians about what to expect when traveling abroad will have to be developed by the central government and disseminated to prospective travelers. This will assist in alleviating the plight of those Ghanaians who travel abroad only to find that they are not welcome or experience economic and social hardships at the intended destination. By itself, the government of Ghana does not have the resources to ensure that Ghanaians who travel abroad receive assistance when needed. The effective management of the human resources of the country calls for a concerted effort on its part to implement strategies and programs that will culminate in the guarantee of safe travel and abode for all Ghanaians who travel abroad.

International Migration and the Re-shaping of Ghanaian Society

The forces that trigger the exodus of skilled and unskilled Ghanaians to the West in search of greener pastures are complex and varied in their nature. The international migration of Ghanaians is a necessary evil. The opportunities that the migrants seek in the West are not abundantly available in Ghana. As might be expected, the opportunity to earn higher wages relative to the wages of most Ghanaians is a primary motivating factor pushing people to look elsewhere for better economic opportunities. However, each migrant who leaves the country deprives the country of a skill, a talent, and a contribution to the national development effort. Ultimately, international migration holds the key to the reshaping of Ghanaian society, especially in the political and economic domains. The changes that have come about in Ghana post-1966 following the overthrow of Nkrumah have been driven in large part by the human capital that present and past Ghanaians who were domiciled in the Western capitals remitted to the country. The failure of the central government to establish a sustained process of national development to improve the lives of ordinary Ghanaians has proven costly for the country. This cost can be measured in terms of the persistence of stymied economic growth, poverty, and a decline in the basic standard of living of Ghanaians.

A solution to the chronicity of rural poverty, illiteracy, lack of access to healthcare, electricity, pipe-borne water and other amenities in Ghana has eluded almost all the governments that have come to power in the country since 1966. The ultimate cost is people are forced to flee so that they can avail themselves to opportunities abroad, with the hope that one day they too can become partners in the short and long-term national reconstruction of the motherland. The capital flows coming into the country in the form of remittances and machinery, coupled with the new ideas that the returning immigrants bring with them upon repatriation have become a potent force in the development of the country. Recent governments of Ghana have come to recognize the potential contributions of Ghanaian immigrants in shaping the future of Ghanaian society and are beginning to implement measures and policies to mobilize the resources of migrants to raise the living standards of native Ghanaians. Examples of this growing recognition include government-sponsored programs to assist immigrant returnees by providing them with tax incentives and business planning assistance to identify sectors of the economy where to invest the capital resources they bring home from abroad. The provision of governmental assistance to support the business initiatives of the private entrepreneurial class stems from the recognition by the central government that private capital ventures must be supported if they are to create jobs for Ghanaians. The assistance given by the government to private capital investors is based on the recognition by the government that it alone should not be the sole provider of jobs in the country. Supranational organizations and multilateral economic assistance in resuscitating Ghana's economy while critical are not the total panacea to bring the country back on its feet. In many respects, the private resources amassed by Ghanaian immigrants while abroad must also be mobilized toward the economic and social development of the country.

Once Ghanaian migrants arrive at their destinations and find attractive economic opportunities that are relatively better than what they have left behind, they perceive that these attractive opportunities must also be extended to or replicated at home. Their individual and collective efforts in spreading the benefits of the economic opportunities they encounter in the West back to Ghana have become the driving force behind investment and capital formation in the country. While this effort is admirable and necessary to propel the country to greater economic heights, it is not sufficient to ameliorate the country's economic problems. A combination of centrally planned government initiatives and international assistance along with private capital ultimately holds the key to the economic and industrial self-sufficiency of the country. A key component of the development process is an understanding of the macrosociological factors that affect globalization, transnational migration, and the segmentation of labor. The full impact of the growing internationalization of capital and the temporary or permanent movement of people across national barriers will continue to influence the direction of Ghana's march to become economically self-sufficient.

Micro-capital resources and skills transfer by Ghanaians living in the West will continue to dominate the flow of investments into the country. The management of these resources by the central government will prove critical in the revitalization of the nation's economy. A seamless institutional mechanism designed to harness these resources for maximum efficiency is sorely needed. The creation of a stable financial climate to attract Ghanaians abroad to bring foreign investments back into Ghana is also imperative. Current industrialization and manufacturing strategies initiated by the government to support light manufacturing have been successful in attracting capital into targeted export-driven industries such as the processing of agricultural raw materials and mining. The sources of the capital investments have come from both international donors and also through remittances and savings accumulated by Ghanaians living abroad. Remittance flows, the return migration of Ghanaians abroad, and changes in the financial structure of the country to accommodate the formation of small and large scale business establishments, coupled with reforms in the educational and labor sectors would certainly contribute to a stronger conceptualization of the relationship between international migration and economic development in Ghana. The continued expansion of economic and industrial activities in the country is beginning to have an impact on the retention of returned immigrants, especially the returnees who transfer all their foreign assets to Ghana and use the assets as leverage to secure loans and capital from state and private financial institutions.

Assisted by donor countries, particularly Britain and the United States, the current government of Ghana has managed to temporarily stop the economic hemorrhaging of the country by taming hyperinflationary cycles, debt reduction, promotion of national fiscal transparency, and a push for the promotion of export-driven commodities. However, systemic structural imbalances brought upon by the continued lack of sufficient foreign reserves, stymied manufacturing base, poor feasibility studies which mar the economic viability of projects, and persistent institutionalized corruption all continue to impede any sustained economic growth and increased productivity. In the end, efforts to create and sustain long-term economic growth will hinge on the implementation of economic projects by the private sector and the concomitant promotion of investment strategies and initiatives that will encourage indigenous manufacturers and their foreign counterparts to invest in job-creation enterprises. The role of the state in this regard is to expand the infrastructural facilities of the country to provide economies of scale for the private sector to launch and direct micro development projects across the country.

Theoretical and Methodological Implications of the Ghanaian Diaspora

Ghana has become a transnational migrant-sending country. The migration of the country's skilled and unskilled population will persist as the country becomes more integrated into the global economy. The form and structure of the diaspora and its continuity has some theoretical implications for the formulation of paradigms of migration, particularly from the developing countries to the developed countries. Previous theoretical models explaining migration have emphasized both macro and micro variables to account for the flow, direction, and volume of migration from the sending to the receiving countries. These models have postulated and highlighted the structural characteristics of places, particularly the economic and politico-social factors that serve as the push-pull factors that motivate people to engage in voluntary migration. The study of Ghanaian migration has followed the classical theoretical models by highlighting the role of economic conditions in the developing countries as contrasted with the high standard of living and wage differentials in the developed countries.

In constructing theories to explain the underlying structural contexts of Ghanaian and, by extension, African migration, we sorely need a paradigm that incorporates specific elements of African social structures and institutional frameworks (normative systems, family organization, multiple household relationships and the networks they establish, age and gender specific cohort roles and statuses). The linkage(s) between household decision making regarding internal, regional, and international migration within the African contexts and the global labor marketplace are not well grounded in existing theories of international migration. In Ghanaian and African migration decision-making, extended family networks and webs of friends play a major role in facilitating migration. Theories of international migration will have to incorporate information gleaned from communication exchanges among relatives of immigrants and attempt to explain how these exchanges are rationalized in the implementation and formation of the decision to emigrate. Such theoretical models will have to identify the structural and non-structural proximate determinants families and networks of friends make regarding where to migrate, the cost involved in embarking upon the journey, the incentives given to prospective migrants to migrate, and the social–psychological expectations and meanings that the extended family and networks of associates attach to migration. In this regard, the formulation of new models of international migration that incorporate the economic structure of the household and characteristics of the family with regards to the production of goods and services is warranted.

In Ghana, the family is a primary economic producer. As families assume a greater proportion of economic production and explore ways to create wealth and expand their sphere and range of economic services, international migration of selected family members will become pivotal. To shore up its economic base and implement measures to alleviate or reduce the poverty that confronts it, the Ghanaian immigrant community utilizes the assets of all its members who are expected to make financial and non-financial contributions to strengthen the economic base of the extended family. Above all, the social processes involved in how families in Ghana make decisions about who to sponsor for international migration are not well understood. The evidence presented in this study suggests that the decision as to which member of the family to sponsor to go abroad is a consultative process involving the rank and file of extended family members. While educational attainment in Ghana appears to dominate the selection process, other structural factors, such as gender roles, age or birth order, marriage rites, inheritance, and the overall financial standing of the extended family, are equally significant covariates worthy of empirical attention. Psychological variables, such as how well prospective migrants who are selected for family sponsorship will fare in the West, coupled with their commitment to extended family goals as opposed to individualistic norms are important considerations in the modeling of the determinants of family sponsored migration. To date, theories of international migration of Ghanaians to the West have yet to incorporate and recognize the saliency of family dynamics in the formulation of migration decision making. Furthermore, the understanding of the relative importance of how the migration decision making process is influenced by family relationships is equally critical in the modeling of theoretical statements to account for the decision not to move.

The decision not to move or engage in transnational migration is also mediated through the existing structures of extended family relationships. When some family members elect to stay home rather than to migrate, this decision is often overlooked in the modeling of migration theory. Relatives of immigrants who stay at home play a significant role at various points in the migration process. Though they may elect to stay home, non-movers are not passive actors or agents. They often choose to stay home to manage the remittances and the business transactions of their relatives who are domiciled abroad. They serve as a link between the relatives who are abroad and those who are left behind. Information flows from home to the immigrant point of destination are often gathered and shared with relatives who are abroad. Decisions regarding family organization and economic production (child socialization and rearing, family residential patterns, household budget and management) are often made by the non-movers and communicated to relatives abroad. In essence, the non-movers keep those who have moved away anchored in the happenings at home. Migration theories have often dismissed this important aspect of the transnational migratory process. The nature of the Ghanaian family, its organization, and the web of relationships that it engenders become salient in developing modules of migration that are broad enough to encompass multiple dimensions of Ghanaian social life.

In explaining Ghanaian and African migration to the West, there is a tendency to explain it from the perspective of the nation state as a political entity. In other words, the tendency is to describe Ghanaians as a group without paying regard to internal differences in culture and expectations regarding the outcome(s) of international migration. This approach tends to mask differences and variations in the patterns, volume, flow, and direction of international migration for the various ethnic, tribal, and clan groups represented in the country. Theoretical statements that link the causes and outcomes of international migration to the ethnic, tribal, or clan membership or affiliation of the prospective immigrant are imperative to understand the experiences of the immigrants. Differences in the patterns of international migration among Ghana's ethnic groups will have to be ascertained and incorporated into the formulation of robust theories of migration.

Anecdotal evidence from Ghana suggests that though Ghanaians from all parts of the country tend to engage in international migration, the bulk of those who leave the country come from the southern tier of the country. While a plausible explanation for this trend may lie in the uneven cultural and economic opportunities between the northern and southern tier of the country (for decades, economic and cultural development programs have favored the southern over the northern tier), what is not known is whether this discrepancy in patterns of international migration is actually caused by the differences in the level of development in the two tiers. A micro-level case study approach that examines the migratory patterns of specific ethnic groups from different geographic regions of the country may shed light on ethnic variations and patterns in specifying the determinants of international migration among Ghanaians.

The formulation of postulates to account for Ghanaian migration to the West must also be approached from the broader perspective of Third World migration to the developed countries. Though forming a very small part of this global or transnational migration of skilled and unskilled population to the West, Ghanaian migration adds a significant dimension to the theories of international migration, particularly the aspects of their migration that deal with stepwise or chain movement of people from the developing nations to the developed countries. Stepwise or chain migration informs the literature on migration by highlighting the fact that international migration is not a linear process where those who aspire to migrate simply move from point A to point B. The tendency to engage in multiple migrations before reaching their destination suggests that in forming the decision to go abroad, prospective migrants tend to define short and long term goals, which are then rationalized within the contexts of cost, physical barriers and impediments of moving from point A to point B, how long each step of the migration will last, and its intended outcomes. Theories of international migration based on the Ghanaian example must incorporate and delineate the factors that shape the implementation of the motivation to migrate at every juncture of the chain or stepwise migratory process. This way, a holistic approach to the unraveling of the determinants of international migration from the perspective of immigrants who engage in piecemeal migration can be ascertained.

Furthermore, the development of diaspora organizational structures and institutions by Ghanaians to maintain the transnational interconnections and networks that the immigrants establish is an important yet often overlooked aspect of the migration of Africans to the West. The importance of these organizational structures was recently observed in a seminal report compiled by the Centre for Migration, Policy and Society (COMPAS) in the UK. These diaspora organizational structures include the web of interlocking transnational networks the immigrants form to stay connected with their country of origin while at the same fostering inclusion in their newly adopted country. These organizations include the immigrant money transfer cooperatives; non-governmental, charitable organizations set up to provide capital or financial assistance to public and private organizations in Ghana; immigrant town or ethnic associations; alumni groups; national associations; religious organizations; and political party organizations. The role of these immigrant agencies in facilitating or hindering international migration is yet to be fully grasped, though anecdotal evidence suggests that increasingly they are becoming vital links in the construction of transnational identities among African immigrants, particularly those who are domiciled in the UK, USA, and Canada. The immigrants rely upon these agencies to ameliorate the problems caused by the inherent contradictions they encounter as they create and recreate newer identities and negotiate the complex terrain and vicissitudes of transnational ethnicities while at the same time anchoring themselves in Ghanaian culture and matters at the home front.

In documenting the contours of the Ghanaian diaspora and its implication to the development of migration theory, a number of methodological issues come to the fore. Chief among these is the dearth of data on the subject. At the central government level in Ghana, data on the volume and extent of migratory movement are hard to come by. When they arrive at their intended destinations in the West, access to official data on the immigrants is usually gleaned from census reports and official immigration data. The diaspora is highly fragmented and undifferentiated as Ghanaians engage in multi-stage migration until they reach their desired or intended destination; therefore, social scientists find it difficult to gather data on Ghanaian immigrants. With the exception of a few countries, particularly the USA, UK, Canada, Australia, the Netherlands, and Germany where Ghanaians have managed to form viable diaspora communities, there is not much data about the migratory experiences of Ghanaians who migrate to other parts of the world. This leaves significant gaps in the understanding of the migratory behavior of Ghanaians, rendering the development of robust theoretical models about their migration behavior difficult. However, survey data collected by social scientists have contributed immensely to an understanding of the Ghanaian diaspora and its transnational contents. Increased collection and utilization of survey data will garner valuable information about multiple dimensions of the migration decision making process. Such data will supplement official data on Ghanaian migrants by moving beyond the demographic and classificatory data that census and official information provide on Ghanaian migrations. Data on migration currently collected by administrative agencies of the government in Ghana do not provide adequate information beyond descriptive variables such as age, educational attainment, gender, and occupation. To move beyond the baseline data, sample surveys tapping into the full range of the migratory experiences will have to be initiated. This will provide full comprehensive data on migration and help in the formulation and implementation of policies designed by government and non-government agencies in planning models of economic development for the country. The added value is that the collection of survey data, however expensive it might be, will facilitate the incorporation of the human resource dimensions of international migration into models of national economic development. This will fill a void in current economic development planning schemes in Ghana and in many other migrant-sending countries in sub-Saharan Africa. This way, a symbiotic balance can be struck between theories of international migration and their methodological implications.

A case study approach to the study of the Ghanaian diaspora has the potential to offer scholarly insights into the complex processes involved in the transnational migratory behavior of Ghanaians. A theoretical approach emphasizing how these micro-level characteristics of Ghanaian immigrants influence family and individual decision making can shed light on the motivations behind Ghanaian migration. While quantitative information, including census data, has proved valuable in advancing theoretical insights about the Ghanaian diaspora, the sole reliance on such an approach masks the complex but contextually rich information about the causes of Ghanaian migration. A systematic effort geared toward the understanding of the economies of Ghana's rural communities and their role in the production of goods and services can aid in the formulation of theories on Ghanaian transnational migration by focusing on the existing but unexplored links between rural to urban migration in Ghana and international migration. Thus, an understanding of the rural economies of Ghana (where about 60 per cent of the country's population reside) and how these areas trigger migration is pivotal. By the time many Ghanaians leave the rural areas to come to the urban centers in search of jobs, education, and cultural enrichment, many of them have already formed the intention of migrating to the West. The migration to the urban scene is a stage in a series of calculated strategies, conceived with family input, to maximize human capital resources of the entire family through transnational migration. The decision to emigrate resonates and finds actualization once the migrant arrives in the city. After all, it is from the urban centers that prospective migrants are able to implement the decisions they have already made about emigrating. While in the urban areas, employment is sought, money is saved, and contacts are established and reinforced with extended relatives who have already embarked upon the journey. The flow of information about the entire migratory process in terms of what the potential immigrant should expect is handled formally within these urban centers. Information about how to secure a passport, visa regulations, fiscal exchanges, and medical requirements to undertake the journey are all obtained in the urban centers of administrative governance. The social and cultural context of the urban scene in Ghana is where the motivations behind the urgency to migrate are played out, within the broad parameters of subcultural and normative belief systems that justify the imperative of international migration as the only possible panacea to cope with the economic malaise dominating both the rural and urban scenes in Ghana. Theories seeking to understand the dynamic forces that continue to shape the diasporic and migratory behaviors of Ghanaians must acknowledge the small networks formed in both rural and urban Ghana that provide the nexus within which decisions to implement migration are formed. The same approach could assist in the development of a theoretical model to account for why others choose to stay and not migrate.

The transatlantic immigrant experiences of the Ghanaians living in the USA and the UK present opportunities and challenges to sociological theories of ethnic immigrant and diaspora communities in the West. While the majority of the immigrants tend to cluster in larger metropolitan communities, their concentrations in specific geographic locations do not completely conform to patterns of residential preferences and community organization established by Hispanic and Asian immigrants in the USA, and Indians and Pakistanis in the UK. The Ghanaian model of residential ethnic community formation is more akin to what can be termed a disaggregated residential pattern, rather than an ethnic enclave model, which has become characteristic of the new ethnicities in immigrant receiving societies in the West. Not having the critical mass of population to form their own ethnic enclave and self-sufficient communities, Ghanaian immigrants tend to disperse in a mixture of urban and suburban localities where they blend in with immigrant and non-immigrant populations alike. The fragmented diasporic identities they portray mean that their ethnic communities cannot be geographically or spatially defined in a fixed category or location. While this residential pattern of desegregation makes it very difficult at times to study them as an ethnic immigrant group, it raises interesting sociological investigations into why a growing number of Ghanaian immigrants opt for a pattern of residential settlement that distances and separates them from native-born blacks but yet they vigorously pursue identification with African and Caribbean black immigrants. Scholarly attention must be given to inter and intra-black diaspora social and cultural interconnections and how these interconnections shape the continuous formation of the global black diaspora.

The UK and the USA have become the epicenters of the Ghanaian diaspora and transnational communities. As the immigrants create their cultural communities and seek membership and integration into their host societies, a greater understanding about how their migratory experiences follow patterns of immigrant settlements and social processes is warranted. Key to this understanding is a number of theoretical issues that speak to the cultural patterns that the immigrants establish. An issue germane to this discussion is the persistence of Ghanaian immigrants' cultural identities. Despite encounters with racism and discrimination, Ghanaians in the UK and in the USA have been successful in stressing their unique cultural traits while also affirming an institutional affiliation with the core values of the host societies. However, the form of black ethnic adaptation they forge is an infinitesimal aspect of their transnational identities. Theories connecting their ethnic identity with their political participation are sorely needed. Also needed are theories that model the sociological patterns of their economic and civic participation as well as their location in the social structures of the host societies. Aspects of their migratory sojourn in the West dealing with intergenerational patterns of integration are absent from the theoretical formulations of their transnational migratory experiences. There is a growing interest in the crosscurrents that define the pathways that immigrants follow to achieve naturalization, citizenship, and incorporation. This aspect in the transformation and broadening of their global identities has yet to yield any theoretical linkages with the experiences of other immigrant groups to the West, particularly Caribbean blacks and Latinos. Despite the growing interactions among America's native-born blacks and black immigrants from Africa and the Caribbean, not much is known about the nature, patterns, or forms of these interactions. The shared cultural and historical experiences are similar as these groups have been subjected to persistent discrimination and denigration. But there are significant differences in the patterns of their diasporic adaptations in the Western countries. These differences span economic, political, and cultural spheres. Often, when they have formed alliances or mobilized themselves for collective action, it is to affirm their civil and human rights. Understanding of how these alliances can be extended to the political and economic domains is useful in mapping out the pathways that blacks in the diaspora in general can follow in seeking full membership and inclusion in the affairs of their respective host and national communities.

In specifying the factors that spur the migration of Ghanaians to the West, the role of women in the process is often overlooked. Historically, family decision making regarding the sponsorship of family members to go to the West favored men over women. As indicated in this study, when women have migrated to the West, they often traveled to be with a partner, spouse, or a male family member. However, as more women in Ghana gained access to primary, secondary and postsecondary education, Ghanaian women have joined the stream of immigrants leaving Ghana to come to the West for other reasons. Despite the increasing number of women who embark upon the journey to the West, there is a dearth of literature about the impact of this movement on a wide range of issues affecting the lives of these women. The findings from this study suggests that although Ghanaian women in the diaspora have achieved upward social mobility comparable to their male counterparts and have forged egalitarian relationships with their partners, not much is known about how international migration impacts women's fertility behavior, relations with men, child rearing, labor force participation, property rights, and inheritance. Whether they undertake the journey to the West alone or migrate to reunite with a partner, a growing number of Ghanaian immigrant women are joining the ranks of factory workers and food processing plants across the United States. Here, many of them compete with immigrant women from Latin America, Asia, Eastern Europe, and the Caribbean. Rigorous and sustained research is needed to delineate the effects of international migration on how Ghanaian and African immigrant women in the West manage their households and intra-family relationships, mobilize resources for collective economic action, and create networks of kinfolks and social acquaintances to express gendered identities.

Looking ahead, we conjecture that the UK and USA will continue to be the main "buckle" in the migration of Ghanaians to the West. The economic and political fragility of the country's burgeoning democracy has yet to be put to the test. A major upset in the form of civil disorder, economic crash, or an environmental disaster will create a tidal wave of displaced Ghanaians who once again will look to the West for assistance. And though some Ghanaians may initially travel to countries outside of the West, eventually several of them will engage in chain migration which ultimately will bring some of them to the USA or UK. These immigrants will continue to strive to create cultural communities that manifest their normative character and sense of who they are, first as Ghanaians, and second as Africans. While sojourning in the West, most of them will continue to hold on strongly to Ghanaian and African identities. The centrifugal forces that define and shape the volume and the direction of Ghanaian migration to the West are going to be affected by the reconfiguration of the motives that underlie the formation of the intent to migrate. Pivotal to this is the current ongoing formulation of the reasons why Ghanaians migrate. The need to affirm and feel secure in their home country as well as in the destinations of their migration will continue to become a significant aspect of the continuity of the transnational identities of the Ghanaian immigrants. Coming from very diverse backgrounds, the Ghanaians who are shaping and defining the immigrant experience in the UK and USA are trail blazers. The outcome of their experiences and the underlying sociological ramifications are pivotal in the delineation and construction of what it means to be Ghanaian in a foreign context. And while different factors may have compelled most of them to leave Ghana, over time, their stay in the West and interactions with British and American ethos and value systems ultimately affect their outlook on life. Their differences diminish and begin to erode the longer they stay abroad and more particularly as they project an outlook that has at its core an economic and transnational foci. The confluence of political, economic, and social developments in Ghana coupled with shifts in immigration policies in the UK and USA converge to dictate both the short and long-term prospects of Ghanaian migration and the formation of transnational immigrant cultures communities across the West.

The Ghanaian diaspora in the West is an unfinished story. Over half of the population of Ghana is under 30 years old and they will continue to look to the Ghana government to create better economic opportunities for them and improve upon their standards of living. Long-term sustainable economic development will be needed to assure Ghanaians that they all do not have to look abroad for greener pastures. Public and private economic initiatives backed by the promotion of strong political culture based on transparent democratization will be need to forestall hope among Ghanaians and renew their confidence in their government. This will entail the nurturing of civility, the rule of law, and the creation of an environment that is conducive for the thriving of democratic institutions. For those Ghanaians who are skilled, the West will continue to be a magnet continually drawing talents from all over the world. For the unskilled, the motivation to look for better opportunities beyond the shores of Ghana will persist. Economic desperation may motivate some of them to engage in risky, unconventional migration such as crossing the Sahara to get to the Mediterranean and subsequently to the European Union despite the tightening of visa controls and immigration. Measures at the bilateral and multilateral levels may have to be implemented to safeguard the security of those who will embark upon the perilous crossings across the desert. For those who are barred from the West due to lack of credentials and skills, other destinations will continue to be attractive, such as the Middle East and Asia.

Bibliography

Abella, D. (1989), "A Note on the Money Courier Industry of the Philippines," *Philippine Labour Review* 13 (1), 99–107.

Addai, I. (1999), "Does Religion Matter in Contraception use Among Ghanaian Women?," *Review of Religious Research* 40, 259–277.

Addai, I. (2000), "Religious Affiliation and Sexual Initiation among Ghanaian Women," *Review of Religious Research* 41, 328–343.

Adepoju, A. (1991), "South-North Migration: The African Experience," *International Migration* 29, 205–221.

Afolayan, A.A. (2001), "Issues and Challenges of Emigration Dynamics in Developing Countries," *International Migration* 39:4, 5–35.

Amin, S. (1974), *Modern Migrations in West Africa* (Oxford: Oxford University Press).

Ammassari, S. and Black, R. (2001), *Harnessing the Potential of Migration and Return to Promote Development. Applying Concepts to West Africa*, Prepared for International Organization for Migration. Centre for Migration Research, University of Sussex, UK.

Appleyard, R.T. (1989), "Migration and Development: Myths and Reality," *International Migration Review* 23 (3), 486–499.

Arthur, J. (1991), "International Labor Migration in West Africa," *African Studies Review* 34(3), 65–87.

Arthur, J. (2001), *Invisible Sojourners. African Immigrant Diaspora in the United States* (Connecticut: Praeger).

Atkinson, J. (1964), *An Introduction to Motivation* (New York: American Books).

Ayitey, G. (1992), *Africa Betrayed* (New York: St. Martin Press).

Berg, B. (1998), *Qualitative Research Methods for the Social Sciences*, 3rd edition (Boston, MA: Allyn and Bacon).

Birmingham, David (1998), *Kwame Nkrumah: The Father of African Nationalism* (Ohio: Ohio University Press).

Brown, L. and Longbrake, D. (1970), "Migration Flows in Intra-urban Space: Place Utility Consideration," *Annals of the Association of American Geographers* 60, 368–387.

Brown, L. and Moore, E. (1970), "The Intra-urban Migration Process: A Perspective," *General Systems Yearbook* 15, 109–122.

Buzan, B. (1980), "Chican Community Control, Political Cynicism and Validity of Political Trust Measures," *Western Political Quarterly* 33, 108–120.

Cardenas, G. and Flores, E. (1977), "Political Economy of International Migration," In A. Rios-Bustamante (ed.), *Immigration and Public Policy: Human Rights for Undocumented Workers and Their Families* (Los Angeles: Chicano Studies Research Center).

Cashmore, E. and Troyna, B. (1982), *Black Youth in Crisis* (London: George Allen and Unwin).

Chambers, I. (1994), *Migrancy, Culture, and Identity* (London: Routledge).

Cohen, A. (1955), *Delinquent Boys: The Culture of the Gang* (New York, Free Press).

Cohen, R. (1992), *Migration and the New International Division of Labor.* In Malcolm Cross (ed.), *Ethnic Minorities and Industrial Change in Europe and North America* (New York: Cambridge University Press).

DaVanzo, J. (1976), *Why Families Move: A Model of the Geographic Mobility of Married Couples* (California: The Rand Corporation).

DiPalma, G. (1970), *Apathy and Participation: Mass Politics in Western Societies* (New York: Free Press).

Ebaugh, H. and Chafetz, J. (2002), *Religion and the New Immigrants: Communities and Adaptations in Immigrant Congregations* (California: Alta Mira Press).

Foner, N. (1997), "The Immigrant Family: Cultural Legacies and Cultural Changes," *International Review of Migration* 31(4), 961–974.

Fong, H. (1971), "Immigration and Naturalization Laws: Today's Need for Naturalization Law Reform," *International Migration Review* 5(4), 406–418.

Fuchs, L. (1992), "Migration Research and Immigration Policy," *International Migration Review* 26:4, 35–50.

Garcia, F. (1973), *Political Socialization of Chicano Children* (New York: Praeger Publishers).

Gold, S. (2001), "Gender, Class, and Network: Social Structure and Migration Patterns Among Transnational Israelis," *Global Networks* 1:1, 57–58.

Goldring, L. (1996), "Blurring Borders: Constructing Transnational Community in the Process of Mexico–U.S. Migration," *Research in Community Sociology* 6, 69–104.

Goldscheider, C. (1971), *Population, Modernization, and Social Structure* (Boston: Little, Brown and Company).

Gordon, A. (1998), "The New Diaspora – African Immigration to the United States," *Journal of Third World Studies* XV:1, 79–103.

Herberg, W. (1960), *Protestant, Catholic, and Jew: An Essay in American Religious Sociology* (New York: Double Day).

Hirsch, H. and Gutierrez, A. (1973), "The Militant Challenge to the American Ethos: Chicano and Mexican-Americans," *Social Science Quarterly* 53, 830–845.

Holtzman, J. (2000), *Nuer Journeys, Nuer Lives. Sudanese Refugees in Minnesota* (Boston: Allyn and Bacon).

Jenkins, R. (1985), "Gold Coasters Overseas, 1880–1919," *Immigration and Minorities* 4 (3), 5–52.

Johnston, R. (1971), "Resistance to Migration and the Mover/Stayer Dichotomy: Aspects of Kinship and Population Stability in an English Rural Area," *Geografiska Annaler Series (Human Geography)* 53B (1), 16–27.

Kandil, M. and Metwally, M.F. (1999), "The Impact of Migrants' Remittances on the Egyptian Economy," *International Migration Review* 37 (1), 159–169.

Keely, C. and Tran, B.N. (1989), "Remittances from Labor Migration: Evaluations, Performance and Implications," *International Migration Review* 23 (3), 261–287.

Kennedy, D. (1996), "Can We Still Afford to be a Nation of Immigrants?," *Atlantic Monthly* (November issue) <http://www.theatlantic.com>.

Kibria, N. (1993), *Family Tightrope: The Changing Lives of Vietnamese Americans* (New Jersey: Princeton University Press).

Koltyk, J. (1998), *New Pioneers in the Heartland: Hmong Life in Wisconsin* (Massachusetts: Ally and Bacon).

Konadu-Agyemang, K. (2000), "Travel Patterns and Coping Strategies of Ghanaian Immigrants in Canada," *Ghana Studies* 2, 1–20.

Konadu-Agyemang, K., Takyi, B. and J. Arthur (2006) (eds), *The New African Diaspora in North America: Trends, Community Building, and Adaptation* (Maryland: Lexington Books).

Lianos, T. (1997), "Factors Determining Migrant Remittances: The Case of Greece," *International Migration Review* 31:1, 72–87.

Mabogunje, A.L. (1970), "Systems Approach to a Theory of Rural-urban Migration," *Geographical Analysis* 2:1, 1–19.

Martin, P. and Midgley, E. (1994), "Immigration to the United States: Journey to an Uncertain Destination," *Population Bulletin* 49 (2): 2–47.

Massey, D. (1994), "An Evaluation of Migration Theory: The North American Case," *Population and Development Review* 20 (4), 699–751.

Nkrumah, K. (1970), *Neo-Colonialism* (New York: International Publishers).

Nuako, K.K. (2006), "'Still Praisin' God in a New Land: African Immigrant Christianity in North America," In Konadu-Agyemang, K., Takyi, B.; and J. Arthur (eds), *The New African Diaspora in North America: Trends, Community Building, and Adaptation* (Maryland: Lexington Books).

Ouattara, A. (1997), "The Challenges of Globalization for Africa," Address at the Southern Africa Economic Summit sponsored by the World Economic Forum, Harare, May 21.

Owusu, T. (1998), "To Buy or Not to Buy: Determinants of Home Ownership Among Ghanaian Immigrants in Toronto," *Canadian Geographer* 42(1), 40–52.

Oxfam (1999), *IMF: Wrong Diagnosis, Wrong Medicine* (Oxford: Oxfam).

Oxfeld, E. (1993), *Blood, Sweat and Mahjong: Family and Enterprise in an Overseas Chinese Community* (New York: Cornell University Press).

Peil, M. (1986), "Leadership of Anglophone Tropical Universities, 1948–1986," *International Journal of Education Development* 6, 245–261.

Peil, M. (1995), "Ghanaians Abroad," *African Affairs* 94: 376, 23–34.

Portes, A. (1995), "Children of Immigrants: Segmented Assimilation," In *The Economic Sociology of Immigration* (ed.) (New York: Russell Sage Foundation).

Portes, A. and Curtis, J. (1987), "Changing Flags: Naturalization and its Determinants among Mexican Immigrants," *International Migration Review* 21, 352–371.

Portes, A. and Zhou, M. (1993), "The New Second Generation: Segmented Assimilation and its Variants," *The Annals of the American Academy of Political and Social Sciences* 530, 74–96.

Pryor, R. (1983), "Integrating International and Internal Migration Theories," In Kritz, M., Keely, C. and S. Tomasi (eds), *Global Trends in Migration: Theory and Research on International Population Movements* (New York: Center for Migration Studies) pp. 110–129.

Ravenstein, E. (1885), "The Laws of Migration," *Journal of the Statistical Society* 48, 167–227.

Ravenstein, E. (1889), "The Laws of Migration," *Journal of the Statistical Society* 52, 214–301.

Rodrigo, C. and Jayatissa, R. (1989), "Maximising Benefits from Labour Migration: Sri Lanka," In Amjad, R. (ed.), *To the Gulf and Back: Studies on the Economic Impact of Asian Labour Migration* (New Delhi: ILO/ARTEP), pp. 255–296.

Rogler, L.H., Cooney, R.S. and Ortiz, V. (1980), "Intergenerational Change in Identity in the Puerto Rican Family," *International Migration Review* 14:2, 193–214.

Russell, B.H. (1994), *Research Methods in Anthropology: Qualitative and Quantitative Approaches*, 2nd edition (California: Sage Publications).

Russell, S. (1992), "Migrant Remittances and Development," *International Migration* 30 (3/4), 267–287.

Stock, R. (1995), *Africa South of the Sahara: A Geographic Interpretation* (New York: Guildford Press).

Sutcliffe, D. (1982), *British Black English* (Oxford: Basil Blackwell).

Sutton, C. and Makiesky, S. (1975), "Migration and West Indian Racial and Ethnic Consciousness," In Safa, H. and du Toit, B. (eds), *Migration and Development: Implications for Ethnic Identity and Political Conflict* (The Hague: Mouton).

Suval, E. (1972), "Selectivity in Migration: A Review of Literature," *Technical Bulletin #209*, Raleigh, North Carolina: North Carolina Agricultural Experimental Station.

Takougang, J. (1995), "Black Immigrants to the United States," *The Western Journal of Black Studies* 19:1, 50–57.

Thomas-Hope, E. (1975), *The Adaptation of Migrants from the English-Speaking Caribbean to Select Centres of Britain and North America.* Paper presented at the Annual Meeting of the Society of Applied Anthropology, Amsterdam.

Todaro, M.P. (1976), "Internal Migration in Developing Countries," *A Review of Theory* (ILO: Geneva).

Uhlenberg, P. (1973), "Non-economic Determinants of Non-migration: Sociological Considerations for Migration Theory," *Rural Sociology* 38 (3), 296.

Ungar, S. (1995), *Fresh Blood: The New African Immigrants* (New York: Simon and Schuster).

United States Bureau of the Census. (2000), *Current Population Survey. Table 7:1* (Washington, DC: US Department of Commerce).

United States Immigration and Customs Enforcement Statistical Yearbook (2000), *Table 3* (Washington, DC: US Department of Justice).

United States Immigration and Customs Enforcement Statistical Yearbook (2000). *Table 2* (Washington, DC: US Department of Justice).

Vickerman, M. (1999), *Crosscurrents: West Indian Immigrants and Race* (New York: Oxford University Press).

Warner, R.S. (1993), "Work in Progress Toward a New Paradigm for the Sociological Study of Religion in the United States," *American Journal of Sociology* 98, 1044–1193.

Waters, M.C. (1994), "Ethnic and Racial Identities of Second-Generation Black Immigrants in New York City," *International Migration Review* 28:4, 1–15.

Watkins, K. (1995), *The Oxfam Poverty Report* (Oxfam: Oxford).

Whyte, W.F. (1943), *Street Corner Society: The Social Construction of an Italian Slum* (Chicago: University of Chicago Press).

Wilson, W. (1980), *The Declining Significance of Race* (Chicago: University of Chicago Press).

Wolpert, J. (1965), "Behavioral Aspects of the Decision to Migrate," *Papers of the Regional Science Association* 15, 159–169.

Wuff, H. (1992), "New Mix, Mew Meanings," In C. Palmgren, K. Lovgren, and G. Bolin (eds), *Ethnicity in Youth Culture* (Stockholm: University of Stockholm).

Zachariah, K. and Conde, J. (1981), *Demographic Aspects of Migration in West Africa* (Washington, DC: World Bank).

Index